BEN BEHIND HIS VOICES

BEN BEHIND HIS VOICES

One Family's Journey from the Chaos of Schizophrenia to Hope

RANDYE KAYE

ROWMAN & LITTLEFIELD PUBLISHERS, INC.
Lanham • Boulder • New York • Toronto • Plymouth, UK

Published by Rowman & Littlefield Publishers, Inc.
A wholly owned subsidiary of The Rowman & Littlefield Publishing Group, Inc.
4501 Forbes Boulevard, Suite 200, Lanham, Maryland 20706
http://www.rowmanlittlefield.com

Estover Road, Plymouth PL6 7PY, United Kingdom

Copyright © 2011 by Rowman & Littlefield Publishers, Inc.

British Library Cataloguing in Publication Information Available

Library of Congress Cataloging-in-Publication Data
Kaye, Randye.
  Ben behind his voices : one family's journey from the chaos of schizophrenia
to hope / Randye Kaye.
    p. cm.
  ISBN 978-1-4422-1089-9 (cloth : alk. paper) — ISBN 978-1-4422-1091-2
(electronic)
  1. Kaye, Benjamin, 1982– —Health. 2. Paranoid schizophrenics—New York
(States)—New York—Biography. 3. Paranoid schizophrenics—Rehabilitation—
New York (States)—New York. 4. Kaye, Randye. I. Title.
RC514.K334 2011
616.89'80092—dc22
[B]
                                                                    2011004622

∞™ The paper used in this publication meets the minimum requirements of
American National Standard for Information Sciences—Permanence of Paper
for Printed Library Materials, ANSI/NISO Z39.48-1992.

Printed in the United States of America

For my children, who had to learn so much, too soon

To Geoff, who took us all in as family, with his love

And with thanks to Joyce Burland, PhD, who had the foresight and courage to create a program that has educated and empowered countless families affected by mental illness

Don't quit before the miracle.

—Anonymous

CONTENTS

Part III: Dealing with Catastrophic Events

Part IV: Recovery and Acceptance

FOREWORD

To help me help myself up a mountain . . .

Schizophrenia is an illness that has devastated the lives of countless individuals and families. For decades, people have suffered in silence due
to stigma, shame, and lack of knowledge about the biological basis of the
illness. Indeed, organized psychiatry played a major role in fostering stigma
with its early theories regarding family and parenting styles as potential
causes of psychotic states. Too many affected individuals have suffered silently, and families have been torn apart by the disease.

Over the past ten years, however, research has generated new and
important information about schizophrenia, and more effective treatments
have emerged. Most importantly, families are recognized as the most important support persons in an individual's treatment and recovery. Stigma
is beginning to wane, and patients, families, and behavioral health clinicians
are together mounting a fight against the illness.

Randye Kaye's book provides a vivid description of the highs and
lows experienced by families of individuals with schizophrenia. Like other
published works, this book details the chaos of the early stages of the disease, the difficulties of recognizing the illness, and uncertainties regarding
treatment options.

Ms. Kaye's story is different, however, with its vivid description of her
family members' efforts to maintain a thread of hope throughout a tortur-
ous several-year process, and to face the difficulties and tragedy of the illness

head-on. The reader is heartened to see each family member, including Ben, find a level of courage that none felt they possessed.

Thomas Smith, MD
Medical Director, New York City
Mental Health Care Monitoring
Initiative, New York State Office of
Mental Health
Associate Professor of Clinical
Psychiatry, Columbia University
College of Physicians and Surgeons,
New York State Psychiatric Institute

AUTHOR'S NOTE

This is a true story.

Other than my full name and the first name of my daughter, Ali, all of the names of people, hospitals, schools, and other institutions included in this book have been changed. Some identifying characteristics have also been altered—and please note that neither of my children shares my last name.

This memoir is an accurate recollection of events as re-created from recorded conversations, hospital records, correspondence with Ben's providers, my journals, and my own memory. This book is not intended as a manual or complete guide to handling schizophrenia; however, some facts and resources are provided to help the reader understand the progression of the illness as it unfolds in the story, and to guide the reader toward books and organizations that can provide support, education, and help.

Our story is not unique. One out of every four families in the United States has been affected by mental illness. Schizophrenia affects one in every one hundred people, worldwide.

INTRODUCTION: 2010

My son, Ben, knows the lyrics to every song I've never really noticed on the radio. He's the one who teaches me to appreciate the poetry in songs by Led Zeppelin, Pink Floyd, and the Grateful Dead. He's my favorite companion for performances of Shakespeare in the Park, because just at the point when I'm starting to think *why don't they just speak English already?* he invariably whispers something like, "Wasn't Shakespeare a genius, Mom? Listen to the music in the way he wrote those lines." Shame on me.

In October 2010, he proudly served as groomsman and toasted his sister, Ali, and her new husband, Marc, as they celebrated their wedding day. He ad-libbed an unscheduled speech that was concise, funny, and full of both nostalgia for the past and hope for the new couple's future. Like Ben, it was loving and sweet.

He's a really nice guy. If you accidentally give him too much change at the cash register, he'll point out the error and give it back to you without hesitation—even if he has to walk a mile back to the store to do it. His face lights up whenever he gives someone a present—especially Ali, whom he has always loved deeply. Ben proudly shows his anniversary tokens from Narcotics Anonymous—marking his years clean and sober. He ends every phone call to me with "Love you, Mom." He gives great hugs. He always remembers my birthday.

Ben loves nature, children, fantasy video games, helping others, the Indianapolis Colts, Thanksgiving with the family, and vegetarian Thai food. He has made the dean's list at college three semesters in a row. He kills at Scrabble. He has offered to counsel my best friend's nephew, who is still lost in the world of drug addiction.

Ben is twenty-eight years old. And—oh, yes—he has paranoid schizophrenia.

Ben is not "supposed to" care about others—that's one of the symptoms of schizophrenia. But he does. He is full of love, and we're grateful for his presence. Our family has learned to live in the moment; there are, thankfully, many moments to treasure these days. But it wasn't always like this, and we know all too well that tomorrow could bring more change. Still, we have found hope and love that we once thought might be lost forever.

When Ben was hospitalized five times in 2003—the height of his crisis period—for symptoms of this illness, no one in my life really knew how to react. No one showed up with casseroles at our door—especially not by the third or fourth hospitalization. People don't really know what to do, how to support the patient and the family. Unlike a physical illness like a broken leg, there's no timetable for recovery from something like schizophrenia. There's no sure moment of getting better. There is no cure; there is only management. As is also true with cancer, there's always a chance for recurrence after remission. But unlike most cancers, the patient's very *soul* seems to be affected by mental illness. The organ it affects is the brain, and that's the window to our personality, perhaps to our soul. People are frightened of mental illness; they're uncomfortable visiting someone on the psych floor. The family feels isolated, stigmatized, and often very alone. But there is hope. Ben is in recovery. He is not "cured," but he can be kept in careful balance. He is part of our family. He is worth knowing. He deserves to be understood and accepted, the same as anyone else with a disability.

Every morning and evening, Ben takes medication to keep his brain in balance. He doesn't agree that these meds do anything to help him, even though if he stops taking them he winds up back in the hospital within days. All he knows is that they make him feel mentally cloudy and physically exhausted. Ben tells me that he feels like a blanket has been thrown over his mind when he's on his medication; he loves the initial feeling of clarity and energy that comes if he stops taking it. *I* know that this euphoria lasts only a day or so, but by the time Ben's brain has raced past that first phase, he's too symptomatic to realize that anything's wrong. He generally just thinks that "people are treating him differently" for some reason. Sure we are. When Ben shifts focus to his inner world, we try like hell to bring him back to us.

Without the medication that restores the chemical balance in Ben's brain, he has to fight to remain connected to what's happening around him instead of within him—and the strain of that effort is heartbreakingly apparent. Ben wants, with all his heart, to prove that he doesn't need the medication that we know has brought him back to us—at least halfway back.

Because of this desire to feel energetic and creative again—and a wish to not really need medication at all—Ben sometimes tries to "cheek" his medication; that is, he pretends to swallow his pills but actually hides them in his cheeks, under his tongue, in his pockets, down his shirt sleeve. Therefore, he's painstakingly supervised when he takes them—usually by the staff at the group home where he lives, and sometimes by me if he's staying overnight at home. Most of the time this works—Ben has been stable, and out of the hospital, for almost five years now.

But we can't let down our guard, not really. Not yet. If we aren't watching for signs of returning symptoms, Ben may wind up needing to be hospitalized until his balance is restored. No one in Ben's life wants to see that happen ever again, including Ben. He just hasn't accepted the connection yet between going off his meds and winding up in the emergency room.

He doesn't even agree that he *has* schizophrenia, for to accept that would mean many things that he doesn't want to be true: that he has an illness, that he's different, that he has to take meds for the rest of his life. That because of this illness, he may never catch up to his friends; his childhood plans and dreams may never, ever come true.

Ben began to change in his midteens. No one seemed to know what was wrong, though there were plenty of guesses, both professional and personal. We tried everything from therapy to ToughLove, but nothing helped for long. As I look back now, I can see in the clarity of hindsight that someone should have, could have diagnosed Ben before he had that first severe psychotic break. Perhaps with early treatment, his road would be easier now. Maybe some of his brain cells would be in better shape. I can't prove it or even know it for sure, but I believe it to be true. There are things I wish I'd known then; maybe this book will alert another family to the need for early treatment.

Ben's recovery began when we finally found the medication regime that worked for him and got him to take it. These years of recovery, after Ben's stabilization on Clozaril and Depakote, are told in present tense in Part Four in this book. Although recovery is far from the end of the story, it is certainly a vastly different chapter once the right treatment has been found. Each year of stability increases his chances for improvement; some research shows that brain cells that may have been destroyed during periods of psychosis can actually regenerate when balance is maintained.

Okay, so everyone used to think Ben would wind up at Yale. He used to get straight A's; he used to have so many friends that I couldn't keep them straight. I won't say that I don't miss the son I used to have, the promising future I used to dream about. I won't say that I don't get a lump in my throat when I look at old pictures of him with Ali, their faces alive with laughter. The *used to*'s fill a long list. But I've learned not to look at it anymore. So, in a way, has Ben.

Ben has never lost us; the love of his family has been part of his recovery. But there were times I wished I *could* give up on him; there were times I just wanted our lives to be free of continuous crisis. We may never be out of the woods entirely, but my family found its way through this new reality: Ben with schizophrenia. The good days are easier, of course, but we also know we'll somehow handle the situation if Ben relapses again. We've done it before. In the meantime, we've learned to live in gratitude instead of focusing on fear. Still, we hold our breath, just a little bit. Five years since his last full relapse and counting—and counting our blessings.

Those years of being in the dark, finally leading to a correct diagnosis and an effective treatment plan for Ben, were hell. Now we're halfway back from there, and it will have to do. It is what it is. I've come to accept it. His sister has come to accept it. The road to acceptance has been a long journey through many stages: confusion, repeated crisis, denial, anger, recognition, grief, hope. Along the way, we learned a lot of lessons, including how to love Ben again, to see the value in his life as it has been redefined by the illness we hate.

It's our new normal.

SNAPSHOT: THE TURNING POINT

It's the night of the Great Northeast Blackout, August 2003. I sit in a hopelessly stained plastic chair in St. Mary's Hospital emergency waiting room next to my son Benjamin, twenty-one, recently diagnosed with paranoid schizophrenia. I watch Ben, aware that if he were a stranger I'd be afraid to sit this close to him. He stares at his feet, mumbling to himself, possibly talking to voices only he can hear and whose existence he always denies.

Only three weeks have passed since Ben's last release. If he's admitted today this will be his fifth psychiatric hospitalization this year. I pray that they will let him in, that he qualifies as "sick enough." These days, the only time I feel that Ben is safe is when he's behind the locked psych unit doors. Nothing can happen to him there. Someone is watching over him.

Today was a day of record high temperatures. I picked Ben up from his roach-infested apartment this morning so he could spend the day at home. I could tell right away that he wasn't having a great day. He was lethargic and unfocused, taking slow plodding steps to the car and responding to conversation only with great effort. I hoped it might be just the heat affecting him. He had *promised* he'd stay on his medication this time. I wanted to believe him.

Maybe a swim will help, I thought. *Once he cools off, he'll be able to focus again.*

So Ben took a swim in our small backyard pool. He'd said he wanted to be alone, so my daughter Ali and I watched from the kitchen window as Ben dived in, swam a few laps, and then got out of the pool. He pulled himself slowly up the ladder and stood, his bathing trunks heavy and drooping low off his body. Instead of reaching for the towel hanging two steps away on the fence, Ben turned around as if moving through mud and stood

xvii

motionless for a long moment, staring at the water. He brought his hands up and stared at his knuckles. He turned his hands over and stared again, at his palms, entranced. Other than that, he stood perfectly still.

The swim hadn't helped, clearly. This wasn't about the heat. I felt the tears rise in my throat, my mind searching the crisis action list for my next steps. *Dear God. Not again.*

Ali, my baby, looked at me, her lips and eyes tightly set so she wouldn't cry this time. "Mom, get him to the hospital. He's not doing well. He's acting crazy again," she said.

And then—the power went out. Fans stopped, the air conditioner got quiet, and before long the news came over the portable radio: power was out everywhere. For me, this was a godsend; the Great Blackout provided me with the perfect excuse to transport Ben quietly to the hospital on my own. No ambulance, no handcuffs this time.

Ben came back inside and got dressed. He had been complaining all day of stomach pain. The perfect excuse. "Ben," I said, "I think we'd better get you to the walk-in medical center to see about your stomach."

"Oh. Okay, Mom," he said. It was that easy to get him into the car. Ben spent most of the ride staring at his hands, mumbling into the air, laughing occasionally at some private joke he might be sharing with an invisible friend. Still, he was alert enough to notice that we were not headed to the walk-in medical center. He looked at me with a spark of suspicion. "Mom," he said, "you're going the wrong way."

Please don't grab the wheel. Please believe my lie. "I know," I said. "They're closed because the power's out. The only medical center that's open is in the hospital." Ben seemed to accept this. It worked. He bought it. Maybe he wouldn't run in fear as he had once before; maybe I wouldn't need the five security guards to chase him down and escort him back into the ER this time. The hardened look left his eyes, and he nodded calmly.

"Oh," Ben said. "Okay." And that was it. We parked in the emergency room lot, and I led my dazed son into the waiting room for this fifth time.

And now, we wait in these chairs. Me, my son, and his voices.

Ben glances up at me now and again, his lips in a faint smile but his eyes clouded and unreachable, and then returns to his inner conversation. Suddenly he looks up once more, this time to address the elderly woman seated in another hard plastic chair across from him, coughing violently.

"Excuse me, ma'am, are you all right?" Ben asks. His voice is suddenly clear, his expression interested and serene.

The woman looks up, eyeing Ben's disheveled hair, his rumpled clothes, his momentarily kind eyes. She considers him, then finally smiles. "Yes, son, I'll be okay. Thanks." She takes a sip of bottled water; her coughing calms. Not until then does Ben return to his own internal world of psychosis. Only then does he abandon the battle to stay focused on the outside world; he gives in to the voices. His expression seems to crumble inward, back to the world inside his brain. The mumbling starts again. This, I can tell, is a relief for him. But he'd made the effort to connect, even though it had taken more strength than I can imagine.

This day is to become the turning point, the start of Ben's return from the confusion of medication roulette. With the right treatment, Ben could find his way to a quieter place, perhaps some relief from the tricks his brain had been playing on him for years. This would mark, for me, the end of the hell of not knowing what was wrong, not knowing what to do, desperately trying to force Ben back, somehow, into the person he had once been. I would learn my lessons of recovery, and Ben would have to learn his. We would find our way back to a new normal, step by painful step. And our love would be the most important part of that journey.

He's still in there, I think. *He is worth saving.*

The nurse calls his name at last, and the double doors to the admitting area slide open. Welcome back.

I

WARNING SIGNS

REFLECTIONS

TIME: THE PRESENT

I sit among doctors, patients, and family members at Columbia University in New York; this conference is designed to provide CMUs (continuing medical units) for mental illness professionals, and information for the rest of us. The presenter is talking about early detection of schizophrenia, about patterns in childhood and early adolescence that seem more prevalent in those who later develop adult schizophrenia, as Ben did. The reason for this research is so that professionals can be on the lookout for signs that may—but, they quickly point out, may not—signal upcoming symptoms of mental illness. Early detection and treatment, they say, can prevent the psychotic breaks that cement the diagnosis of mental illness but may also cause brain damage in some patients, making recovery that much more difficult. Early detection, early treatment, maybe early *prevention*.

I look at the list of patterns, and the changes during Ben's high school years suddenly seem so obvious as they drift into focus. I even find myself questioning his personality from the day he was born. *Was schizophrenia looming there all the time? What if I had known all this while Ben was going through it? Would I have known what to do? Would he be having an easier life now?*

Why didn't anyone see it? Why didn't anyone tell me?

Are we too late?

3

1

BEGINNINGS

It all started, or so I thought, with marijuana.

Or did the trouble really begin when Ben dropped out of high school, with plans to travel cross-country, search for his father, and knock on doors to ask for work if he needed money?

Maybe I should have recognized schizophrenia when Ben was fifteen, the night he broke down in sobs after a huge fight with me and said, "What's *wrong* with me, Mom? Please, please, find me someone to talk to. I don't know what's happening. I used to be so *happy*."

Or maybe earlier, during the first month of high school, when Ben came home and announced, "Nobody likes me at school anymore. I kissed a girl the first week and she liked me, but she doesn't talk to me anymore and all the kids are against me now."

But how was I to know? All I could see was my teenage child in turmoil, my sweet son caught in a really difficult stage of growth. Hormones? Stress? More than just adolescence—adolescence squared, then cubed. Everyone told me he'd grow out of it. All I had to do was hold my ground, set limits, be firm, keep loving him.

But there's no loving someone out of mental illness. Love is a major factor in dealing with the illness, in helping the recovery process, but it can't change the fact of the illness itself any more than hugs can prevent the flu. All I knew then was that Ben kept tripping, stumbling, and then falling—and I kept catching him. Always, between episodes of crisis, there was an oasis of calm and promise that made me fall in love with my son all over again.

Perhaps the illness was there from the day he was born, waiting to spring into action, to take over my son's brain like the vines that snake through my maple tree every year no matter what I do. How far back do we search for the answers?

My baby. Benjamin was born on April 30, 1982, nine days late, after a natural labor and delivery. No drugs. See, even now I remind myself, *this is not my fault.* I did everything right during the pregnancy, I swear— unless you count the Pepto-Bismol during the first week of what I thought was a stomach virus but turned out to be morning sickness. I even got my husband, William, to change the cat litter.

There were no wails of outrage as this child was brought into the light from my womb; there was only a deep breath of life followed by fascination. His face was perfect and somehow wise. He was beautiful, so beautiful. From his very first moment in the world outside my womb Benjamin was alert and assessing the environment through those intent brown eyes that later would so resemble my own. In the hospital room, I stared at this new life, living the first page of his history, and imagined what else would be written there.

I promised my sleeping little baby that I would always do my best, always stick by him. Little did I know how fully, and for how long, those intentions would be tested. Never once, with no history of it in my family, did I expect a mental illness would steal his life from him later on. You imagine cuts and scrapes, broken arms, broken hearts, even car accidents or kidnapping—but never schizophrenia.

2

BEN DROPS OUT

and above the content soul flies to meet the morning
At the dawn of a newly rising sun
Where in the distance the grains of sand cling together
And sift through the holes
Relying on the wind to bring them closer to God.

—Ben (age sixteen) as printed in the
Trumbull High Literature and Art Magazine, 1999

I've tried to come up with the amusement park ride that would come close to representing the four years that should have led to my son's graduation from high school. Roller coaster? It's all anticipation of fear, and then the terror mixed with the thrill. But you know you'll be okay, because you know it will end. And you have no false illusion of control: the tracks are laid, the speed is set. Merry-go-round? No. The same view awaits you each time you go around. Which is the ride that takes you from crisis to crisis, with periods of calm and hope in between? Where each crisis escalates so that you develop *immunity* to it—so that you long for the previous incident, which seemed so difficult then but now seems a breeze in comparison? Which is the ride that raises your threshold of fear each time you ride it? Which ride keeps you blindfolded, so that you can't figure out what is happening or why, which makes abnormal seem normal?

The phone call came at about eleven o'clock one morning in late March. It was from the nurse at Trumbull High. "Can you come in right away?" she asked. "Your son Ben is here and says he is having a nervous breakdown. He does seem rather agitated, and I told him to lie down on the cot."

I exhaled strongly through my nose, an attempt to stay calm. A sound of frustration, anger, fear. *A nervous breakdown? What does Ben mean by that? Is this a new excuse for not going to class? Or is he really breaking down?* "Of course," I said. "I'll be right there."

When I got to the nurse's office, Ben was sitting up in a back room. Other adults were there with him. The nurse told me that Ben had arrived late to class and then could not sit still. He'd said he didn't feel well. His stomach hurt. His head hurt. And then he'd said he thought he was having a nervous breakdown. Now he was talking with the other adults in the back room. I could see him through the glass portion of the door; he alternated between talking animatedly and staring quietly down at his sandals.

I went in. The room was bare except for the posters on the cinder-block wall: "Just Say No to Drugs"; "This Is a Healthy Lung. This Is a Smoker's Lung." Ben sat on a cot, the scratchy brown blanket unused. The room smelled of bacterial soap.

Two men were in chairs, facing him. One, tall and thin with thinning brown hair, introduced himself as Mr. Kozinsky, a school guidance counselor. The other, Mr. Donofrio, was an assistant principal. He wore a brown sport jacket, unbuttoned. His gray beard was neatly trimmed. His face was lightly wrinkled, like his jacket. His eyes were brown and kind.

"Hi, Mom," Ben said.

I sat down in the empty folding chair. *Stay detached*, I willed myself. "Hi, Ben. What's going on?"

My child's eyes peered at me from a hard, unshaven face. "I didn't feel well. I feel better now, but I want to go home."

"What about your classes?"

"I don't want to be here. There's just too much pressure. I can't take it anymore."

I was exhausted. I had heard this all before. *Of course you can't take it anymore*, I thought. *You haven't done your homework in months. Midterms are coming. Why didn't you listen to me?*

And then Ben started to cry.

I looked at my son, sighed, and sat back. I looked at the two men in the room. No one seemed to know what to say. Mr. Donofrio looked at Ben for a minute and waited until the tears stopped. "What's really going on here, Ben? Your teachers tell us you've stopped trying, because you think you're leaving high school anyway. Is that true?"

"Yes," said Ben. His tears turned to defiance. "I'm over sixteen, and I don't have to be here anymore."

"We know you don't *have* to be here, Ben, but it's really best for you. It's a very difficult world without a high school diploma, you know."

"Not for me," said Ben. "I'll be fine. I'm smart. I already know what I need to know."

There was that superior attitude again. Lately I'd seen it a lot. I hated it.

Mr. Donofrio looked at me. I held his gaze and raised my hands in surrender. A small motion, a sign of helplessness. I had heard this before; I'd fought this battle on many fronts. I was out of ammunition. He shifted his focus to Mr. Kozinsky, then back to Ben. "All right," he said. "So, then, what are your plans? Are you going to work? Do you plan to ever complete your education? What?"

Ben looked at each man and then at me. He hesitated.

The dynamic had changed somehow. *Three adults to one Ben,* I thought. *He's outnumbered for the first time in ages. Maybe he'll listen to reason now that it's coming from a united group of grown-ups.* I felt protected. For a few blessed moments, I was not alone. The power had shifted.

Ben seemed less sure of himself—for a moment. Then he took in a breath, sat up straighter, and spoke. His expression hardened, his eyes seemed to stare through me now. "Well," he said, "I want to travel. I want to go around the country and meet people. I think *that* is a real education, not high school classes."

"Ben," said Mr. Kozinsky. "Where will you sleep? How will you eat?"

"I'll go to the ATM machine and get out money when I need it."

What? This was it; I'd reached my limit. "Oh, you will, will you?" I was trying hard to sound calm but inside I was a knot of frustration. I'd heard this plan before from Ben, but never thought it was so real to him that he'd tell the guidance counselor about it as if it could really happen. I lashed out. "If you don't finish high school, there will *be* no money to take out from the ATM. Not from *my* money. I *work* for my money."

"So I'll earn my own money!"

Mr. Donofrio and Mr. Kozinsky exchanged glances. Then Mr. Kozinsky said gently, "And how will you do that, Ben?"

"Easy. I'll knock on people's doors and ask if they want any chores done. I'll dig a ditch. I'll watch their children." His voice was confident but his eyes were empty. His words were meant to be reassuring but they frightened me. "Don't worry," Ben said. "I've got this covered. I'll be fine."

But I *was* worried. In my head I considered a number of choice responses, all designed to point out the lack of logic in this scheme. I envisioned my son, dirty and unkempt from his wanderings, knocking on random doors asking for work. I imagined what my own response to such an uninvited visitor would be. I'd lock all the doors. I'd tell him to go away. I'd call the police if he didn't leave.

What is happening to my son? When will he get over this? Is this Ben talking, or is he stoned? He didn't seem stoned. He seemed focused, convinced of the success of his spotty plan, and ready for a heated debate. He looked stubborn. He looked obsessed.

He looked a little bit—crazy.

3

THERE MUST BE A
REASONABLE EXPLANATION

> My father was an alcoholic. Each day when I would come
> home from school, I would find six-packs of beer piled up in
> the refrigerator. He got divorced from my mother when I was
> six. One morning I saw my mother crying. She told me that
> my father left a message on our answering machine saying that
> he loved us, and goodbye.
>
> —Ben, ninth-grade essay,
> "After All These Years," November 1996

It's hard for me not to see Ben's life in two parts: before the illness, when everything seemed manageable with normal parenting skills—and afterward, when all hell broke loose. Hopefully, now he's in a third phase: recovery. I remain so grateful that he's doing well. But I am still, on occasion, haunted by the child he was, the child we lost. That person is still inside of Ben, peeking through the cloudy veil of schizophrenia and the medications that keep it under control. Like all parents, I miss the baby I once had. But there's more. I also mourn the man he might have become, if not for the illness that crashed into his path, forcing him to take other roads—unknown and sometimes terrifying roads.

There are predictable stages families go through when a member begins to exhibit signs of mental illness. One of the earliest of these is called *normalizing*. We look for reasonable explanations for the changes in the person we love. We think it is under our control. We believe we can fix everything, change the person back, if only we can figure out the logical reason for what's happening.

This much I know: a boy whose father disappears without a trace is bound to have a harder time growing up. For the first fifteen years of Ben's life, I believed that any rough spots could be fixed with patience, structure, therapy, and our love.

William disappeared from our lives when Ben was six, and we didn't know where he was or even if he was alive, for eight years after that. It took four additional years before Ben and Ali saw their father, broken by his addictions but hoping to begin again, in person.

I had wondered, even walking down the aisle in 1981, if I had chosen the wrong man to marry. I wonder, to this day, if maybe his genes were somehow flawed and I should have been able to see the signs. I'll never know the answer to that, but it's the question I am asked most often: "Does schizophrenia run in the family?" I'm not even sure why it matters, except that the questioner wants some kind of assurance that it can't happen to his or her child.

The answer to that question is no. It does not run in my family. My parents, grandparents, eight aunts and uncles, and twenty-six first cousins are all mentally healthy. Of all the many children in the next generation of second cousins, only one has the same illness, but attributed to a birth injury. On William's side, there's no way to tell. He was an orphan, born during World War II, and his father's identity is unknown. He has two children from a prior marriage, and both are fine. William's only symptom of imbalance is his alcoholism, and I was too inexperienced with that illness to see the truth until well after our wedding.

The short story of our marriage and divorce, then, is only significant in that the lack of a father seemed to be the most logical explanation for any symptoms of anxiety in Benjamin as he grew up. Could Ben's sensitivity, his difficulty with transitions, his inconsistent focus have been early signs of the mental illness to come? Could we have started treatment earlier, caught the illness in the early stages? Psychiatrists are still debating this point, and so am I. For how were we to know? And would I have believed such a diagnosis?

William and I met in Los Angeles in February 1981. He was charming, attractive, British. At the party where we met, he was the only grown man who got down on the floor to play with the hostess's toddler son.

I was in L.A. to try to make a living as an actress and singer, feeling the uncertainty of show business very strongly by that point. My heart kept telling me that there had to be more to life than just booking your next gig. I was emotionally ready for more, for a real life offstage. I wanted babies even more than I wanted a husband. Husbands scared me; motherhood did not. Still, I longed for the whole package of a conventional family.

Six months later we were married and had moved to the East Coast for our new life together. My family was in Connecticut, and that's where we settled. I wanted to give my new husband the gift of my family, of my roots. We both also wanted to start a new family. It didn't take long; before William and I marked our first anniversary, we celebrated the birth of our gorgeous baby boy.

I search now through my mental snapshots of Ben's childhood to see where it might have begun, some signs I might have missed in the earliest years of his life, and all I come up with are reminders of the sweet boy I miss so much. A little anxious at times, perhaps; a little needy after his father disappeared from his life at age six, but who wouldn't be?

This was a baby with a quick smile, a hearty laugh, and a desire to stay awake as much as possible. A toddler whose brown curly hair, warm brown eyes, and incessant curiosity consistently drew smiles from strangers. He was funny, loving, and unstoppable.

Ben's intelligence was clear almost from the start. At three years, he grew bored with any dot-to-dots that had fewer than a hundred numbers— too easy. He dumped puzzles onto the floor for the challenge of reconstructing them without the frame for help. Like most children, he saw the world in his own unique way. Once he told me that he knew where the end of the world is ("the place where you started"). He wanted to know if I could look in his ear and see the ideas he kept in his head. When he saw one of our cats rest his paw on the other cat's head, Ben declared that "he's putting his friendship into her."

Alexandra (soon nicknamed Ali) was born when Ben was almost three. My parents proudly brought Ben into my hospital room. He wore "big brother" scrubs with little cartoons of trains on them, and he held a pink carnation tightly in his chubby hands. Ben immediately asked, "Where is my sister?" and took the flower over to her bassinet. He got up close to his new sister, nose-to-nose. "Hello, my baby," he said. She was *his*.

Ben adored Ali and delighted in making her laugh, building her towers of blocks to knock over, showing her the colors on her mobile. When she was almost one, Ben tried unsuccessfully to help Ali out of her swing and she fell. She was fine, just a bit scared; she quickly stopped crying and moved on. Ben, however, was inconsolable. Even though I assured him everything was okay, he insisted, "But I hurt my little sister. I hurt my little baby." He seemed to feel so much of his world resting on his little shoulders.

So serious, this sense of responsibility. Still, I loved Ben's sensitivity. My friends told me how lucky I was to have such a sweet and generous boy. "He's so good-natured," they said. Later on, that would be his saving grace.

And he would need it. Not long after Ali's first birthday, William's drinking began to escalate. Our marriage had gone through ups and downs, most often related to the degree of William's drinking habits. As his alcoholism progressed, everything went with it: his work, his commitment to being a husband and father, his financial and moral behaviors. Our bank account suffered, and our relationship disintegrated. It wasn't until years later that I found out he had been using cocaine as well as alcohol and pot. All I knew was that our marriage was falling apart.

William and I separated when Benjamin was five years old, and our divorce became final a few months later. William's addictions were beyond my control, and I couldn't see any way out. There was no way to remain married to William and keep my family functional. The divorce was not contested. The court date was the easy part.

Soon after that, it became increasingly clear that William's addictions were running his life. He lost it all: his job, his house-sitting situation, his address, his phone number, his self-respect. Though I was struggling with the mortgage and three jobs, William was much worse off: he was reduced to living in his car. I felt powerless to help him.

His visits to the children became more inconsistent; I always checked his breath for the smell of beer before I let him spend time with them. For weeks that fall, we could not contact him, but occasionally he left messages on our answering machine.

One day in October, not long after a school picnic he had attended at Benjamin's school, he left another message. "Hi, kids, it's Daddy. Just called to tell you that I love you." Little did we know that we would not hear his voice again for more than eight years, nor see him for another four years after that. William simply disappeared from our lives the night he uttered that sentence into our machine. Was he even alive?

When I realized he was gone, I tried to find out where he was. I found William's old date book in a carton he'd left in the garage, and I called everybody in it. While I made these calls, Benjamin sat across from me at the kitchen table, the answering machine between us. My son was hugging his father's datebook, rocking, crying, and pushing the play button on the machine so that he could hear his father's voice—over and over and over. I will never forget it. I hated William for doing this to him.

In the months that followed, I sometimes found myself wishing that he *had* died. I didn't know how to explain this disappearance to my babies. The open-endedness of it was without ceremony, without recovery stages.

There had been no clue, no real farewell. There was no closure for us, as there might have been had William passed away. There was no child support money, and little emotional support from anywhere. People didn't know what to say to us. The kids were always left wondering. They were always left hoping, especially the first year or two after the disappearance.

"Don't worry, Mommy, I'm sure Daddy will call for Christmas," Ben would say. Then, months later, "I'm sure Daddy won't forget my birthday." But of course he did forget—or ignore it. And the questions got harder as the years went on and there were still no answers. Until the big question became: "Do you think Daddy is dead?"

Ali's response was less open than Ben's. No heart on her sleeve. She didn't talk much about her father, but one day soon after his disappearance, when we had the wrong kind of animal crackers in the house, she cried uncontrollably for forty-five minutes. This was not like Ali at all, my girl who had never had a temper tantrum, rarely been without a smile. She didn't go near any men for months after William left, and she wouldn't even hug her grandfather for a while. But she couldn't say why. I don't think she knew why. She was only three and a half.

Ben's emotions, however, never went unexpressed. He'd wake up and tell me he had "dreamed about Daddy coming home and now I hurt all over again." He asked for me to come to Fathers' Visiting Day instead of his grandpa, because "I'd rather have a real mommy there than a fake daddy." A few months later at summer day camp open house, he said he felt shy because "I don't want to make friends that I can't keep for the rest of my life."

Ben kept trying to make sense of his sorrow. One day when he was six years old he told me, "It's like one quarter of my heart loves you, another part loves Ali, and a third part is where I love myself. Those parts feel fine, Mommy. But then there's a part that loves Daddy, and that part hurts all the time. I can't close it up."

It was to be a long twelve years of unanswered questions ahead. The trauma of this open wound in Ben's heart became an easy explanation for any behaviors to come. Any signs of anxiety that appeared as Ben grew up could be explained, in my mind, by the fact that one of his parents had disappeared without a trace.

So if he was a little bit anxious, who could blame him? Lots of children are afraid of the dark. So my son worried sometimes that the house might catch on fire. So transitions were hard for him—from walking through the door at Kiddie Gymnastics or being picked up from nursery school to a predictable bout of anxiety at the start of each school year until he knew his teachers. So what? It always passed, always turned out fine. Not every child with monsters in the closet grows up to develop a mental illness.

Besides, Ben's character remained constant: kind, sensitive, loving. If a child was left out at a birthday party, Ben was the one who went over to say hello—and then made sure the child was included in the next game or activity. During recess, he protected the girls from the bullies who teased them. From fifth grade on, Ben was in constant demand as a babysitter and often as a tutor. He was most effective, in fact, with the children who were considered difficult by others.

The school Ben had attended since first grade was called Nouvelle. One of my jobs was as their drama teacher. Ali started in Nouvelle's pre-school program, and so all three of us went there together. The small white building on a country route in Connecticut became our second home. Nouvelle was small and personal; Ben's entire grade had only sixteen students in it.

In the sixth grade, he was one of a handful of students in his school to be awarded a certificate for his math and verbal skills from the Johns Hopkins University Center for Talented Youth. His IQ score was 148.

Okay, so sometimes he had a hard time focusing. His brain was often in overdrive unless he was fully engaged. In fourth grade, the school suggested Ben be evaluated for attention deficit disorder (ADD). We went to a child psychologist; after eight visits the final verdict was that Ben was (and I quote) "ADD-*ish*," with no need for medication. The therapist said, "I'll talk to the school and tell them what Ben needs to succeed. We'll just work with some behavior modification and special teaching techniques. He's so bright that he'll compensate for any attention deficit, and when he grows up he'll do just fine"—he smiled at me—"as long as he has a good secretary."

I was thrilled. *See, there's nothing really wrong. Ben can't really have ADD if no Ritalin is prescribed.* This strategy worked pretty well for a while. Ben's teachers knew him well and adjusted to his behavior patterns. *See, no problem we can't handle,* I'd said to myself.

I now know that schizophrenia can seem to arrive suddenly, often in the early twenties, in the form of a clearly defined psychotic break from reality—what used to be called a "nervous breakdown." In Ben's case, however, it was to develop as *gradual onset schizophrenia.* That basically means that changes start slowly, looking like symptoms of something else, until the illness finally makes itself clearly, heartbreakingly evident. Two of the symptoms that can be part of the childhood pattern are anxiety and attention deficit.

CHAPTER GUIDEPOSTS

Is Schizophrenia Inherited?

Like many other medical illnesses such as cancer or diabetes, schizophrenia seems to be caused by a combination of problems, including genetic vulnerability and environmental factors that occur during a person's development. Recent research has identified certain genes that appear to increase risk for schizophrenia. Like cancer and diabetes, the genes only increase the chances of becoming ill; they alone do not cause the illness. (From the National Alliance on Mental Illness website, www.nami.org.)

What Is a "Second Hit"?

The epigenetic theory, or the "two-hit hypothesis," is one recent theory about schizophrenia's development. Basically it suggests that genetic or environmental factors (such as frontal lobe damage due possibly to heredity, birth complications, a virus, toxins, or head injury) disrupt early central nervous system development. These structural brain abnormalities set the stage for the possible later development of schizophrenia or other mental illnesses, usually later in life (typically in late adolescence or early adulthood, when cortical connections in the brain fully develop). This tendency can be affected by a "second hit" at that time, such as a major life event or episode of stress. Although stress does not cause schizophrenia, many researchers seem to agree that it can affect the timing of its onset and of subsequent relapses.

Attention Deficit Hyperactivity Disorder (ADHD)

The principal characteristics of ADHD are inattention, hyperactivity, and impulsivity. These symptoms appear early in a child's life. Because many normal children may have these symptoms, but at a low level, or the symptoms may be caused by another disorder, it is important that the child receive a thorough examination and appropriate diagnosis by a well-qualified professional.

All children are sometimes restless, sometimes act without thinking, sometimes daydream the time away. When the child's hyperactivity, distractibility, poor concentration, or impulsivity begin to affect performance in school, social relationships with other children, or behavior at home, ADHD may be suspected. (From the National Institute of Mental Health website, www.nimh.nih.gov.)

Gradual onset can take years and doesn't really begin to escalate until the midteens. That's when the tornado begins to take shape: years of confusion, years of explaining it as something else, years of sticking fingers in the dike, one after another, until you have nothing left to stop the flood. The illusion of control is strong, seemingly hopeful but actually quite hopeless. You can't see what's on the other side of the dike. But in your child's earlier years, you have no reason to suspect any more than what seems obvious. I had no doubt that my son would be fine, that there were just a few bumps in the road, easily explained and manageable.

Ben graduated from eighth grade with several awards of excellence. After eight years in the same school, with the same friends, it would be time to move on. *The end of an era*, I thought. Little did I know. High school was ahead, with changes that I could never have imagined, even in my worst nightmares.

NO ANSWERS

> I was so nervous I was jumping around the room. I have been empty all these years, not knowing much of my father except what my Mom has told me. I was going to have a father again. I hoped that he would come back to live with us again. I knew it wouldn't happen, but I wouldn't let myself believe it.
>
> "Hello?" I said rapidly.
>
> "Hello, Benjamin," he said very politely.
>
> —Ben's ninth-grade essay, "After All These Years"

A psychiatrist I know once told me, "It's extremely hard to diagnose schizophrenia during adolescence. With all the changes in their hormone levels, all teenagers are a little bit mentally ill." He smiled as he said it, but it really wasn't a joke. That statement had a great deal of truth in it. What parent hasn't said, as the high school years begin, "Who are you and what have you done with my child?"

And so, the events of Ben's first two years in high school may not seem extraordinary. They can be, and were, explained away as a result of teenage rebellion, hormones, growing pains, experimentation. In retrospect, however, they seem more significant. In light of what I later learned about early signs of mental illness, the changes in Ben now form a classic picture of predictable trouble. At the time, I knew nothing about that. Neither, it seems, did any of Ben's teachers, advisers, or psychologists. We all, instead, tried to handle the challenges in conventional ways: discipline, consequences, limits, academic advice. And doesn't that make sense, after all? Who would ever witness a series of adolescent mood swings and jump straight to mental illness as the explanation?

Hormones, changes, stress. Three strikes, all at once, as high school began for Ben. A new school, in a new town, with a brand-new set of teachers, friends, and academic expectations. And, that first year, we finally answered the question of what had happened to Ben's father. That year, we located William. Be careful what you wish for.

When Ben left the safety of his K–8 experience at Nouvelle, he begged to go to the Fieldstone School, an exclusive private high school about a half-hour's drive away in New Haven. This school was known for its direct path to the Ivy League. Ben not only passed the competitive entrance requirements but also managed to get a substantial scholarship under a work-study program. There had been other changes, too: both of my parents, Ben's only grandparents, had died. Ben's friend Simon, from the Big Brothers program, had moved to Los Angeles after five years of being involved in Ben's life. Many losses in a short time.

Orientation went fine . . . until Ben tried out for the soccer team and didn't make the cut. At Nouvelle, all he'd had to do to play a sport was express an interest in it. Reality check number one. Then, there was the stress of making new friends. It took only two weeks for the anxiety to set in, for Ben to say he didn't like the other kids and they were "all against me." *All against him?* That sounded so strange to me. I reassured myself: *It's got to be just a temporary phase.*

But it wasn't. My popular, sociable child began to withdraw at school. He was invited to parties, but never seemed comfortable. Academically, he continued to be rather disorganized, and now the faculty concessions that had been made for his "ADD-ish" tendencies at Nouvelle were perceived as babyish. He was expected to motivate himself, go for help if he needed it, figure it out.

There was plenty of help if he asked for it, but he seldom did. When Ben failed to write a proper thesis essay, his English teacher met with him after school and carefully explained the process from outline to finished product. Ben listened patiently, said "Thank you," then came home, ripped up the teacher's notes, and threw them away. "Those were her ideas, not mine," he said. "I have to do it my own way."

I chalked all of this up to attention deficit, which technically it was. I read book after book on how to help your child work with these tendencies. I was on the phone often with Ben's academic adviser as we tried to find a way to communicate to Ben that help was available and not a source of shame. But the academic stress was getting stronger, and all the stories I'd heard about success with ADD medication now convinced me that this might be the right move after all. I tried without success to get Ben to consider the idea. He wouldn't hear of it.

"I'll figure it out my own way, Mom. Don't worry. I've got it under control."

"Stubborn" was the word used over and over to describe Ben's reaction to any suggestions for help. Somehow, he managed to get decent grades at first, but it was clear that he still lacked the organizational skills—and, perhaps, the motivation—to achieve consistently. More importantly, the stress he was creating for himself by doing so many things at the last minute was making him difficult to live with at times. He was his good self—kind, sweet, cooperative—if the topic was anything other than school. When it came to academics, however, his defenses were up and his temper flared.

I figured that since Ben was struggling academically, he simply wasn't feeling good about himself in that particular world, and that he was just one of those kids who found his true acceptance outside of school. Luckily, Ben did find a place to belong, the youth group at our temple. So, while he was struggling at Fieldstone, he was thriving on the weekends. The phone rang constantly for him, and he was invited and welcomed everywhere within youth group activities, both official (meetings, events) and unofficial (parties, sleepovers).

So, I thought, *he's just one of those kids who find their niche elsewhere. Perhaps it's just a matter of time before he gets comfortable at school, too.*

And always underneath, there was that gaping hole of uncertainty for our family: what had happened to William? Eight years after a death, there might at least have been some closure. There might have been a timetable for recovery to alleviate the sense of loss that never seemed to heal in Ben. There were only a few people left in our lives who had even known William. My children didn't have the warmth of stories to keep their father's memory alive. Other than some pictures, a few moments of video footage, and the birthday cards he'd signed when they were babies, he was an unreal figure, a dim memory.

If I could just find him, or find out what happened to him, maybe there could at least be some closure for all three of us. In the eight years since he left, we had called everyone we knew, given information to the investigators hired by the companies to whom William had been deeply in debt. He seemed to have left no trace.

"This is like widowhood, without the emotional support and without the Social Security benefits," I told my friends. One of them answered, "Well, why don't you have him declared legally dead? Maybe at least the kids could get survivors' benefits." This possibility spurred me into action. It was after a long wait in line at the Social Security office that I got the news that made me feel as if a ghost had risen from the grave: William was not only alive, he was in this country. After eight years of no activity in his official records, a loan application had just been filled out using his Social Security number.

So many feelings fought for attention inside my head: shock, anger, gratitude, curiosity, relief. But I knew one thing for sure—I had to find him.

It took only $155 and one Internet search by a private investigation firm to locate him. William was in Oregon, and the firm had even found his phone number. I held it now in my hands. My shaking hands.

That night, after the children were asleep, I dialed the number. I didn't think. I couldn't think. I just punched those numbers, like plunging into a cold swimming pool instead of edging in from the ladder. William answered the phone. This was too strange to be happening.

"Hello?" The voice was unmistakable.

"William?" My throat was dry.

"Yes, who is this?"

"It's Randye."

"Randye? *Who* is this?"

He doesn't even remember who I am? Now some color came back into my ghost-white feelings. Now I was angry—and also oddly amused. Now I could talk. "Your ex-wife, remember? The mother of Benjamin and Ali?"

The briefest of pauses. Caught by shock. Still, I had the upper of two very weird hands. "Where did you get this number?" he asked. I heard the suspicion in his voice.

I took a breath. "It doesn't matter. I just want to talk to you. I don't want anything from you. I just thought you might like to know how your children are."

A longer pause. I could almost feel his relief over the phone. "Of course, luv. How are they?" As if he'd just spoken to me last week.

William and I talked for over an hour. I did not think, I didn't let myself feel. The story of where he had been for the past eight years? Back to England, where it "didn't work out," off to Greece to "keep a mate company on holiday," then back to the States. Yes, he'd been working for cash under the table. Yes, he thought about us every day, but he felt too guilty to call. Yes, he was living with a woman, but she was "impossible to live with." Yes, he kicked himself all the time for what he had done. In the end, he thanked me for calling him. He said he'd love to speak to the children if they were willing.

We hung up. I finally breathed, then had a surge of energy propelled by too many conflicting thoughts. I paced around the house, letting them wash over me.

How am I going to tell the kids? What does this mean? Will the closure help Ben? Can it heal him? Will it open Ali up to feelings she's hidden for almost all of her life?

I waited for a day to get these thoughts—and a plan of action—together. I decided to begin with a sort of starter thought, like a vaccination against the shocking news. Casually, in the car on the way to the mall, I told Ben and Ali that I had found a new Internet service that might be able to locate their father.

"Really?" Ben asked.

"Yes, and I think I'm going to talk to them. It may not work, but it's worth a try."

"Cool."

That was the easy part. I let two more days pass. I sat the kids down on my bed that evening and said, "I have something to talk to you about, guys."

Ben looked at Ali, then at me. "What did we do wrong *now*?"

"Are we in trouble?" Ali asked.

"No." I laughed. "Not this time. It's about that search I told you about. Remember?"

They nodded. Ben picked at a thread on my comforter. Ali was inspecting her fingernails.

"Well, it worked," I said. "We found your father."

They both looked up at the same time, and at each other. Then they both burst out laughing at the same time. "You're kidding!" said Ali.

"Nope." I filled in the details, then, as best I could.

"Can we call him right now? Can we?" Ben said.

"If you want to."

Ali's face was suddenly still. "I don't want to talk to him."

"That's okay," I said. "You don't have to. But you can listen if you want." We went into the kitchen, and I dialed William's number. Ben was right beside me, ready to grab the phone from my hands. *What if William won't answer the phone? Is this too soon? Should I have set up a time for this?*

But William was there, and Ben excitedly took the receiver from me. I picked up the extension phone to listen in. There was no way I was going to let this man say the wrong thing to my son.

The conversation was awkward, at first. William had no idea what to say. It was Ben who took over and tried to make William comfortable. "I like your accent, Dad," he said. "You sound like John Lennon." Then they talked about the Beatles for a while. "So, do you have any pets? What's your girlfriend like, Dad?"

William laughed then, and said, "Whoa! Hold on, son!" But he answered all of Ben's questions. And Ben continued to ask them, in a manner that was curious, polite, and charming. Not the least hint of anger or resentment. He was just glad to be talking to his dad. *I am so proud of this boy.*

Halfway through the phone call, I saw Ali pick up an extension phone, too. She kept her hand over the mouthpiece and listened.

William and Ben talked about school, and Oregon, and our cats. They kept talking. Suddenly William said, "Benjamin, I have to say something to you."

"What, Dad?" It seemed as though he couldn't say that word often enough.

William hesitated, took in a breath, and plunged. "Listen, Ben. I know I've been a terrible father to you. I'm so sorry that I left you the way I did. I was wrong, and I think about you and your sister all the time. Your mummy was very brave to call me, and I'm glad she did. I'm going to keep in touch with you now."

Ben glanced at me, then turned away as if to keep his father all to himself for a moment. "That's okay, Dad."

That was worth every penny of the hundred and fifty-five dollars. No matter what else happens.

Then William asked, "Is Ali there? Can I talk to her?"

Ali looked at me, uncertain. I nodded. "I'm here," she said, in a thin voice very unlike her.

"Sweetheart!" said William. "How are you?"

"Fine, thanks." She let our cat climb into her lap and stroked him. That seemed to soothe her.

William repeated his apology to Ali, and she said, "Thanks." That's it. But she had a smile on her lips—a little one—and looked a bit more relaxed. "I love you, sweetcakes," her father then said, using the babyhood nickname he'd called her back when he'd been a real father.

Ali's face froze. "Um . . . okay. That's good." Later on she told me, "I didn't know what to say to that, Mom. I wanted to say something mean

like, 'Yeah, well I don't love you,' but I didn't want to hurt his feelings."
My babies. They took the high road.

Ben wrote about this, too, in his essay for English class:

> Ali didn't have much of a reaction, except silence. I could see on her
> face what I felt at the time. We were confused. He appeared to be a
> loving man, and I wondered why he hadn't called us earlier. I knew.
> He was *sober* now, and that was why. It was the disease that stopped
> him from calling us. He thought he could run away from it all, and he
> couldn't. I still sometimes wish that he would come back, sobered up,
> and we could live happily ever after, but it won't happen.

The mystery, at least, was over. *Now*, I thought, *my children can begin
their healing. Ben's got to feel better after this breakthrough.*

But although getting some answers about William was a good thing,
for sure, it worked no magic. After that night, we received an occasional
letter or phone call, but more often than that he was unreachable again.
Still, I hoped that the answer to the question of what had happened to William would at least serve to help Ben's self-esteem. I thought I'd found an
answer. But it made very little difference, after all.

As the end of his freshman year approached, Ben was given the option of transferring to our local public high school, or of making a plan to
help him succeed in the tenth grade at Fieldstone. To my great surprise, he
opted for the latter. Together with his adviser, the three of us formulated
a plan that would put Ben in regular math instead of honors, and include
an acting class instead of an extra academic one. We were all hopeful that
he would learn from the "mistakes" of his first year and make good use of
a fresh start in the fall.

So ninth grade was not really a crisis but definitely a warning. It seemed
to be under control. My only nagging doubt was this: *What if he really does
have ADD, and what will happen if it goes untreated?* Ben would not even consider the idea. "Stop telling me there's something wrong with me!"

That summer, Ben spent lots of time with his nonschool friends and
also worked in the Fieldstone bookstore as part of his work-study scholarship arrangement. *Anything that isn't academic*, I thought, *will be a relief.* He
worked hard in the store but remained withdrawn on the Fieldstone campus. And even without the pressures of homework and performance, he
didn't make many friends at work. When I'd come to pick him up, he was
almost always off by himself.

I scraped together the money to take the three of us to Club Med for
a week. Ben managed to find a group of friends: the ones who slept all day

and spent the evenings drinking alcohol if they could find someone willing to buy them drinks.

Ben is drinking. I was livid. *With an alcoholic for a father, you'd think he'd know better. What is happening to him?* One more change. One more step away from the Ben I thought I knew.

At home, arguments became more frequent. I set rules; Ben hated them. He wanted to apply for a job at the mall; I said there would be no job if he could not get his grades up. Another reason to hate me. He started sleeping down in the basement, claiming he needed the privacy; I let him.

It's just a phase. But this seemed so extreme. Changes were coming faster than I could absorb them, react to them. *Is he sad? Is he lonely? Is he drinking? Despite all my careful parenting, will he end up like his father?*

Sophomore year started, as they all did, with new resolve and the promise of a clean slate. The first set of report cards in November reflected that Ben was eager to please and to do well, but that his anxiety about doing so was getting in his way. One teacher suggested that Ben might have a reading disability. I thought she was right, especially after the night I'd looked in on Ben, lying on his bed, actually trying to get through a chapter in his British History textbook. Twenty minutes later, I'd checked in again, only to find Ben still on the same page—and in tears. "Mom," he said, "I keep reading the same page and I don't understand it. I can't remember one thing."

He sounded so frustrated, and I felt his hurt along with my own relief that he was, at least, admitting he was having some trouble. "Well, Ben, let's get you some help with that. I'm sure you just need to go over it with someone who does understand it and can help figure out how you can, too."

Ben's eyes flashed instantly with anger. "No, Mom," he replied. "I am *not* doing that. I only tried to read it in front of you tonight to *prove* to you that no matter how hard I try to study, it's *impossible* for me to get this. I am not reading this again. I'll pass the course myself."

Why, oh why, is he so stubborn?

Ben refused to be tested for a reading disability, turned down the very idea of getting help. Although many teachers still praised his "keen intellect and delightful enthusiasm" that year, Ben's grades continued to fall. So many ways for me to feel helpless.

Now there were two additional concerns: teachers began to comment on Ben's increased mood swings and on his need for isolation. He seemed to swing from a desperate need for approval, during which he would be overly enthusiastic, to a desire for solitude, when he became overly withdrawn.

This was scary. Ben needed help, and he was refusing it again. How do you force your child to accept help he says he doesn't need?

So here was the list of worries: ADD, reading disability, isolation, rebellion, mood swings, and alcohol use. Then, in February, a new item to add to it: getting high.

Marijuana became the new "reasonable explanation" for the next couple of years, as the Ben I knew began to disappear even more deeply behind too many layers of strange.

MARIJUANA: 1998

Ben had been looking forward to a temple youth group trip to Washington, D.C., where his class would join many from the state and around the nation for a weekend of education, lobbying, and being with other teens in hotel rooms without their parents (the main attraction). I sent him off with great hopes. He was always at his best when around these kids, and he always returned more like his old self. The chaperones on this trip, including our rabbi, were among Ben's greatest fans.

We didn't hear from Ben the entire weekend, which I took to be a good thing. *No news must mean he's doing well.* I expected to see Good Ben getting off the bus when I picked him up—laughing, joking with his friends, and hugging them good-bye. But no. Instead, I saw an exhausted Ben with eyes at half-mast, sharing just a few half-hearted farewells.

There was also on our rabbi's face an unmistakable look of disappointment. He pulled me aside and told me that we had to talk about Ben's behavior over the weekend. Evidently Ben had stayed up through most nights, and he was so disdainful of the lobbying process and so tired that he had *fallen asleep* on the floor of the congressman his group visited. I was shocked, embarrassed, and livid. Club Med I guessed I could justify: the wrong crowd, too much freedom on vacation. But an educational trip to Washington with his "good" friends? How could he blow it like this? This was not my son.

It wasn't until a few months later that I found out that Ben had discovered pot on this weekend. Still, while drug use explained his behavior, I couldn't explain the sudden drug use itself—especially not in this situation, which had always been such a source of joy and pride for Ben. This was the only group of friends and superiors in which he had felt totally accepted. Now, even this was changing. What was left to hold on to?

Getting desperate to find another place for Ben to feel some success, I gave him permission to take the job he had been offered at Discs, a local record store, after school. *If he does well there, his increased self-esteem might transfer to his academics.* I was starting to sound like a broken record, even to myself.

At first, it looked like it just might help. Ben was so enthusiastic about work, about a new chance for success, that it was almost a miracle. He dressed carefully, showed up on time, welcomed the responsibility, and earned Employee of the Month the first time at bat. He had charmed more customers into purchasing a Discs membership card than any other employee there. Thinking that maybe all he had needed was this hint of manhood, I breathed easy for a few weeks. *If only there were a crystal ball to show me he'll grow up to be fine, no matter how nuts he makes me on the way there. I can manage anything if I know he'll come out of it all right.*

But then the complaints and excuses began. First: "They don't pay me enough. Why am I just getting minimum wage? It's not fair." Or: "It's okay if I'm a few minutes late." Then: "There's a meeting of all employees this morning. I don't think I should have to go. The meetings are stupid." And: "I don't like the dress code. I should be able to dress any way I want to. It's a free country."

This same pattern, yet again. *Why doesn't anything stick?*

Then there was Lindsay. Ben had found a girlfriend, and they were becoming each other's entire world. Lindsay was a slight, rather shy girl, one year older than Ben. She wore little makeup and her light brown hair was parted simply in the middle, long and straight. She dressed in retro-hippie style: long skirts or simple jeans and T-shirts, necklaces and bracelets made of beads. She was not just a vegetarian, but a vegan—so she ate nothing derived from animals: no milk products, no eggs, not even honey.

Lindsay attended our local public high school; she and Ben met at a party. Their relationship seemed normal enough; it seemed like something I could handle. I knew the rules for teenage love, after all: *Set the limits, and then let them have their love. Don't turn them into Romeo and Juliet by saying anything negative. Let it run its course.* I thought, in fact, that having a girlfriend might help Ben. He seemed under so much stress all the time, much of it self-created. Perhaps this would help him settle, be less anxious. Of course, I had said that about Discs, too. And youth group.

By that April, Ben's track record at Fieldstone had settled into a familiar pattern: homework completed always at the last minute, if at all. Teachers could not understand why Ben wasn't learning from the stress he caused himself. He was well liked by many of these teachers, though, and everyone seemed to be rooting for him to succeed. His English teacher summed it up in the most positive way she could:

> Ben is a bright, original boy battling tension, disorganization, distraction, and plain worry most of the time. He needs calming and reassuring influences to help him achieve a suitably quiet mental setting.

No kidding. My child was not learning from his mistakes, and things at home were getting even worse. Despite being in love with Lindsay, Ben's anxiety level was high, his mood swings frequent. He was argumentative almost all the time now. I never knew what to expect. If I told him to take out the garbage, he might do it cheerfully or he might insist that he wasn't my slave. If he told me his homework was done, I could no longer believe that he had told me the truth. I was losing the son I'd known, more and more.

Most of the time now, Ben didn't seem to respect me. Even worse, he sometimes didn't even seem to *care* about me. Perhaps the most disturbing thing of all was that he seemed not to care about anything. If I took away his allowance, he coped with less. If I refused to let him practice driving, he had Lindsay drive him. If I grounded him, he just stayed in his room. I was running out of ammunition for discipline.

Ben completed tenth grade at Fieldstone, but he failed British History despite our best efforts. Somehow he managed to pass the other classes, with grades ranging from B− to D+. But all along the way, he refused help. He knew better than anyone else. He was *fine*.

His English teacher was brutally honest. She gave Ben a C+ but evaluated him this way:

> Ben likes ideas, he likes to fight for them, and he likes the whole process of getting fired up for interesting debate. Given such strengths, Ben should be and could be an excellent English student. Problems beyond his school life get in the way and distract him so much that there are times when he can't concentrate at all. He needs tending. He's alone too much and can't find his way to seek help. Whenever he has come for help, he's been surprised at how efficiently he can take and use it. He has so much promise and so little joy of it. He shouldn't be left to struggle as much as he does.

She had hit the nail on the head—but it felt to me as if she had hit me on the head, too. *What does she think I'm doing, not tending my own son? Sometimes I think that's all I do. Who does she think she is?*

The teacher clearly cared about Ben. I was grateful for that. But she had also judged his family life without once talking to me about it.

Ben himself wasn't willing to talk anymore, and he was getting through by the skin of his teeth. His choice was to transfer to our local high school, where he reasoned things would be a cinch for him, compared with the rigors of private school.

We met with the Trumbull High School adviser to plan for the fall. Mr. Zachowski was a gentle but no-nonsense man who fortunately had Ben pegged from the first moment they met. Ben wanted to "convince" everyone of how fine he was, but Mr. Zachowski was no pushover. Ben seemed interested in nothing except getting through with school, getting by.

"Want to play saxophone in the band next fall, Ben?" Mr. Zachowski asked.

"No thanks, that's for dorks."

"Do you have any interests?"

Ben stared at his lap. "I like to think. I like to write."

Mr. Zachowski glanced at Ben's transcript. "I see you took acting performance at Fieldstone. Would you like information about the drama club?"

"No, thanks. I'll be fine."

Ben stepped out of the office, and Mr. Zachowski said, "He's very isolated, isn't he?"

That hurt—because he was right. My social son, whose saving grace had always been his love of and for his friends, was showing no interest at all in connecting with anyone. This change was the most frightening thing of all. Ben's *personality* seemed to be disappearing. Nothing came to mind to explain this one, except perhaps marijuana. Could Ben be using more than occasionally? I was watching him carefully, but I couldn't do it every second. Most of the time he didn't look stoned; he just seemed distant. Yes, *distant*. That was it.

But I still wanted to believe Ben when he told me, "I'll be fine, Mom. I'm going to do better. I just need this new start." Another new start. He was beginning in this new school in the fall, and before that he planned to go with our temple to Israel. *Maybe the trip to Israel will bring him back to himself. A month away from me. A month with his old friends. A taste of manhood. Maybe some of it will stick.*

Maybe. Maybe. My world was full of maybes, of hopes, of small victories. In focusing on each day, on each battle, I'd won a few. Ben had finished tenth grade. He had gotten confirmed with his class. He had been supportive at his sister's bat mitzvah. He had some friends left. He had a girlfriend who seemed to love him, and wasn't it natural in first love to cross the line a little, even into obsession?

I had gotten him this far. Only two more years of high school. *Two years until we're out of the woods. There's only so much I can control; let go of the rest. Trust the process.*

If only I could believe the things I was telling myself.

Summer was ahead, and then the new school year. Ben was looking forward to his trip to Israel, and so was I. It might be just the thing to mark a new, and brighter, chapter. *Please let the trip bring him back to the way he used to be. Please.*

4

THE WAILING WALL

With every breath I accept my Judaism.
With every breath I breathe in millions of souls feeling what
     I feel
Asking what I ask . . .
I see with my eyes and heart
Destruction conquered by unity,
And as I left I felt my eyes change from light to darkness,
Leaving me with views of others
And with more knowledge within me than I could imagine.
I grew from experience
As a Jew, as myself, and I slowly become one.

> —Ben, poetry from the Wailing Wall,
> Jerusalem, summer 1998

Ben left for Israel two weeks after he finally broke apart and cried out to me for help. It was as through the iceberg of distance that had frozen around him had finally, painfully, cracked.

It was finals week for Ben. Late one evening, I was reading in my bedroom, propped up against my pillows. Ben came upstairs from the basement, where he was still sleeping at night. He stood in the doorway, facing my bed.

"Mom, can I ask you a question?" Many of our worst conversations began with this opening line.

I put my book down. "Okay."

"How come you still think it's your business whether I do my homework or not?"

Choices occurred to me: *Answer the question or deflect it? Detach or get involved? Humor or anger? Logic or authority?* I settled on my standard answer. "Ben, it's 1 a.m. I am not going to answer that question again. Do your homework. That's the rule. That's your job. If you don't do your job in this family, you don't get to have the privileges."

Ben put his hands on his hips, bracing for the argument. "What if I don't care about the privileges? It's my right to live my life the way I want to."

Here we go again. "Not under my roof it isn't. Go to bed."

"You can't tell me what to do." Louder, angrier.

"Oh yes I can. Go to bed. We'll talk about this tomorrow."

"No," he said. "You always tell me there's no time like the present."

"Ben. Go to bed!" I said, my volume now up to his.

"Hey, don't yell at me! I'm being calm here and you are freaking out."

This is a line I heard from him way too often lately. *Stay calm, in control. Take a deep breath.* I did. "I am not freaking out, Ben. I am angry. I am tired. Go to bed."

"I can't help it if you have an anger management problem."

"I do not have an anger management problem. You have a *responsibility* problem. You have a *listening* problem. *Get to bed.*"

Ben's face was tight, tensed with conflict. He shouted, "You always freak out over nothing. I hate you! I don't want to live here anymore. If you can't respect me and my choices, I'm leaving!"

So I lost it, too. "Go! There's the door."

"I hate you, Mom!" By now, he was crying.

I looked at him for a long minute. The tears seemed manufactured to me, designed to manipulate. Still, it hurt to see them. "Ben, what is this about?"

"You're a terrible mother. I'm moving out. Right now."

"It's the middle of the night, Ben. Where are you going to go?"

"It doesn't matter. You don't care about me. I'll be gone when you wake up."

Oh, God, here we go. This is what everybody warned me about: the intensity of teenagers. Everything will be exaggerated, every rule a matter of life or death. Don't buy into it. Be the sensible one. Breathe. Act neutral.

"Okay, I guess I can't stop you. Good luck. Call me if you change your mind or when you want to come home. But the rules are the rules, and they'll still be here when you return." *Nice and calm.*

He stood there, momentarily robbed of the momentum of the argument. Then: "How can you act so calm, Mom? You don't even *care* about me." A change in tactic.

"I do care, Ben, and I hope you don't run away. But I guess I can't stop you." *Textbook calm. Good.*

"You'll never see me again!" he screamed, and he ran downstairs to the basement. I sat there, stunned. As soon as I heard the door slam, I began to sob. *How long can I keep up this charade?*

I tiptoed to the basement door and heard Ben sobbing on the phone to a friend. I went back to bed and tried to read; I took out my journal and began to write, but the written word was no match for the turmoil I felt. Ben's not doing his homework had been forgotten, but the issues behind it were wearing a tremendous hole in the fabric of our family life, growing ever more ragged as we pulled at them. When would it stop unraveling?

After an hour, Ben came back upstairs and knocked on my door. He was calm, even contrite. "Mom," he said. "I'm sorry. I decided not to run away, and that your rules aren't so stupid after all."

Thank God, a reprieve. Is this the same child who ran downstairs an hour ago? I put my journal aside and looked at Ben. "What made you change your mind?"

"I called Jason and he talked me out of running away." Jason, a friend of Ben's, had gone through some issues of his own a few years before. He was, with help, doing better in school and in life. Ben had been Jason's voice of reason in middle school; now it seemed the tables had been turned. "Well, what did Jason say to you?"

"He reminded me that if I left you, I'd be deserting you just like Daddy did. And I decided I didn't want to hurt you the same way he did." That was the last thing I expected to hear. Ben didn't want to be like his father, whose addictions to alcohol and drugs had driven away any feelings he might have had about deserting us. This was almost worth it.

Then Ben burst into tears again. This time it was different; these weren't tears of frustration and anger. Ben seemed genuinely distraught; he heaved uncontrollable sobs. I was so surprised by this that I couldn't move toward him. I just watched to see what would happen. I hadn't seen him cry like this since he was a child. Ben's body shook. He let out a moan of despair. "Mom, I need help," he said, and he collapsed to the floor in my doorway.

Help. This was the word I'd been praying to hear. I leaped out of bed and went to Ben, putting my arms around his trembling shoulders. "Please help me," he went on. "I think I need someone to talk to. I need to talk about my feelings, but not to you. Please. Help me. I need *someone* to talk to."

I'd waited so long to hear these words that I'd almost forgotten how much I'd hoped for them. *Does Ben mean it, and will he still mean it in the morning? Where do I find the right person to help him? What if I pick the wrong one? Will we have to start all over again?*

I brought Ben over to the edge of my bed where we sat together with my arms around him until he calmed down. Then we talked; I promised him we'd find the right therapist, someone he could relate to. *This could be the breakthrough. This is huge. We're going to be all right.*

The next morning I began the search for a therapist, preferably a male role model who would be there to help guide my son to manhood, along the bridge I had never crossed. And maybe, just maybe, this one could get inside Ben's increasingly isolated world.

We finally found Art, a man with an ex-hippie persona (complete with ragged jeans and ponytail) and a gentle manner that appealed greatly to Ben. Things were looking up. But still, there was a very long way to go. Art had a lot of work to do.

In July 1998, Ben set off on the trip to Israel. Five weeks of freedom for me, if I could just get him on the bus. Always, those last-minute fears. Always, nothing for certain. But he kissed Lindsay good-bye, boarded the bus, and my burden became immediately (temporarily) lighter.

I heard from Ben only twice while he was away. The rest of the phone card I had given him was spent on phone calls to Lindsay. *That's normal*, I thought. *Don't worry: he needs to "not need you" right now.*

Ben returned home in August with the rest of his group. He got off the bus, safe and sound and completely filthy. His hair was long and uncombed, his clothes dusty and wrinkled. All of his friends looked exhausted from the trip, too, but they didn't wear the same blank expression that I saw on Ben's face. He seemed to be looking inward, lost in some private thoughts, while the other teens were shouting excitedly to their parents and hugging their friends good-bye. A few of them hugged Ben, but these farewells were far less emotional than I'd hoped.

In fact, very few seemed to seek him out at all. One of his best friends, Carrie, told me, "Oh, Ben became a real *thinker* on this trip. He was always off in a corner, writing poetry."

"He was? Off by himself?"

"Yeah," she said. "We called him the Deep Thinker. He was different from the Ben we're used to. We still love him, though! Sometimes he read his poetry to us. It was awesome."

This was not the report I had been used to, or wanted. These youth group friends were always the ones who had brought out the most social side of Ben. Among them he'd always been funny, talkative, and affectionate. Whatever this new phase was, I didn't like it. The changes had begun to spill over into his friendships.

Ben, who had previously prided himself on being a good, reliable pal, began to let his friends down after that trip. He made promises he didn't keep. He forgot plans. He didn't return phone calls. If he meant something one day, you could never be sure he would still mean it the next. He was argumentative with them. Ben, who had once lived for his time with these friends, seemed not to care about anyone except his girlfriend.

Ben laughed less, much less. That was the scariest thing of all.

CHAPTER GUIDEPOSTS

More Early Symptoms: Mood Swings and More

Mental illness is often classified as either a mood disorder (such as depression or bipolar disorder) or a thought disorder, such as schizophrenia. The difference between the two types is often exhibited in the cognitive defects that accompany a thought disorder, such as difficulties with concentration, organization of thoughts, and memory.

Symptoms, however, can and do often overlap.

Schizophrenia also affects mood. According to the National Alliance on Mental Illness (www.nami.org), while many individuals affected with schizophrenia become depressed, some also have apparent mood swings and even bipolar-like states. According to the British Columbia Schizophrenia Society (www.bcss.org/2008/07/resources/early-warning-signs), some of these signs are:

- Extreme mood swings
- Noticeable social withdrawal
- Irrational plans and ideas
- Unexpected hostility
- Extreme reactions to criticism
- Shift in basic personality

What to Do

- Be alert.
- Remember that the key is the extreme changes in behavior.
- Educate yourself.
- Get help if symptoms continue.

NORMALIZING

> We decide all this is not really happening and/or there is a
> perfectly logical explanation for these events. We normalize
> what is going on.
>
> —National Alliance on Mental Illness (NAMI)
> Family-to-Family Handout: "Predictable Stages of
> Emotional Reactions among Family Members"

Ben started his junior year at Trumbull High in August. Ali was entering eighth grade then and had grown into a loveliness that always surprised me. Tall now, almost my height. New curves. A wickedly funny laugh. Brown eyes with flecks of light, not at all like the dark brown eyes Ben had inherited from me. "She's such an old soul," said one teacher to me. "Such wisdom in those eyes."

Now there were two adolescents in the house. I braced myself for a double struggle, but Ali's mood and changes never seemed to be unmanageable. Not perfect by any means, but just, well, *normal* trouble. Tears that spilled without warning followed by sweetness and teddy bears five minutes later. "You never let me do anything!" followed by "I love you, Mom," as if nothing had happened. Questioning the rules, but then reluctant acceptance after the law was laid down. Pouting, but only small explosions of emotions.

I must be getting better at this, I thought. *Maybe my expectations are more realistic. Perhaps it's easier for a single mother to raise a girl than a boy. Or Ali just has an easier personality.*

During the summer, we had closed on a new house in the same neighborhood. It was a colonial, with four small bedrooms upstairs. Though I loved our old ranch, I had always wanted to be in a two-story home. The fantasy I'd always had included coming downstairs for breakfast, or Ali or Ben dressing upstairs for the senior prom and then making a grand entrance down the staircase. I could picture those scenes in this house.

The kids had also been thrilled to discover that there was an in-ground pool in the backyard, and plenty of level space there for basketball and soccer. Now we could really be the house where all their friends gathered. I envisioned laughing young men in sweaty T-shirts shooting hoops in the driveway, kicking a soccer ball across the backyard, coming into the kitchen for cookies and milk. I saw teenage girls and boys gathered by our pool, throwing each other in the water, flirting and splashing.

This way I can keep the kids home. I will know where they are. We'll be the gathering place. At the time, this seemed like a really good thing.

There was also a bedroom downstairs in the finished basement. Ben fell in love with the idea of living down there, even though he would have to come upstairs to use the bathroom. "It'll feel like having my own apartment!" he said.

The illusion of independence, I thought. *That just might work.*

We didn't actually move in until our ranch sold in October. This gave us time for transition, for packing up the memories of the past ten years of our lives. For Ben, this brought with it a revelation.

When Ben was packing up his things, he came to me with a picture he'd found in his desk drawer. He said he had stared at it for a long time. It was of him with his friends from youth group. In this photo, Ben was smiling, his face open and full of life. He had his arms around his friends, and theirs were around him. Had this been taken only a year ago?

Ben looked at me, his younger self in his eyes, and said, "I forgot how happy I was then."

This was true. He *had* been so happy. And he did seem to have forgotten. "Mom, I'm going to take a walk. I don't know why I'm not spending time with these kids anymore. Because I want to. I really was so happy then. I just can't figure it out."

I can't either. "Okay, honey," I said.

Ben put the photo on the kitchen table, staring at it for a few more seconds. Then he looked up at me. "Mom, what is *happening* to me?"

This hurt more than any outburst of his ever had. *Oh, honey, I wish I knew.* "I don't know, sweetie. But I know you can be happy again. Let me know what you come up with."

Ben went out for that walk but didn't come back with an answer; he called Lindsay instead. He did not go back to youth group after that day. Despite his own discovery of the happiness he had lost, despite his desire that day to reclaim it somehow, he never found the way. Instead, his behaviors continued to grow more unpredictable.

Ben's year at Trumbull High went quickly from promising, to bad, to worse. Different place, increasing problems. Ben's grades started out high and then fell. With just a few exceptions—Lindsay and a few of her friends—he became more and more isolated. Sometimes he came out of his shell to talk to me. He loved endless discussions about God, the state of the world, or philosophy. Once we spent an hour dissecting Bob Dylan's lyrics; on another evening he read me some of his poetry. At those times he would say, "Mom, you're really smart. I'm so lucky to have a mother I can talk with about real ideas, not the bullshit everyone else talks about."

Cool, I would think. *My son appreciates, at least, my intellect. I'll take what I can get. Maybe that's the one connection we can rebuild on when he gets over this phase.*

I hung onto that hope, because the "bullshit" we *couldn't* seem to talk about included the practicalities of his real life: grades, plans for college, ideas for his future, the fact that his entire roster of friends had been replaced by a single girlfriend.

The changes in Ben rolled ahead: strange behaviors, more excuses. The clothes on his bedroom floor were getting wrinkled, filthier by the day, sometimes even moldy. His answer was, "What does it matter if my clothes are clean? It's not fair for the world to impose that rule on me. I can dress the way I want to." Ben was also showering less and less, refusing even to wash his hair, much less to cut it. "I'm growing dreadlocks, Mom. They need the oil from my scalp to form right."

The need to study? "That's just stupid. It's under control, Mom. I don't need to do the homework. I already know everything I need to know. There's not much high school can teach me anyway."

Ben was angry almost all the time now. Even when we had called a truce, even when I was refusing to engage in battles over the rules, he sometimes had a *hard* look about his eyes when he looked at me. This scared me. Nothing seemed genuine about him anymore except his anger—and while that was genuine, it was mainly unfounded.

I missed our humor the most. It was just gone. Completely gone. The laughter had flown from our relationship. The warmth had disappeared, too. The only people Ben seemed warm to now—this child of mine who had been the most loving child on the playground—were his girlfriend Lindsay and his sister Ali.

In fact, Ben's love for Ali was the most consistent emotion he had within our family. Art, his therapist, had said that this was Ben's saving grace, his love for both of us. It was hard to connect with his love for me, so covered with anger and resentment. But as the threads of his relationship with me grew thinner, this one with his sister seemed unbreakable. I was very grateful for that. At least I had done *something* right as a parent, if they loved each other so much.

Other than that, however, there were no signs that this phase was ending any time soon. Ben's behavior was only becoming more confusing, and not just to me. My brothers and sisters-in-law started to ask why Ben wouldn't "listen to reason." It seemed he had a negative answer for everything, from why he ought to wash his hands or go with the majority vote on a restaurant we chose, to why it was important to stay in school and do well.

If only I could find the reason for the changes. If only I could point my finger at something, some cause, then I would know what to do. There had to be something I could do. I was sure I could fix it, if I only knew why.

So when I discovered that Ben was smoking pot again, it almost seemed like good news. Maybe this was the explanation for everything that was happening. If there was a reason, there had to be a solution.

The smell of incense coming from the basement was the first tip-off. Though Ben claimed to just "like the incense smell," I knew how well it could cover up the more telltale odor of pot. I searched his room and his backpack, whenever either was unguarded. I hated this. I *hated* this. And, in October, I found the evidence. *Shit. I was right.* I did not want to be right.

"Mom, it's not mine!" Ben said. "I was holding it for a friend!"

"Uh huh."

"Really. I was! I have to give it back to my friend. You have no right to keep it. It's not yours!"

"Ben. Let's get this straight. Pot is illegal. It does not belong in my house, no matter who it belongs to. You could be arrested. I could be arrested. Your friend put you in a very dangerous position, even if the pot *is* his, and therefore he's no friend. You will not be getting the pot back, and neither will your friend. It's against the law."

"I hate you! You stole from my room!" Ben said. He ran out the front door.

About an hour later, Ben returned. He had taken a walk, thought about things, and come up with a confession (yes, the pot was his), an apology, and many promises ("I'll never do it again. I promise I'll do my homework. I'll clean my room today, too.").

And he did. For a few wonderful days, Ben kept those promises and seemed to want to make a fresh start with me. I couldn't believe how much better life was when he was behaving like a normal person. We had conversations. He did things the first time he was told. Communication took place without manipulation.

But the pattern had not been left behind. By the end of that month, we were back to more frequent episodes of fighting, tears, reinforcement, and retaliation. I wanted to trust that Ben's future would be brighter, but it was more and more difficult to envision this. It seemed as though things were only going to get darker. There was no reasoning with him, not about school, not about his growing obsession with Lindsay as his only joy in life, not about anything.

And now he was taking refuge in a new cave: his own sense of superiority. "Other kids have to do homework, but I don't. I have a photographic memory. I know everything just by listening in class." Or: "I don't have to practice saxophone. I'm good enough without it. I'm gifted."

I kept searching, and hoping, for that reasonable explanation. One I could wrap my brain around. One I could do something about. *Maybe it's Lindsay. Maybe she's a bad influence. That's it! Lindsay. He has changed in order to please her. It's an unhealthy, codependent relationship.*

Ben had now been dating Lindsay for over six months. He'd begun to change his eating habits to match hers, eventually giving up all animal products, including eggs and dairy. I let it go even though I thought it way too extreme. Pick your battles. Part of me was glad to see that he was, at least, still capable of loving, since very little of his love was coming directly my way.

I really wanted Lindsay to be the problem. I really wanted pot to be the problem. Teen identity crisis. Stress of having no father. ADD. The new house. The new school. Reading disability. Anything. Anything, just so long as I could pinpoint it and know where to search for a solution—and support. I really wanted to believe that this would pass, especially if I found the one thing that would get us through.

Nothing made sense, though. Our confrontations were getting not only more heated but also stranger—and predictably repetitive. Changes in behavior were short-lived, if they happened at all. While Ben was obeying the basic rules such as curfew, manners, and chores, I found myself having to explain and justify them over and over.

But beyond discipline, there were the other changes that frightened me even more. My warm and loving son was becoming even more withdrawn and cold—and not just with his family. This is where his behavior differed from what was considered "normal teenage rebellion." Even Ben's friends commented on how he was changing. It wasn't entirely consistent, which fed my hope that he would come around someday.

I was grateful for things that happened in increasingly rare moments: sincere smiles, hugs, conversations, laughter. Especially laughter. But these things, these traces of the old Ben—they weren't happening often enough.

January passed in relative calm. Ben went to school and got by somehow. He continued to go to therapy with Art. I tried once again to find William, who had by then moved again with no forwarding address. It had been almost three years since that last phone call and letter, and Ben had started asking if he could talk to his father again.

"I just want to call someone Daddy and mean it, Mom," he kept saying.

So maybe that was still the explanation for all this. William's disappearance, still unresolved. That, at least, was something that made sense to me, and something I could try to accomplish. *Maybe that's all Ben really needs*, I told myself once again. *This will be the thing that helps him. This will make the difference. He just needs more closure.*

I sent letters, and made a few calls. Nothing. Then at the end of January, William called us out of the blue.

Ali, now almost fourteen, answered the phone; her eyes widened when she heard who it was. "Mom," she said, covering the mouthpiece. "You'll never guess. It's Daddy!" And she laughed and rolled her eyes. *Yeah. Big joke.* But, to her, it was. She had always chosen humor and indifference as her coping mechanisms, at least externally. She always told me we were just fine without a father in our family.

Ali was polite to William. "Yes, thanks, I'm fine. How are you?" Then she handed the phone to me. William sounded sober, and so we chatted carefully for a while. His ex-girlfriend had forwarded our letter to him, and it had taken him a while to work up the courage to call. I then handed the phone to Ben, who'd been hovering impatiently next to me.

The last time William had called, I'd monitored every moment of the phone conversation for my kids' emotional safety, but this time I let them talk alone when Ben deliberately took the phone down to the basement. *He needs this*, I thought. *This taste of what the other boys have—their father's voice.*

A half hour later, Ben emerged upstairs with a smile on his face and questions to ask me. He seemed almost renewed by the phone call, as though having to report to his father made him more aware of how his own life plans measured up. All this opened the door to a remarkably reasonable discussion about Ben's feelings about William, his hopes and plans to stay in touch with him. Ben also became receptive to hearing what I expected of him, and what was needed to get his life together. I hoped against hope, once again, that a magical turnaround would occur. I had done something right. I had found William once again, and made it possible for a relationship there, no matter how distant or small. Ben seemed happy, even optimistic. I relaxed again, for another week or so.

Once again, that's all the time I got. Ben's moods returned in full force—and worse.

In therapy, Art told me that Ben was "angrily dependent" upon me. That seemed the perfect explanation for his attitude, for his mood swings. But it only made a tiny dent in the difficulty of living with Ben's grandiose and unrealistic plans, his growing though sporadic contempt for me, and those outbursts I could never fully predict or handle.

The bright spot, still, was that he was always nice to his sister. Not exactly close in the way they had once been, since Ben was becoming increasingly self-centered and didn't listen to Ali with the same compassion he had always had. He was full of advice, though—he was always full of advice, because he thought he now had all the secrets of life figured out. The problem was, this advice sounded more and more like bullshit.

It had to be the pot. It *had* to be. I searched his room again, I rifled through his backpack and pockets. I never found any more evidence. Ben swore he had stopped. I never saw him smoke it. But he seemed unfocused almost all the time now, and conversations were more difficult because he strayed from the subject. His eyes seemed clouded over, focused inward. This sure seemed like stoned to me.

If I can just get him off the drugs, I thought, *everything will be all right.* I threatened; I made him sign written contracts. I waited, and I hoped, for him to outgrow this, to learn these lessons himself. But it was not happening. In fact, things were still growing stranger. Ben didn't seem just rebellious anymore; he seemed troubled. His logic began to move further and further from reality.

Ben became obsessed with certain books: *Lost Horizon*, *Siddhartha*, and *Ishmael*, about a gorilla who can communicate his wisdom telepathically. Now, when he engaged me in discussions that were not about his choices, his behaviors, my rules, or my parenting, he talked about philosophy. What is God? How can we change the world? He told me how happy he was that we could talk about ideas and concepts. At first, I welcomed this change. I thought that we had finally found a way to connect. Ben's ideas, however, seemed to be going down only one avenue, and they were seldom backed up by reason.

I approached Art with my concerns about Ben's high dose of philosophy and low dose of reality, and he told me it seemed all of Ben's ideas were straight out of the *Ishmael* books. This was another explanation I could grab onto with relief. *He's just impressionable. It's these books he's reading.* Maybe Ben was just grasping at another straw. He was clearly struggling, but at least I knew where he was getting his ideas. At least he was reading. At least he was interested in *something* other than rebelling against me.

CHAPTER GUIDEPOSTS

More signs I wish I had understood earlier:

- Hyperactivity or inactivity—or alternating between the two
- Inability to concentrate or to cope with minor problems
- Deterioration of personal hygiene
- Extreme preoccupation with religion or with the occult; bizarre behavior
- Irrational statements
- Drug or alcohol abuse
- Rigid stubbornness*

*British Columbia Schizophrenia Society, "Schizophrenia/Psychosis Early Warning Signs," www.bcss.org/2008/07/resources/early-warning-signs.

At Nouvelle, where I was still teaching drama part-time, I was surrounded by other teachers who'd had Ben as a student and loved him. Many of them had, as parents, also nursed their own children through the difficult teen years, and their advice to me was plentiful. They assured me that while Ben was giving me a hard time, he had always been a little off the beaten track and would be fine as long as I was clear about my limits and also trusted him to learn from his own mistakes. They laughed with me about some of his idiosyncrasies and odd ideas. "Ah, that's our Ben," they said. In those moments, I didn't feel quite so alone.

This minor confidence left me in April, when the next crisis struck. Ben decided to drop out of school, two months away from completing his junior year.

IS THERE LIFE AFTER HIGH SCHOOL?

There we sat in the nurse's office: two school officials, one helpless mother, and the son who was slipping away from us all. The three of us tried to reason with him. We pointed out the problems with his plan, the social and educational consequences of dropping out of high school. We presented other possibilities: dropping some difficult classes and making them up in summer school; transferring to the "alternative" high school, where other kids who had lost their way were finding it again; night

Is marijuana use connected with the onset of schizophrenia?

There has been a lot of attention to this question recently. One study from Australia, published online in 2011 in the *Archives of General Psychiatry*, concludes that people who smoke marijuana are more likely to develop mental illnesses, like schizophrenia, faster than they would otherwise. The study specifically states that the onset of the mental illness will be 2.7 years earlier in a marijuana smoker.

In this study, Dr. Matthew Large pointed out that marijuana may hasten the onset of psychotic symptoms in people who are already vulnerable to such illnesses. Marijuana use can also make the symptoms worse.

However, others believe that it's difficult to tell which comes first, the early symptoms of schizophrenia which may drive sufferers to self-medicate, or the drug use itself.

According to *Time* magazine, Marie-Odile Krebs, professor of psychiatry at the National Institute of Health and Medical Research (INSERM) laboratory in France, and her colleagues published a study in June 2010 that identified two broad groups of people with schizophrenia who used cannabis: those whose disease was profoundly affected by their drug use, and those who were not.

school; home schooling; tutoring. I let the two men do most of the talking. I didn't want Ben's automatic "If Mom says it, it must be wrong" response. Nothing got through. Ben seemed more convinced than ever that his plan was brilliant.

"Look, Ben," I finally said. "Maybe you're right." *Am I really saying this to him?* "Maybe you do need some time away from school to figure things out in a different way. But at least finish this year. At least pass the courses you're enrolled in. And then, if you ever do go back . . ."

"But I won't!" he said. The two men looked at me. I saw only exasperation on their faces. They'd used up all their arguments. *Welcome to my world*, I thought.

"Maybe, maybe not. Still, I'd like you to be prepared in case you do decide to return to school. And if you do finish this year, you can take some time off to figure out what you want to do. If not, you're on your own."

"But, Mom!" he said. "You have to support me until I am eighteen. That's the law!"

I'd been warned about this line of thinking at ToughLove meetings. I searched my memory for the right answer. "That only means room and board under my roof, nothing more. Whatever your plan is, you'll get nothing else from me to make it happen—law or no law. If you don't like it, call a lawyer when you can afford one."

I hoped my information was correct. I hoped he didn't call my bluff. I wished this conversation wasn't happening. I sounded tougher than I felt. I wanted to take Ben by the shoulders and shake him until he made sense again. "Finish out the day, Ben. I will think about this at home and we'll talk later."

Ben went back to class, and the adults stayed to talk. Although neither of these men had dealt directly with Ben before, they'd heard a lot about him recently from very concerned teachers. All of them had said they loved Ben but were increasingly worried about him. Ben's behavior was unpredictable. He could not sit still. He spoke with enthusiasm in class but often pushed his ideas onto others instead of engaging in dialogue.

"Ms. Kaye," said Mr. Kozinsky, "I'm so sorry it has come to this. Although we've spoken about Ben to his teachers, we never realized before today just how troubled he really is."

It was a relief to have others in this situation with me, even if only for half an hour.

"All right," I said. "So now you know how bad it is. What can we do?" *We. I love the sound of that word.*

"Well, we have lots of help available here—school psychologists, tutors, alternative programs." Mr. Donofrio took off his glasses and pinched the bridge of his nose between his fingers. "In fact, the options have been presented to Ben several times. But Ben always says he doesn't want them. He seems to think he has all the answers. I haven't seen anyone this stubborn in years. He says he doesn't need help from anyone. He keeps telling his adviser that he's fine."

"Fine." *Hardly.* "Are you telling me that I can't really forbid this from happening?" I said. "What if I get a lawyer?"

"I'm afraid there isn't anything you can do legally. At the age of sixteen, a child in Connecticut has the right to drop out of school."

"Well, can I threaten to kick him out of the house, then? There has to be some consequence I can use to stop this."

"I'm afraid not. Legally, you're responsible for his room, board, and behavior until he is eighteen years old."

I had to support Ben, but I could go to jail if he broke the law. "But that's not fair!" Now I sounded like a child.

"No, it isn't very fair. You're right. I agree, but all we can do is try to convince him to stay in school. We have to reach him somehow."

But I had tried that so many times. I knew how impossible this was. I left the room, dropped my visitor's badge off at the main office, entered my car, and began to sob. Ten minutes later, I blew my nose, started the car, and went home. I spent the week bargaining with Ben; nothing worked.

One week later, his adviser, Mr. Zachowski, called Ben and me into the office to sign the release papers. Numb at heart, I signed off on the end of Ben's high school career. I knew this was idiotic, that it made no sense. I also now knew I had no real say in the matter. Ben was dropping out, no matter what I wanted, what I did.

It was the first of April; in twenty-nine days Ben would be seventeen years old, and no longer a student. I cried in the adviser's office, I cried all the way home while Ben sat in the passenger's seat. He, on the other hand, was incredibly cheerful. "Mom," he said, "thank you so much! You'll see. I'll work hard and save money now. I don't need school. I'm free!"

I wished I could turn the car around and undo the last hour. I wished I could undo the last year. I dreaded having Ben underfoot now that he wouldn't be at school. I hoped he would take this enthusiasm and immediately start looking for work. I didn't want to have to remind him; I didn't want to have to talk any more sense into him.

Underneath all this was a small hope that was my only source of comfort: maybe leaving school might be the Magic Thing. I was always on the lookout for it—the key to what might magically fix Ben. It might be medication for ADD, it might be tougher limits at home, it might be just the right words from the right person at the right time. *Maybe this will turn out to be a great lesson for him. Maybe this will turn his life around.*

But Ben did not look for work the next day. Or the next. Or the next. He claimed he was at a disadvantage because he didn't have his driver's license yet. He said he needed a rest from the stress of school. He said not to worry, he would handle it.

He slept late. He spent time with Lindsay. I told him he now had to be busy forty hours each week. He walked to nearby stores and asked about work, but he was usually dressed in ripped clothing and was not clean-shaven, or even clean. Reminders about proper dress were ignored. "If an employer can't like me for who I really am," Ben said, "then I don't want to work for him. People shouldn't judge you by your appearance."

He was so idealistic. He was so rebellious. He was not going to get employment this way. I wondered if Ben had regrets. He was so unpre-pared for life. He seemed so far removed from reality. I watched and waited for reality to set in somehow, for his money to run out, for him to *suffer* enough.

"But I can't find a job! I don't have a car! Or my license!"

"Well, that's because you let Lindsay drive you everywhere. You haven't been to driving school in weeks." *When did he stop caring about even that? Driving?* I remembered taking the day off from work on his sixteenth birthday so that we wouldn't wait even one extra day to get his learner's permit. He'd been insistent and excited. *Was that really less than a year ago?* "Well," I said, "you need some kind of job you can walk to, then. How about the supermarket?"

"The supermarket? That's beneath me, Mom. I don't want to pack groceries all day in a stupid apron."

"Dunkin' Donuts?"

"No, all my friends hang out there."

"The bank?" *Maybe he could start as a teller. He's so good at math.*

"They won't hire me without a high school diploma."

Is this really the same boy who, a few years ago, willingly and enthusiastically took any job? The same one who babysat, shoveled snow, even learned to make balloon animals so he could work at birthday parties? He was once so ambitious. No job was beneath him. Where is that child? Ben was disappearing, bit by bit, and I couldn't tell when it would stop. I just assumed, somehow, that it would stop sometime. If things got bad enough, Ben would recognize the truth—no matter how stubborn he was.

Finally, things began to look up. The shock of Ben's withdrawal from school subsided, and acceptance slowly took its place as we redefined our family life. Ben found work at last, in a pet store. He seemed to be doing well there even though he kept telling me the chores were beneath him. I accepted a promotion at the radio station where I worked, a shift from afternoon drive time to the morning show. Ben's reaction reassured me; it showed a glimpse of the big brother he still wanted to be. "Mom, that's so great! Go for it. And I'm home in the mornings now, so Ali won't be alone." *He's thinking of someone else for a change,* I thought. *This is a good sign.*

Ben also pursued his passion for writing, something else that seemed like a sign he might be getting better. He worked on his poetry when he wasn't at work, and he and Lindsay began to attend poetry readings at a local coffeehouse called Laszlo's. One night, after Ben had once again told me I wasn't really "in his corner" because I had no belief in his future as a great poet, I softened. I wanted his new life to make at least some sense to me. *Maybe our relationship needs some friendship in it. I can show up for at least one of his dreams.*

So I drove to Laszlo's one night when Ben had said he'd be reading. The place was pretty empty. The decor was Early Greenwich Village. Mismatched chairs and tables, seating for about thirty. Homemade tablecloths. A small stage in the corner, with one barstool and a lone microphone stand. On the wall were paintings and drawings by local high school students; there was even one painted by a girl who had once been a best friend of Ben's. *So he's not alone. Lots of kids hang out here and think it's cool. This could be his community. Maybe he feels at home here.*

The young girl behind the counter, in a long, flowing, hippie-style skirt and peasant blouse, told me that she knew Ben, that he and Lindsay came in there often. His poetry, she said, was hard to understand but sounded very intellectual. She seemed to like Ben, found him both interesting and pleasant. This cheered me.

CHAPTER GUIDEPOSTS

Symptoms Increase

- Irrationality
- Sleeping excessively or inability to sleep
- Excessive writing without meaning
- Indifference
- Dropping out of activities—or out of life in general*

What the Family May Experience at This Stage

- *Crisis/chaos/shock*: Feeling overwhelmed, confused, lost . . . Something catastrophic is going on and we do not know how to deal with it.
- *Denial*: We decide that this is not really happening, or that there is a perfectly logical explanation for these events, and/or it will pass, and so on.
- *Hoping against hope*: The hope that . . . if we make a huge effort it will change everything and our lives will go back to normal.†

An Important Step to Take If You Do Suspect Schizophrenia:

A complete physical to rule out other medical conditions sometimes confused with schizophrenia, such as brain tumors, temporal lobe epilepsy, multiple sclerosis, AIDS, and others.

---

*British Columbia Schizophrenia Society, "Schizophrenia/Psychosis Early Warning Signs."
†Joyce Burland, NAMI Family-to-Family Education Program, class 1 handout, "Predictable Stages of Emotional Reactions among Family Members."

I waited there and drank a cup of tea. Ben didn't show up that night, but at least I'd tried. I'd gotten a glimpse of his new world, and I'd seen that it wasn't so bad. In fact, it brought me back to my own college days, singing folk songs in coffeehouses. I felt a bond with Ben. That was rare. Maybe *here* was a place we could reconnect.

Later, at home, when I told Ben I'd gone to hear him read, his face actually lit up. I hadn't seen that expression in his eyes for quite some time, much less been the reason for it. "Really, Mom? You came to Lazslo's? Thank you! That is so cool."

"You're welcome, sweetheart." For once, the endearment came easily to my lips. I felt normal. It didn't last long. One week later, I gave my son a black eye.

5

THE BLACK EYE

I had never hit Ben before, except once back when he was three. That slap had been an almost involuntary reaction when, from the baby seat of a supermarket cart, he'd grabbed a box of cookies off the shelf and tossed it into the cart where his baby sister was sitting in her infant carrier. Ali wasn't hurt, but she could have been—and I had *warned* him. So I smacked him then, breaking the taboo. I'd chalked this up to primal protective motherly instincts and had never hit him again. Until now, when he was seventeen—and pushed me over the edge.

I'd been holding on for dear life to the thought that somehow we could get through this awful stage of Ben's life. I took comfort in my list of "at leasts":

At least he is working part-time.
At least he has a dream.
At least he has a girlfriend.
At least he talks about getting a GED someday.
At least he takes out the garbage.
At least he is respectful to me in public.

When I lost that final "at least" one afternoon, I lost my fragile sense of control at the same time. We went to the dentist where Ben had been a patient since toddlerhood, for a routine checkup a few weeks after he'd dropped out of school. His teeth, which had been perfect after years of palate expansion and braces, were moving right back to where they'd been before treatment. This time the dentist, Dr. Berman, was insistent.

"Ben," he said, "this is really your last chance here, buddy. If you don't start wearing this retainer again—and wearing it every night—there's no chance that your teeth will stay straight, and we'll have to start all over again with treatment. You don't want that, do you?"

Oh, good, I thought. *Ben responds best to emergencies. Now he'll agree to do this. After all, he doesn't want to start all over. He likes Dr. Berman. He'll listen to him—he always has before.*

Ben looked at the bow-tied dentist and said, "I'm sorry, Dr. Berman, but I don't care. It's my mouth and my teeth look fine to me."

Dr. Berman opened his mouth but no words came out. He looked to me for a response.

"Ben," I said, "you'd better listen to the doctor. Don't you understand? All those years of braces, and all the money I spent, will be for nothing. All you have to do is wear the retainer at night. No big deal. You have to wear it."

Dr. Berman nodded. "She's right, Ben. Come on, think about it."

Ben's eyes took on a hard edge. I'd seen that look before, but never in this office. "Mom," he said, "it's my mouth, and they're my teeth. This is none of your business." Then he added, "I'm sorry, Dr. Berman. You did a great job. Let's go, Mom."

I looked at Dr. Berman and at the receptionist who had overheard this exchange. They looked as shocked as I felt. Ben was already out the door. I followed him out and into the car.

I wanted to make him feel guilty. We drove down Main Street and I reminded my sullen passenger that I had *slaved* to make the monthly payments for his beautiful teeth. "The very least you could do is to not lose ground. All you have to do is put in a stupid retainer at night! I can't be your policeman. What am I supposed to do, check your mouth after you go to sleep and make sure you have the retainer in? Why don't you ever listen to reason? What is the point of rebelling against your own health?" I couldn't seem to help myself. I hated the way I sounded.

I glanced over at Ben; he was smirking. Smirking! He was looking at me like I was a lunatic, and he was the calm one. The superior one, tolerating my unreasonable mood, and just barely. It was all too much. All the months of patience, of waiting for him to come to his senses, of excusing his behaviors, came barreling in. My right hand reached across and slapped him. On the cheek. Hard. *How did that happen?* "Stop it!" I shouted. "What is wrong with you?"

Ben was stunned. He put his own hand to his reddened cheek and stared at me.

"You *bitch!*" he yelled. "You hit me. You *hit* me! You're crazy, you are fucking crazy!"

And my right hand hit him again. I was nearing a red light and stopped the car, but I could not stop my hand. This time the slap landed closer to his eye. "You earned it!" I heard myself scream. "How dare you call me that?"

"But you *hit* me!" he said. "You *abused* me. I'm getting away from you!"

"Fine," I shouted. "Get out of this car. Now. Find your own way home. You want independence, you got it."

"What?"

"Get out. Now."

"Fine!" Ben slammed the car door hard as he ran into the nearby parking lot of a strip mall next to the traffic light. The light turned green and I tore away. I drove for five more blocks and then pulled over. I was shaking. *What did I do? I hit my son! I never hit my children. What did he make me do?*

But I still felt awful. For my own peace of mind, I had to apologize to him. He was acting like an asshole, but that was no excuse for what I'd done. I drove back to the parking lot where Ben had disappeared and caught a glimpse of him; as soon as he spotted the car, he ran and hid behind a building. I waited to see if he'd come out, but he didn't. *Fine. At least I tried.* I drove the fifteen miles home alone, then waited to see what would happen. Maybe a long walk home would bring Ben to his senses.

But Ben got rescued; actually he got *enabled*. He didn't have to walk home after all; Lindsay's family picked him up and took him into their home overnight. There went the lesson. Ben didn't learn anything from this—except now he had more people to take his side. Lindsay's family thought I was a villain and suggested Ben and I go through family therapy. *As though this were* my *fault!*

The next morning, I found myself in my living room facing Ben, Lindsay, and Lindsay's mother. Underneath Ben's left eye was the faint but unmistakable evidence of yesterday's slaps. Yes, there it was: a black eye. There was no swelling, and it looked as though it would clear up within a day or two, but still . . . I had caused visible, physical damage to my baby. He now sported a tangible reason to decide I was an unfit mother. Holding Lindsay's hand, he said to me, "But, Mom, I'm afraid to live here now. I never know when you might hit me!"

I suppressed the urge to scream at him, with difficulty. Still, I found myself surprisingly empowered. For the first time since he had grown taller than I, Ben looked at me as if I were worthy of *respect*—or at least some sort of fear. I rather liked that, to my surprise. This felt *good*. "Ben," I said, "be afraid, then. Be very afraid." *Did I really say that?*

Ben backed down right away.

CHAPTER GUIDEPOSTS

What Is an Enabler?

noun: one that enables another to achieve an end; especially: one who enables another to persist in self-destructive behavior (as substance abuse) by providing excuses or by making it possible to avoid the consequences of such behavior

—www.merriam-webster.com/dictionary

What Is Tough Love?

noun: the use of strict disciplinary measures and limitations on freedoms or privileges, as by a parent or guardian, as a means of fostering responsibility and expressing care or concern

—*American Heritage Dictionary*

With Lindsay's mother serving as mediator, we reached enough of an agreement to allow Ben to return home. We went through another week without incident but with no discernable improvement, either. Just another crisis, followed by a period of peace. But the crises were escalating.

I kept hoping and watching for signs that my son was finally coming around. They always appeared, but how could I know that the hope they provided would turn out to be false, every time? How could I know that something was happening so deep within my son's brain that no matter what solution we tried, we were nowhere near the source of the real problem?

I wanted so much to believe Ben would grow out of this, that it was only a tough phase. Tougher than what other kids seemed to be going through, but still just a phase. It was too hard to think that whatever was going wrong with Ben couldn't be fixed. By me. By a role model. By maturity, natural consequences, tough love, therapy. By anything. By anything.

RUNNING AWAY

There were still two things to try that I thought might fix everything. One was to somehow find a way to reunite Ben with his absent father. What if all this could be cured by getting some closure? The other was to let Ben carry out his plan to live on his own; only then would he learn from the natural consequences of his actions. Then, maybe, he'd stop blaming me for everything.

I'd heard many such stories at ToughLove meetings: "We finally let him go, and he came back to us with a maturity he never would have gotten while we were managing his life." I put much of my faith in natural consequences. Sooner or later, Ben was sure to learn from his own mistakes. The thought of letting him go was liberating—and frightening. He was sorely lacking in life skills, and he was drifting further from reality in his plans.

Ben did leave home several times during the next year. My rules were too much for him. He believed he would do better on his own. He wanted to be a man. He wanted to live his own life. He said I didn't understand him. He wanted to find his father. The reasons kept coming. The results were, sooner or later, always the same: back home to me, with no lasting lesson. The first time he ran away it was a shock, and I fought it. By the fourth or fifth time, I could just hold open the door and let him go.

The first time it happened was late in June, at the end of what would have been Ben's junior year of high school. His being home didn't seem so abnormal now that other students were out for the summer. I didn't see school buses going by. I didn't have to think *Why isn't Ben on that bus?*

That afternoon, I returned home and walked through the side door into the kitchen. Ben and Lindsay were talking quietly near the sink. The minute they saw me, they stopped talking and looked at each other with matching "I've-got-a-secret" looks. "Mom," said Ben, "we have something to tell you."

Oh no. She's pregnant. They're pregnant! I put my bags down on the counter. My mouth was dry. "Well," I said, "what is it?"

"You're not going to like it very much," said Lindsay. "But we've made up our minds."

I hate her, I thought. She has ruined my son's life. "Mom," said Ben. "I'm leaving home. For good."

Not pregnant. That's a relief. Then the words penetrated. "Ben, what the hell are you talking about?"

"Mom, there's nothing for me here in Trumbull. I don't belong. I want to start living my life. I *told* you that." He sounded like a seven-year-old with his matchbox cars all packed, ready to run away from home.

This can't be happening. But let's play it out. Maybe this will pass if I don't make a big deal. "All right," I said. I willed my voice to remain even. "When were you planning to leave?"

"This afternoon."

I sat down. "What?"

Lindsay chimed in. "You know Kenny, who lives down the street?"

I did. Years earlier, when Ben had seemed headed for success, I'd thanked my lucky stars that he wasn't turning out like Kenny. Kenny had dropped out of school. He'd spent a full summer camping out in town-owned parks. He smoked a lot of pot. He and his girlfriend had a child out of wedlock when Kenny was eighteen. He'd work just long enough to buy something he wanted and then quit. Now he was twenty-one, and his prized possession was a refurbished old school bus that served as both his vehicle and his home. When Kenny was in town, this bus was parked in front of his parents' split-level home for weeks on end. Neighbors considered it an eyesore and made no secret of the fact.

"Well, he and his girlfriend and baby are on their way to the Rainbow Gathering and they invited us to come along! Isn't that cool?" said Lindsay.

"Cool?" I said. "I don't even know what you're talking about."

They explained it to me, with the forced patience and hidden disdain of the cool talking to the uncool. The Rainbow Gathering was an unofficial but huge event that emerged in a different state park every summer. This year it was to be held in Pennsylvania. It sounded like a throwback to the late sixties: one to two weeks in the park, communal food, music, spiritual gatherings.

Oh, wow. If that isn't right up Ben's alley. "Ben, you are not going to do this. You have to work."

"No offense, Mom," he said, "but you can't really stop me. I'm going with Kenny this afternoon. I'm already packed. I just wanted to say goodbye so you don't worry."

"But what about your job at the pet store?"

"They said I can take the time off if I want. But I probably won't be coming home anyway. I'm going to hitch a ride with someone from there and start going cross-country. I'm going to try and find Daddy."

Oh my God. "Both of you?"

Now, for the first time, even Lindsay seemed confused by Ben's plans. "No, Randye," she said. "I'm coming home after a week. I have to start my summer job. If Ben doesn't want to come home with me"—and she shot him a look I couldn't decipher—"then I can't help that."

Calm down, I told myself for the thousandth time. But I wasn't going down without a fight. I marched down the street to confront Kenny and his parents. I took large angry strides right past that school bus and knocked on their screen door. They were all in the kitchen, where Kenny and his girlfriend were stuffing things into their backpacks.

I first tried enlisting their sympathy, which I got—but only from the parents. They knew exactly why I'd marched in the front door and listened with sympathetic looks and nods. I could see that I had joined their ranks—the parents of the "thank-God-he's-not-*my*-kid" offspring. I hated being part of this new "club," yet I felt a tiny bit better for their company.

Kenny was over eighteen, and his parents were legally powerless to stop him as long as he was paying his own way to this event. They assured me that it was a harmless, gentle gathering of peace-loving souls. Then Kenny spoke up in an oh-so-wise tone of voice. "Maybe it'll be good for Ben," he said. "He could learn a trade; they have workshops on jewelry-making and all kinds of things. Everyone cooperates to make meals and stuff. He'll like it."

How much more can I take? How many more things am I going to have to learn to accept? When are the changes going to slow down, so I can take a breath? "Kenny," I said. "My son is underage. He is seventeen. Do you want the job of being responsible for him? Understand that this is *kidnapping*. If he gets on that bus, it's against my will. Maybe I can't physically stop him, but I do not grant permission and it's on your head if he goes." I wasn't entirely sure if the kidnapping angle was legally accurate, but I thought it might have an effect anyway. It did not.

"Sorry," Kenny said. "I don't accept that responsibility. If Ben comes with us it's his problem. Call the police if you want to, but I think they'll see that Ben is coming along because he *wants* to."

I looked at Kenny's parents, and they just sighed. They'd evidently had this conversation already.

Underneath all the anger and shock I felt were two other emotions that surprised me. One was relief, the other I recognized as hope. *I don't want Ben to go. But—if he does go, I get to have a week or two without him. Maybe he'll learn that this leftover hippie culture isn't all it's cracked up to be. Maybe he'll get a dose of reality that will turn him around.*

So, in the end, I didn't say yes but I didn't enforce my refusal. I walked back home. I didn't stop Ben from going. I didn't call the police. I didn't want to. It seemed useless. I was so tired of fighting. I had no resistance left in me.

Ben took his backpack and stood at the door. He looked at me and waited. "Mom," he said, "aren't you going to kiss me good-bye? I'm going to miss you."

I suddenly felt an ache in the middle of my chest. *He's really going to do this. Why does he have to learn everything the hard way? What will he do after the Rainbow Gathering ends? Will he be safe?* "Okay, honey," I said. I gave him a kiss and a long hug, which he returned. It had been a long time since we'd hugged. Ben walked down to that old school bus and got on board. I didn't cry until he was out of sight.

Numb with worry, disappointment, anger, and shame, I made it through the rest of the day pretending everything was normal. I pushed the fact that I might not see my son again for two weeks or longer—much longer, if he chose to search for William—out of my consciousness. That night, though, it all came crashing back as soon as my head hit the pillow. I lay awake, all manner of possible images haunting me—and then, abruptly, I made a decision to not worry. It wasn't helping, it couldn't change anything. I realized my only choice was my attitude, so I created a new one for myself where all would be well. I pretended that Ben had gone off to summer camp, where he'd be safe and sound and supervised. That way, maybe I could enjoy my freedom.

Ben was supposed to be at the Gathering for two weeks; the day after he left, I heard via Lindsay's parents that they were all right, so I relaxed. When, the following Monday, Ali left on the first of three Monday-to-Friday teen trips, I found myself, blessedly, alone in my own home.

Unfortunately, this vacation didn't last long. That same day, I heard from Lindsay, and also from Kenny's mother, that Ben had left the Gathering. He'd said it was a disappointment and "nothing but a big drug fest." He had, evidently, expected Shangri-La and gotten *Lord of the Flies*. I was pleased and proud that he'd seen through it all, but now I didn't know where he was.

He called me himself the next day. "Mom, it's so good to hear your voice!" he said. "Boy, you were right. This place is just bullshit. All people want here is an excuse to do drugs. They're not interested at all in spirituality, or world peace, or love. I'm coming home. I love you and Ali so much."

I wanted Ben to find his own way back, but Lindsay's parents stepped in again. They paid for a motel room for him and Lindsay—along with a few other disillusioned attendees of the event. They then drove to Pennsylvania to drive them all home—to my house in Connecticut. I suddenly found myself with three young hippie houseguests from Long Island. I made them call their parents and arrange to take the ferry home the next day.

I listened with amusement to the idealistic conversations Ben and his guests were having about peace and love—remembering similar talks from my own adolescence. Ali was home for the weekend, and she joined in their conversation with a guarded and bemused detachment. The house was full of noisy teens, just as I'd imagined it when I saw it for the first time.

After our humbled houseguests left to rejoin their own parents, life was calm—for a whole two weeks. Ben thought I was cool to have let his new friends stay over; suddenly I was Mom of the Year. He showered, shaved, and started wearing clean clothes. He sought my approval for his new habits and grinned when I told him he looked nice. We enjoyed a period of relatively normal family life. I liked my son again.

A big part of me hoped that Ben's decision to run away, and his decision to come back home, might have a lasting effect. By letting go, perhaps I'd gotten my son back for more than a short time. *Surely he learned from this. Maybe we are out of the woods now.* The other part of me, though, was just waiting for the other shoe to fall. And it did.

The Rainbow Gathering was to become just the first time Ben left home, only to return after a period of time with new promises and plans. Running away became just another pattern that happened so often it almost began to seem like part of the normal fabric of our lives. What passed for normal in our home sounded like a bad movie plot when I told it to someone else. The family threshold for normalcy kept moving further away.

Ali began to roll her eyes whenever the subject of Ben came up. Slowly, with each incident, her respect for her brother seeped out of her. She took refuge in her own life, in her own friends. She refused to talk about him after a while. She, too, was always waiting for the other shoe to fall. It seemed that every time he returned home, he would stay stable just long enough for her to hope he might come back to life, be the way he used to be. The minute she began to trust that hope, the cycle began again. My heart would break for both of us. For all three of us.

The next time Ben left home was after the summer. This time, he moved in with another family. He slept on their couch for a few weeks and worked part-time in a store near their home. Ben thought this would be the answer, but it wasn't. Once again, the same pattern: a fresh start in a new place, a few good weeks at his new job, and then the change in Ben's attitude. He lost his job. The family told him to go home, but he wasn't ready to come back to the rules he'd left behind so stubbornly.

Ben spent days begging other families to take him in. Some did, some wouldn't. Late one night I got a call from a parent in the neighborhood. "Randye," she said, "this is a very hard call for me to make, but did you know that Ben was here tonight, asking if he could sleep on our couch? What's going on?" I didn't know this woman very well, but our kids had been in Trumbull High together for a time. I filled her in on what was

CHAPTER GUIDEPOSTS

Final Connections in the Adolescent Brain

For many years it was thought that brain development was set at a fairly early age. By the time the teen years were reached the brain was thought to be largely finished developing. However, scientists doing cutting-edge research using magnetic resonance imaging (MRI) have mapped the brain from early childhood into adulthood and found data contrary to these beliefs. It now appears the brain continues to change into the early twenties, with the frontal lobes, responsible for reasoning and problem solving, developing last (www.edinformatics.com/news/teenage_brains.html).

This is often why schizophrenia appears to emerge in the late teens or early twenties. This is when the final brain connections are supposed to occur. Instead, families see the irrational behaviors and loss of life forces in their ill relative, while it seems that others of that age are moving ahead with their lives and growing up.

ToughLove International

ToughLove® was founded in 1979 by Phyllis and David York, family therapists from Pennsylvania who were struggling to raise an out-of-control teenage daughter. Basically, the Yorks detached from the

happening, and my reasons for distancing myself from it. I felt like the worst parent in the world. Who did I think I was, letting my boy wander around town begging for a place to sleep? "Is Ben there?" I asked.

"No," she said. "I told him to go home to his mother. I said I wasn't going to help him avoid family issues and that he should work it out with you."

I thanked her for saying no. I thanked her for having the courage to tell me. I imagined Ben walking through the dark streets, and I hoped he'd found somewhere to sleep. I prayed he would come to his senses soon. *How did it come to this?* I wondered.

Four days later, on the last day of September, Ben showed up at the door—finally. His hair was matted. His face was filthy and unshaven. He looked completely exhausted. He had been gone for five weeks. "Hi, Mom," he said. "I want to come home. I guess your rules aren't so stupid after all."

situation and allowed their child to determine the pace of her recovery. They concentrated on regaining their own emotional and physical health and prayed for the well-being of their child. Eventually the family was reunited.

Out of this family's solution to a seemingly impossible situation emerged the principles and guidelines of ToughLove, a nonprofit international self-help program with more than seven hundred groups.

ToughLove meetings are highly structured, with parents sharing their "stand" (a long-range goal) and "bottom line" (action they will commit to enforcing that will facilitate achieving this "stand"). (See www.wikipedia.com.)

Rainbow Gatherings

Rainbow Gatherings are temporary intentional communities, typically held in outdoor settings, espousing and practicing ideals of peace, love, harmony, freedom, and community, as a consciously expressed alternative to mainstream popular culture, consumerism, capitalism, and mass media.

Rainbow Gatherings and the "Rainbow Family of Living Light" are an expression of a utopian impulse combined with bohemianism and hippie culture, with roots clearly traceable to the 1960s counterculture (www.wikipedia.com).

I took him back under some new conditions, clearly spelled out in a written agreement between us. Ben ran away a few times after that, but seldom for more than a night or two. I learned to wait it out, numb to the worry I couldn't let in. He always came back home. There was always, then, a grace period of respectful and cheerful behavior inspired by his appreciation, and then the fall from that grace and the escalation of rebellion, until he got so angry he ran away again. But my vision of what odd behaviors Ben was capable of kept stretching and stretching. "Normal" was getting stranger and stranger.

NOBODY'S FAULT

I still thought I could somehow make it stop. I kept trying to locate William again. Maybe this was the missing piece that would bring Ben back.

Ali showed no interest in finding her father, but Ben kept pointing to his father's absence as the reason for his unhappiness.

Later that summer, we got our wish. William came back. And that didn't do it, either.

It was early July, a few weeks after the Rainbow Gathering had proved a bust. I was alone in the house when the phone rang. It was William. "Hello, luv," he said.

I stood motionless. It had been two years since I'd heard William's voice, twelve years since I'd seen him. Still, the voice was unmistakable, as was the use of "luv" instead of my first name. Everyone was "luv" or "mate" to William. There was so much—and so little—to say. I settled for "Hi."

"It's a good thing you're still listed in the phone book," he said. "I almost couldn't reach you." Spoken by the man who'd been in hiding for twelve years.

William was calling from a motel room in the state of Washington. He was staying there courtesy of the charity of a nearby church who'd taken pity on him. He had no money, no identification; his wallet had been stolen. He had nothing but some clothes in a plastic bag, my phone number, and his British pride. He was homeless.

I hesitated, absorbing this information. William, on his last dollar. No wonder he'd called. Still, the tone of his voice told me one thing I hadn't expected: he sounded sober.

He was sober. No accusations, no slurring, no rambling.

"Ben has been trying to reach you," I said.

"I know. I called my ex-girlfriend, and she told me. That's how I knew to call you. I'd like to talk to Benjamin."

I'm sure you would, but you'll have to get by me first. I was glad that I was alone; it bought me some time. "He isn't here right now," I said.

"Oh. That's too bad." He spoke as though we'd just chatted last week.

"William, where have you *been*?"

Silence. I heard the tapping of a cigarette pack against his hand. "Well, luv, I've been sort of camping."

"Camping? Where?"

"Down by the river in Portland, Oregon. I helped out some of the other mates there."

This didn't sound quite right to me; William was whitewashing something. I pressed him for the whole truth, and he reluctantly filled in the details. What he meant by "camping," as it turned out, was really a year of living as a homeless person. He'd gotten his dinner out of Dumpsters.

He had eaten very little but had drunk a lot of beer—or whatever alcohol he could get—until finally he'd collapsed due to a ruptured ulcer and had almost died. This incident opened his eyes, and he decided it was time to sober up.

After three months of sobriety in a rehab facility, he left with an older man who said he needed a travel companion. Always one for a free ride, William had gone with him, but after a few days the old man had stolen his wallet and left William on the side of the road. Any other possessions from William's life had been in a "mate's" storage room back in Portland, and he didn't know how to get them back. He was stuck.

"I need your help," he said. "I'm sober now. I've been so stupid. I want to come back to Connecticut and get to know the kids again. I was so bloody stupid to lose you."

I had no idea what to say. "Are you still there, luv?" he asked.

"Yes."

"So—what do you think?"

I took a deep, slow breath. "Look, William, I'm a little shocked by all this. I have to think about it. Give me your number and I'll call you back tomorrow."

"Okay," he said. "But tonight's my last night here. After that I'll be out on the street."

We were the last resort, of course. "I'll phone you before eleven. I'll let you know tomorrow." I hung up the phone and sat down, trembling.

I spent much of the next twelve hours consulting professionals, friends, and my own heart. *Should I help him? Do I allow this man to come back into our lives? After the way he deserted us, ignored us?*

But there was only one choice, really. I had to do this, for Ben's and Ali's sake. They deserved to meet the man who had been their daddy but was now only their birth father. No matter what happened, it would be worth the risk to have him come back, for the closure alone.

I set up a concrete plan so that I wouldn't slip into enabling William. I wired him enough money for bus fare across the country and some food along the way. I told him that when he got here, I would rent a motel room for him for one week only—and then give him the names of shelters in the area. I told him I hoped he would go to AA (Alcoholics Anonymous) and stay sober. I would bring the kids to him, if they wanted to see him, but it was up to him to try to establish a relationship. I would encourage the children to get to know him, but I would not force them to. After the week at the motel was over, William would be on his own. He was to ask for no more handouts—I let him know I could barely afford the help I'd offered.

He readily agreed to the plan and thanked me profusely. "I know you have no reason to trust me," he said. "I know you're aware that I could take the money and run again. But that's not what I want. Trust me—I will get off that bus in Connecticut. And I'll call you from every stop along the way so you know I'm keeping my word."

And that's exactly what he did. Every time the phone rang, Ben answered it. He was excited to have William coming home. He called him "Daddy" every chance he got. He ended every call with "I love you, Dad." He told everyone that his father was coming home.

One of the reasons I'd insisted on a bus for William, instead of a plane, was that it would buy me time to prepare the kids. This had all happened so quickly, and while Ali was away for the week. Ben, as usual, had jumped right in. I hadn't told Ali yet. She'd have a different way of handling this.

I picked her up from the teen tour bus on Friday afternoon and broke the news in the car on the way home. Ali's first reaction was surprise: "You're kidding! Oh my God!"

Then, as I filled in some details, she listened without further comment until she burst into tears. "I don't care what you say," she said. "I'm not seeing him. I don't want to see him. We don't need him. We've done just fine without him!"

This was pretty much the reaction I'd expected. "Okay, honey," I said. "If you change your mind, let me know." She needed time to get used to this. I was glad she had another teen tour scheduled for the following week. William would be arriving on Tuesday, and I could ease into his appearance, one child at a time.

That day, Ben chose to keep his therapy appointment, and he was already in Art's office while I waited for William at the bus terminal. *Will I even recognize him? It has been twelve years since I saw his face. Were we ever really married?*

An old man got off the bus. His back was stooped and he walked with hesitation. He was cleanly dressed, but all he carried were two plastic bags. And then I realized it was William. He seemed so much smaller than I'd remembered.

I went to him and hugged him. I didn't know what else to do. Up close, he didn't look quite so old. His hair and his body were both grayer and thinner; he was, however, clean and well groomed. "You look pretty good," I said. "I didn't know what to expect."

"I shaved on the bus, and some woman gave me a haircut in Washington. I always want to look my best, you remember that."

I smiled a little. "Yes, I do remember that." I felt like I was in the twilight zone. "Come on, let's go. Ben is waiting to see you."

William got into the car and we drove down the Post Road to Art's office, passing by restaurants and other places we had gone to as a married couple, so long ago. I fought fiercely to stay in the moment, so I wouldn't veer off the road. This was just too weird.

In Art's office, father and son were reunited. They hugged, cried, and went downstairs to smoke a cigarette together. *The bonding moment,* I thought. *First thing they share is a nicotine addiction. Things change in twelve years.*

Art looked at me. "You did a good thing, you know. I think this will help Ben so much."

"God, I hope so," I answered.

When we booked William into his motel, the desk clerk looked at the three of us. "You know," she said to Ben, "I can't figure out who you look like more, your mother or your father." Ben beamed. I thought how wonderful that simple sentence must sound to him. For so long, I'd been his only yardstick. Either you look like your mom, or you don't look like your mom. Now, at last, two parents to measure himself by. Just like normal kids. *Maybe this will make Ben feel whole again. Maybe now he'll want to feel normal. And act normal.*

When Ali came home that Friday, she agreed to meet William, "just to see what he looks like." We drove to the motel, where William was waiting at the open door to his ground-floor room. Ali got out of the car and walked over to her father. William reached out and hugged her. Her hesitation seemed to evaporate, and she hugged him back. Then they both cried. We all walked across the street to the diner for a family dinner. I still felt like this wasn't really happening.

After that, we let the summer—and this new-old relationship—unfold. William found a job near the motel, at a carpet store owned by a friend, and then a house-share within walking distance. He stayed sober for a few months, during which he tried to be involved with Ben and Ali.

It didn't make a huge difference to Ali, as far as I could tell, but there was a subtle change. She said, "At least now, Mom, I have a normal story to tell. Divorced parents, I don't choose to see my dad much. I don't have to say that I don't know where he is." This seemed to satisfy her. Questions were being answered, and William was less of a mystery.

Ben was more willing to let William in, but he quickly became disillusioned. This was his father, but not the father he wanted. Ben left his job at the pet store to work at the carpet place with William, the plan being for

CHAPTER GUIDEPOSTS

The Double-Edged Sword: Negative and Positive Symptoms of Schizophrenia

"Positive" symptoms are behaviors you never saw before in your loved one, which may be *added* as he or she becomes ill. For example:

- Rudeness and hostility
- Inflated self-concept
- Constant tension and nervousness
- And as the illness progresses, hallucinations and episodes of psychosis

"Negative" behaviors are the ones that may be *taken away* from your relative as the illness takes hold. For example:

- Ability to focus
- Capacity for intimacy
- Warmth and thoughtfulness in relationships
- Pride in taking responsibility
- Willingness to follow a treatment plan when ill
- Ability to read social signals such as body language

Why Isn't He Learning from His Mistakes?

Because schizophrenia is a thought disorder, its cognitive symptoms can be very frustrating to live with.

father to take son under his wing and teach him a trade. This plan quickly deteriorated. Even with his father involved, Ben's pattern remained exactly the same. He was a wonderful employee for about three days and then decided that the jobs they were giving him to do—straightening up samples, vacuuming, etc.—were "beneath him." He and William began to argue at work and outside of work. William began to drink again. Ben lost respect for him. There was no fantasy solution here, and the list of options suffered one more loss. This was not going to help much, after all. Where was the missing piece, then? What had I missed?

Nothing Seems to Stick. Why?

The problem, as I understand it, is that the brain affected by schizophrenia is lacking in the ability to make many of the connections that we count on: between cause and effect, between behavior and circumstances.

Cognitive symptoms (or cognitive deficits) are problems with attention, certain types of memory, and the executive functions that allow us to plan and organize. Cognitive deficits can also be difficult to recognize as part of the disorder but are the most disabling in terms of leading a normal life.*

The ill relative is simply not connecting the dots the way we'd like. While there may also be a lot of "interference" in the brain if positive symptoms are present—to my understanding, like a television set with all the channels on at once—the cognitive deficits are just as big a problem. It isn't his or her fault. It may take many repetitions of the same lesson to get the connection to hold. But it can. This requires understanding, patience, and time.

What to Do: Stop Blaming

One of the most important insights for family members is to know which added behaviors and diminished responses occur in their relative's illness, which may look to be under his/her control, but are not. This will help us separate the *person* from the *illness*.†

---

*National Institute of Mental Health, "What Are the Symptoms of Schizophrenia?" www.nimh .nih.gov.
†National Institute of Mental Health, "What Are the Symptoms of Schizophrenia?"

I felt completely stuck, out of ideas now. Therapy wasn't providing any lasting answers. Treatment options were limited, because Ben was over sixteen. Bringing his father back hadn't worked any magic. Ben had made so many choices that only resulted in a more limited life. He had dropped out of school, quit jobs, left home—and now he had strict rules, no money, few friends. None of it seemed to affect him, to matter to him. He didn't seem able to learn. *Why? Why? Is there anything that will get through to Ben?*

All I had left was hope, however unjustified. I still hoped this was just a bad phase, that Ben might go back to school. I still hoped I could salvage some of this very strange summer. I decided to take the kids on a four-day vacation—without William. Whatever went on, it would only be for four days. At least we could pretend to be a normal family, by doing what a normal family might do.

It wasn't too bad. We were together, at least, and away from the argumentative atmosphere of our own home. I was happy to see my two children spending time with each other, even if it was because there weren't too many other options. As for Ben, he was occasionally sullen, but there were no episodes of strangeness or outbursts of anger. It was okay. Okay seemed pretty good to me by then.

II

CHAOS, TRIAL AND ERROR

REFLECTIONS

TIME: THE PRESENT

I'm in Washington, D.C., at the national convention for the National Alliance on Mental Illness (NAMI). Without the education and support I found in NAMI—and the opportunity I now have to guide others as a teacher—I don't know if Ben would be anywhere near recovery. I don't know if our family would have survived the chaos of his crisis years intact. I might have given up on my own son, out of sheer desperation and confusion. We might have lost him. We might have run out of hope.

I'm astonished at the sheer number of people I see and the full calendar of activities. There are workshops, speeches, legislative briefings, and a hall full of exhibits. The keynote speaker is a U.S. senator who lost a son to suicide due to mental illness. There are movies, too: *People Say I'm Crazy*, filmed by the sister of a young artist with schizophrenia, at his request, to document his struggles (www.peoplesayimcrazy.org); *Out of the Shadows*, a 2004 film by Susan Smiley, a filmmaker who grew up in a household dominated by her mother's illness.

I meet people from every state and from several other countries: consumers, family members, and providers. The problems that come along with a diagnosis of mental illness, it seems, are the same no matter where you live. In every town, every city, every country; in every church, mosque, and synagogue; in every school, on every block, someone is trying to cope with the changes that occur when mental illness strikes. So many don't know how, or where, to begin to ask for help. Here, I meet the luckier ones; they have found NAMI.

I recall all too well how confused and alone I felt when Ben's symptoms began to get more extreme. I remember sobbing at the graves of my parents, begging for help. I remember how Ali tried to help Ben, then turned toward her own life and friends, shutting her grief and need inside her competent exterior. I remember how I felt: angry, helpless, frustrated, and terrified. And ashamed. I felt ashamed.

6

FRIGHTENING THOUGHTS

I know I will change the world, for I found it is my destiny through what suddenly came to me. Something around showed me the connection that the OM (breath of life) is what the government has blinded people from . . . and the PRADHANYA (force . . . like chi . . . which carries and sustains life) is what I must do . . . reincarnate the om and show people.

—Ben, letter to Lindsay, fall 1999

I came across the first real evidence of Ben's irrational thoughts in a letter he wrote on our computer. He'd been unreasonable before, of course—I saw it in the way he'd dropped out of school with that insane plan to wander around the country begging for work, in his unrealistic attempts to run away from home, in the arguments he came up with to defend his choices. But the letter I discovered frightened me more than any of that. In it, Ben talked about government plots, about how he knew it was his destiny to change the world and set them straight. He knew this because of a force that showed him what to do.

And yet, even then, I wanted a more acceptable explanation, one that I could fix. There were plenty of those offered to me: it could be drugs, it could be the influence of friends or of literature. And all that probably was true. What I didn't see, what no one else seemed able to see, is that an illness was developing inside Ben that made him even more *susceptible* to those ideas. It was like a creeping vine that hadn't yet broken ground to make itself clearly visible.

There were a few threads of promise that fall, and they kept me going despite all the conflict and mood swings in the house. One was Ben's graduation equivalency diploma (GED). He took and aced the test, despite his months away from a classroom. At last, a success that couldn't go wrong, that couldn't be taken away.

When the results came in the mail, we found that Ben had not just *passed* the test; across the equivalency diploma were the words "With Honors." When Ben saw that, he grinned. He actually grinned. "Mom," he said. "Look! I got *honors!* Isn't that great?"

I smiled, too. "Yes, Ben, it is. Congratulations." *This was too easy,* I thought. *Will he think everything is supposed to come this easily? But maybe this will be the boost he needs.*

Yes, he was proud of himself. He called his aunts and uncles right away and told them. He held his head just a little bit higher. He displayed the diploma in his room. When Ben was acting like himself, that self was easier to be around.

The GED did not change the range of Ben's moods, though. The swings were getting wider and weirder now. For the first time, I began to think that Ben might need treatment for something more serious. Despite all I'd read about ADD and its secondary symptoms of frustration and anger, I considered that he might need medication for a mental illness.

We'd been seeing therapists for over a year now. One for Ben (weekly), one for me (every two weeks), and sessions together (when Ben showed up). I offered Ali the chance to participate, but I always got the same answer. "I'm fine, Mom, I'm fine. Ben is the one who's being stupid. I don't need any help." My son certainly did need help, but I had to face the fact that he was not getting better.

My first thought was that Ben might be suffering from depression. I looked at the facts: how much he was sleeping, how unmotivated he often was, and how all the joy was draining out of him. He hardly ever laughed. He just seemed so sad all the time. I did more research. Yes, this made sense to me. Maybe he was depressed. *Maybe that's what was missing all along, why nothing else seems to work.*

I brought this up privately with Art. "Yes," he said. "That occurred to me, too. I even asked Ben about it, but he refused to talk about it. He won't even consider medication. And we can't force him to take anything: he's over sixteen."

Our hands were tied by the legal system. We couldn't force treatment on Ben; he had to want the help. How would that ever happen?

I kept watching Ben's moods, kept reading about the symptoms I witnessed. There were times when the pendulum swung the other way, when Ben became unrealistic, angry, irrational. I parented in between the tantrums. I kept watch. I kept looking for a new answer in books about mental illness. Just in case. I hoped I could find an answer there—and I prayed that I wouldn't. The symptoms in the cases I read about were so extreme that Ben seemed okay in comparison, most of the time. *He can't have a mental illness. Not Ben. There's got to be another explanation.*

Every time Ben began another of his fresh-start phases, I still hoped this might be the time it would stick. I wanted to put those books away and never look at them again. One such time was when he finally found another job, an *official* job. Ben was hired part-time at our local Starbucks, and he could walk to work from our house.

This time, I thought, *will be different. This is a real job. No one handed him this one as a favor.* But I was wrong. The familiar pattern emerged once again. It only took a few weeks before the superior attitude took hold of Ben. He wanted to be paid more money. He showed up late. He only wanted to make cappuccinos, and he grumbled about taking out the garbage. He received his first warning from the company.

A week later, Ben missed work. I found him still asleep one morning when I knew he was supposed to be at Starbucks. He told me he was sick, but I suspected he was faking. He insisted I should trust him. We argued, and I gave up. *Natural consequences.* He now had two strikes against him at work.

One month later, I found the letter, the one that made me angry at first but then scared the hell out of me. While cleaning out the computer, I found an unnamed document file. When I opened it to see what it was, I glimpsed the opening line of a letter to Lindsay that Ben had written on the day he'd skipped work. It read:

> Since you inquired about the relationship between me and my mother, she is crummy. For example, because I called out of Starbucks one day faking sick (although I wasn't but didn't want to go to work), my mother said I am not permitted to go out even though I am feeling better.

I knew it! He was faking! All that ranting and raving about how I don't care about him, why don't I trust him, and he was faking all along!

I read on. Ben talked about still wanting to go to college but that he wasn't sure; about finally "reuniting with himself" as evidenced by the fact that he now loved to be alone a lot, and that he had started writing a book that was coming to him "unconsciously." It was the next paragraph, though, that stopped me cold. Ben had written:

> The government is onto the fact that I will change the world. I want many people to relate to and not have to put up with bullshit such as a job, which was only created to occupy your mind with meaninglessness and the concept of submitting yourself. They say it's the right way when half the money we "earn" goes to the government to choose how we will live our lifestyle.

The government is onto the fact that he will change the world? Oh my God. Was he on drugs that day? No, I don't think so. I was with him that entire day. Is this what he really thinks?

The rest of the letter was about Ben's new "destiny" with the "OM." I sat still in the desk chair, staring at the computer screen, then clicked "print." I took the printout and carried it with me to read again the next

---

CHAPTER GUIDEPOSTS

Delusions

"People with paranoid schizophrenia may believe that others are deliberately cheating, harassing, poisoning, spying upon, or plotting against them or the people they care about. These beliefs are called delusions of persecution" (National Institute of Mental Health, www .nimh.nih.gov).

The family might be experiencing a mixture of:

- Dawning realization
- Hoping against hope
- Normalizing

Steps to Take

- Keep learning. Check the resources at the end of this book. Read. Go to websites for information.
- Shop for the right professional help—not all are created equal.
- Report symptoms you observe to your doctor, therapist, or psychiatrist. Family members see behaviors around the clock. That information is vital.

day; the shock and fear were still there. There was something very, very wrong.

I called Art, told him what I had found, and faxed a copy of the letter to him. He called me back with his explanation. "These ideas are practically word-for-word right out of the book *Ishmael*, which I recommended to Ben. I thought it would strengthen his relationship to me to see that I had read books that echo his ideas about the world. I had no idea he would take the ideas so literally, though."

My fear eased a little. *At least these ideas are ones that Ben read somewhere, that didn't come out of his own head. But they aren't helping him very much, are they?* I went to Ben's bookshelf, pulled the *Ishmael* book from its place, and hid it in the attic. I felt better, but I was still scared, and still very much on my guard. I was still watching for symptoms.

7

ALMOST ARRESTED

Above the content soul flies to meet the morning
At the dawn of a newly rising sun
Where in the distance the grains of sand cling together
And sift through the holes
Relying on the wind to bring them closer to God.

—Ben, 1999

The fake illness episode had been strike two at Starbucks. A few weeks later, Ben got his strike three: late again. Following strict corporate policy, Starbucks fired him for good; now he was idle and underfoot again, at home way too much. I was getting tired of this. I was getting tired of Ben. And things were about to get worse.

Another crisis. My son almost got me—or himself—arrested.

My schedule that fall was very full, and sleep only came in small pieces. I got up at 3:15 and got to the radio station by 4 a.m. In the evenings, I was performing in a local theater production of *Guys and Dolls*, playing Adelaide. In between, I sandwiched in my freelance voice work and drove the Mom taxi. After so many years of missing after-school hours because of my old radio shift, I was happy to be able to pick up Ali from Trumbull High and be there for her and her friends.

In order to keep my health and sanity, I used my lunch hour to nap. This was not a luxury, but a necessity. If I wasn't near home, I'd pull the car into the nearest parking lot, recline the seat, and grab a few minutes of sleep that way. I was always a little weary around the edges.

One afternoon in November, I was vacuuming the house after my nap. Ben followed me around the rooms, halfheartedly doing the dusting chores I'd assigned to him. He seemed poised for a fight. Maybe he was bored, maybe he was frustrated. I wished he were not there.

"Mom," he said, "why do we have to do this, anyway? I don't feel like it."

"Too bad, Ben," was my automatic response. "It has to be done."

"But why are you so obsessed with cleaning, anyway?"

Obsessed? My mother would be all over me, if she were alive, for how haphazard my cleaning habits are. "Just do it, Ben. I am not in the mood."

"Well, what do you think I am? Your slave?"

My slave? I counted to ten, then to twenty. "Well, Ben, if you were in school or at your job, you wouldn't be here to do this with me. Since you aren't putting in your forty hours at anything, you will use that time to help around the house."

"That's unfair. This is slavery. You can't make me do it!"

What is the big deal? What is his problem? I walked away from him and into the laundry room, to put away the vacuum. If I didn't get as far away as I could, I was going to get sucked into an argument I'd had too many times before. No matter how many times I put my foot down about chores, no matter how many times he said he finally understood and would do better, we always had to start this over from scratch. Nothing ever seemed to stick.

Ben followed me into the laundry room. "Mom, you didn't answer my question!"

"Look, Ben," I said. Now I was sucked in. I didn't want to be, but I couldn't seem to help it. "This is part of living here. We all work together."

"But, Mom," he whined, "Ali doesn't have to do as many chores as I do!"

"Ali is in school," I said. "She has chores, too, but she spends time on homework. It's not the same. You would have the same deal she does if you were back in school."

Now Ben exploded. This seemed exactly the trigger he had been waiting for. "There you go again! Always about school! Why are grades so important to you, anyway? Can't you even *try* to understand me? I don't need school, I don't need work, I don't need chores. You're so closedminded!"

I turned toward him, my cheeks burning. I'd had it. *Enough!* Ben said, "You want to *hit* me, don't you, Mom? Go ahead, just like after the dentist. I know you want to hit me. You are so violent underneath that calm face you turn to the world."

I hate him. Who is this person? He's ruining my day. He is ruining my life. When will this ever end? I picked up the vacuum in frustration and then crashed it back down onto the tile floor. Ben stared at me. Then he started yelling. "See? I told you! You almost threw the vacuum at me! You are *abusive!*"

What? "Ben . . . " I said.

"I'm calling the police! You're an abusive mother." He stormed into the kitchen, picked up the phone and dialed 911.

I can't believe this. If anyone should be calling the police, it's me. "Ben, *stop it!* What are you doing?"

"I'm reporting you to the police! You are flipping out, Mom. I can't live here with you if you're like this." He gave our address to the police before I could grab the phone from him.

Now there was nothing I could do except wait for the squad car. I went out onto the front porch, watching the driveway. I stayed as far away from Ben as I could. Ten minutes later, the police arrived. By that time, Ben had calmed down; I had not, but I had gone into shock mode. I was outwardly all business, but inside I was churning.

I can't believe this is happening. What are the neighbors thinking? Will one of us get arrested? I can see the headline now: "Local Radio Personality Behind Bars." Or worse: "Son of Local Radio Personality Behind Bars." How did it come to this?

The police officer questioned Ben, who now seemed confused and a little contrite. His story lacked the drama he'd thought it had. My picking up a vacuum and then putting it down wasn't enough to warrant the call he had made. Ben began accusing me of a history of bad behavior. "She's *always* flipping out," he told the police officer. "Once she hit me and left me miles from home to find my own way home. I never know what she'll do next."

I kept my mouth shut, but the officer could sense that there was something off in Ben's story and looked at me with raised eyebrows. I shook my head slowly, waving my hands in a gesture of helplessness.

"Get in the squad car, son. I want to talk to your mother alone." The second officer put Ben in the back of the squad car and locked the door. I could not absorb this information, could not process this picture of my son in the police vehicle. "Ma'am, can you tell me what's going on here?"

I explained what had happened as best as I could. The officer looked as if he were trying to figure out how rational I was. I had nothing to protect me other than the fact that I was telling the truth. "Well," he said, "one of you will probably have to go with us today. I'm just not sure who to believe."

This can't be happening. "Officer," I said. I was strangely calm. "My son has been having mood swings for the past six months. I don't know what's causing it. He dropped out of school in April; he works only a few hours a week. He may be depressed. He could also be smoking pot; he may be doing other drugs. I forbid them, but I just don't know how else to explain what happens to him sometimes."

"Do you think your son is on drugs right now?" he asked.

"I have no idea. He doesn't seem stoned to me, but I can't tell if he's on something else. Not anything I can recognize. His moods are so unpredictable and so short-lived. I just don't know what's going on." My professional manner began to crumble. I put one hand over my mouth and breathed in slowly through my nose, willing myself not to cry. Saying those words out loud to this policeman made them frighteningly real.

"Do you mind if we go and search your son's room?"

I exhaled. "Of course not," I replied. "Go right ahead. His bedroom is down in the basement." *Yes, please. Please find something. Find a drug that will explain where my son has gone. Something that will account for that letter he wrote about government plots, for the strange poetry I find all over the house. Let it be a drug. Where there's a drug, there's the chance of rehab.*

It took the two officers about an hour to search Ben's room. While they were in there, Lindsay arrived in her car. She got out, saw Ben in the back of the squad car, and gestured to him through the window that she was going inside to talk to me. "What happened, Randye? Ben called me and said that you were getting crazy or something. I can't believe he called the cops! What's going on?"

After I explained what had happened, Lindsay sat quietly for a minute looking at her hands in her lap, playing with the friendship bracelet on her wrist. Then she looked up at me. "I don't know what's happening to Ben. When I met him he was so *cute*. He was working at Discs and he had this big smile and everyone there loved him. Now—I don't know. He's different."

So Lindsay sees the change in him, too. It's not just me. "Lindsay," I said, "did you want Ben to drop out of school?"

"No!" she said. "I *told* him not to do it! I said it was stupid, that you'd be mad. But he did it anyway, and now he's not even working. I keep *telling* him to get a job. He just doesn't make sense sometimes." She looked at me for an answer but I had none. She looked vulnerable and a little bit frightened.

Lindsay is not the problem, I thought. *She's as confused as I am. Is that good or bad? Now I can't pin the change in Ben on his relationship with her, either. Not the lack of a father, not a tough adolescence, not a bad crowd, not his girlfriend. Maybe not even ADD, maybe not even drugs. Then what? What?*

The police officers came back upstairs. "We didn't find anything there, ma'am. No drugs. So—we're going to let you both go and let you work it out. There doesn't seem to be any real incident of domestic violence here."

I let out another breath I didn't realize I'd been holding. "Thank you, officers. I hope this won't ever happen again." *Please let that be true.*

"We're going to have a talk with Benjamin before we go. Maybe he'll realize he should never have called us without cause. We'll do our best."

"Thanks," I said. *Yes, someone else talk sense to him. Make him listen, make him hear. Please.*

Once again, we entered a period of calm after the incident. I was out of ideas. I was out of theories. Life was about damage control. We went from one crisis to the next. And now the crises were coming around more frequently.

Ben ran away a few more times. He would get upset with me, announce he was leaving home, and run out the door with only his backpack or nothing at all. He'd leave at midnight and plan to "sleep outside the health food store" until the next morning. I became so numb to these outbursts that I'd just say good-bye and go back to finishing the laundry. Often he'd come back in a few hours or even as quickly as ten minutes later.

Sometimes he even had a note of apology he'd written for me, written with sincere regret and promises to change. *This time, maybe he finally gets it.* But these hopes were becoming halfhearted now. I wanted so much to believe, with each extreme, that Ben had finally hit bottom and learned from it, something that would *stay* with him.

Instead, Ben's resentments grew deeper, his theories wilder. Sometimes he spoke about the incident he'd created by calling the police, and he'd scream that they'd had no right to search his room, that I'd had no right to let them do it. I heard him telling Lindsay, on the phone, that he thought his phone had been bugged while the police were there. "Maybe the FBI is listening in," he said. I assured Ben that he wasn't really important enough for a phone tap, but he just smirked at me and said he knew better.

Therapy sessions continued, but all they ultimately did was remind me of how powerless I felt. I couldn't force treatment if we had no diagnosis; even then, we had to get Ben to agree to it. The only reasonable explanation I could still find for his behavior was that, somehow, Ben was still smoking pot and hiding it from me. *But how is he getting it? Where is he smoking it? And how is he paying for it?*

I still prayed that the answer was as simple as drug use. At least I would know where to begin to turn for better help. I had never felt so lonely in my life.

CHAPTER GUIDEPOSTS

Why Do People with Schizophrenia Use Substances?

Same reasons as anyone else:

- to feel better or different
- to relax and have fun
- to be part of a group, to fit in socially
- out of curiosity, experimentation
- for stress relief
- to overcome boredom, isolation, and inhibitions

Additionally, with schizophrenia, motivations may be intensified:

- Self-medication that seems to work temporarily on symptoms
- Fewer vocational, recreational, and interpersonal opportunities in life
- Feelings of powerlessness associated with having a mental illness
- "Drug use can put off the uncomfortable confrontation with yourself that something is wrong—very wrong—with your mind"*

What to Do If the Outbursts Escalate

- Call the police if necessary.
- Calmly explain the situation as best you can.
- Protect the safety of your family but allow the police to do their job.
- Remember: *this is not your fault.*
- "Considerable research has shown that a parent is not responsible for a child's emotional or psychological well-being; past opposing theories were based on faulty premises and are remnants of Freudianism."†
- Be mindful of feelings of confusion and embarrassment in yourself and other family members.
- Take care of yourself.

---

*E. Fuller Torrey, *Surviving Schizophrenia: A Manual for Families, Consumers, and Providers* (New York: HarperCollins, 2001), p. 10.
†Nando Pelusi, *Psychology Today* online, December 31, 2007.

8

THE LAST RESORT

Dear Mom,

    I spend a lot of time here, besides retrospecting upon my mistakes and becoming aware of my problems (except laziness which I now notice and once denied), singing to myself, out loud of course; but the lyrics always apply to how I feel. . . . I still feel the snake bite on the upper left side of my body; it's spread to my *heart*, I can feel it pulsing.

—Ben, notebook journal he kept in Montana,
2000 (found in 2003)

I had Montana on my mind. Maybe, somewhere far away, someone else could save Ben.

For years, I had worked with Mason, an audio producer who frequently used me as a narrator. His children were a few years older than mine, and we'd always shared parenting stories and solutions. A few years earlier, his son David had gone through a terrible change in his early teens: mood swings, the wrong friends, drug use, even episodes of violence. Mason and his wife, Emily, had tried everything, and they had finally sent David to a place called Adventures. It offered a three-week outdoor wilderness assessment program (WAC) to start, which took participants through Arizona and ended on-site in Montana with scheduled family meetings. After the WAC some teens were referred to further programs within Adventures. Mason and Emily had always told me that Adventures had saved their son's life. He'd stayed in their summer program and come back a changed person. David was back on the path to success, and their family was peaceful once again.

I'd mentioned Adventures to Ben once before, as a possible alternative when he'd dropped out of school. Ben had refused to discuss it at the time, but now I was convinced this might be the only option left. I'd run out of ideas. Nothing else was working.

By this time, there were very few people I could turn to for advice or support. Certainly not their father: William had started drinking again, and his life was a mess. No help there. My friends had tired long ago of hearing about Ben's problems. They tried to be sympathetic, but I could almost see their eyes glaze over if I started to tell another Ben story. My brothers, too, were getting tired of it. I didn't blame them—I was sick and tired of it, too. Each had tried to help Ben, especially my younger brother. He had taken Ben out to dinner alone, to talk some sense into him, to talk him out of leaving school. He had come back looking exhausted and shrugging his shoulders. "I tried, but . . . he is the most stubborn, hard-headed kid I have ever met," he said. It wasn't just *my* reasoning Ben was rejecting; it was reason *in general*.

I called Adventures to find out more about the program. I spoke to Larry, who ran the program with his wife, Patricia. "Our program is designed for teens who have lost their way," he said. "It's not a boot camp. Our kids don't have criminal records, but they seem to have lost the feel for things like motivation and accomplishment. They have trouble remembering how important teamwork is. They need structure and a clear path. Sometimes, they also need to get clean and sober." It sounded perfect.

"What if he doesn't want to go?" I asked.

"Well, we usually hope that they will want to come here. Some of them are so happy to be away from their parents that they can't wait. Others, though, refuse to go."

"And then what?"

"We know that for some families, this is the only choice they feel they have left. We do provide an escort service to get their children to our door. We take it from there. Sometimes the most reluctant arrivals find they have gotten the most out of the program. We get thank-you notes all the time—and sometimes apology letters, too."

Larry spent over an hour on the phone with me, and later that week he called and spoke to Ben about it. Ben listened politely and asked questions about the program. After he hung up, I asked him what he thought. "Sounds nice, Mom, but I don't think I need it," he said. *I knew it wouldn't be that easy.*

The cost for this program was over $3,000 per month; however, if this was the way to a happy future, it would be money well spent. The way things were now, Ben might never get to college at all; the money set aside for his education could be better spent possibly saving his life. *Besides—maybe he'll be ready to think about college after they straighten him out. Or he'll go back to high school. He'd only be a year behind.*

Armed with a new possibility, I waited for the right time to spring it on Ben. I did some more research and found out that, legally, I only had to make sure Ben had room and board *available* to him until he was eighteen. If I chose to have him leave the house and arranged another living situation, then I was not responsible if he chose to refuse those accommodations.

So I had the legal right to send Ben to a new living situation—but that didn't take care of the guilt I felt for not being able to fix my child myself. I needed to be sure that this was the best choice, possibly the only choice, for all of us.

Finally, one afternoon, I was pushed too far over the edge to keep hoping I had any chance of handling this by myself. The last thread snapped, at long last. On that day, Ben and I were standing in the family room, locked in another standoff that was in great danger of escalating. Ali sat on the couch, her math textbook in her lap. Every time we raised our voices she looked at us in disgust.

Ben had reverted again to telling me that I was the source of his problems because of my "obsession with conventional things" like earning your own money. I looked at his matted, greasy hair, his ragged, oversized jeans, and a litany of complaints came to mind. I was about to lose control—I felt it coming.

Ali looked up at me, sighed, and started to gather her schoolbooks to leave the room. That stopped me. I took a deep breath. "Ben," I said. "I'm not getting into this. You must work forty hours a week. That is the rule."

"But Mom, you're not hearing me!"

"That's the rule." I willed my voice to remain even and pleasant. I smiled to show him that it wasn't personal. It wasn't easy.

"That's stupid, Mom."

Ben was getting so agitated that I knew I had to get away from him physically. If I stayed, I was going to try to win. I would try logic. I would try reason. I would try every angle, every turn of phrase, every quote I could think of. And then we would get louder and angrier. I didn't want that to happen again, especially not in front of Ali. She'd seen and heard it too many times. I could feel the anger rise in me like lava. I made myself turn and walk away from him, toward the front door. I had to leave the scene, quickly.

"Don't walk away from me!" Ben shouted. "You are just avoiding the truth! That won't help, you know!"

A number of retorts occurred to me, but I ignored them. "I am not getting into this, Ben," I said. I walked outside.

He followed me. "You can't run from conflict, Mom! Didn't you always tell me that?"

Oh, Lord, give me strength. I wanted so badly to turn and fix this. I wanted to argue back. I wanted to push him away. I wanted to grab him in a strong hug and *will* some reason into him. I hated him; I loved him. I couldn't detach from him if he was standing near me. I walked to my car, got in, and started the engine. I didn't know where I would go, but I knew where I could *not* be.

I put the car in reverse and looked back to see if the road was clear. Ben was standing right behind the car. "Don't you drive away from me!" he said.

If I move, he'll have to get out of the way. I'll call his bluff. I took a deep breath and began backing up the car. Ben looked at me in disbelief. He did not jump out of the way. The car's rear bumper touched his knees and he put his hands on the trunk lid. "Are you crazy?" he screamed. "You're trying to run me over! Mom, you're losing it. You're trying to kill your own son!"

Inside, I was screaming: *You're the one who's nuts. I am not trying to kill you. I just need to be away from you. I am trying to* not *kill you!* But I didn't say any of those things. Instead, I set the parking brake and turned the car off. I opened the door and got out, slamming it shut. I walked right past my son, down the driveway, and around our block. Fast. Furiously. I prayed that the neighbors would just think I was on a power-walk.

No such luck, though. Ben began to follow me. He was on a roll—a furious one. I walked at a near-run. Ben was right behind me, screaming at me. "You are the worst mother that ever lived! You don't love me! You tried to run over your own child! I hate you! I can't wait until I don't have to live with you anymore!"

The faster I walked, the closer the tears came to spilling down my face. I remembered walking around this neighborhood so many other times, with my children by my side. I remembered Halloween nights, staying behind them to make sure they were safe while trick-or-treating with their friends. I remembered Ben's first driving lesson with me, on these same streets, right after he'd gotten his permit. Walking around, counting the houses with Christmas lights, looking for the ones with menorahs. We used to play a game: which house would you buy, if you had to choose? Ben used to laugh. He used to *laugh* with me, with Ali.

Ali. Where is she right now? Back in her room, trying to study—or talking on the phone to a friend, complaining about her brother. Maybe crying again, as she'd done so often lately. Maybe missing the way he used to be. I can't live like this anymore. And, God knows, neither can Ali.

Ben seemed to run out of steam as we continued our strange parade around the block. The more I pretended that his words had no effect, the more he calmed down. Finally, he caught up to me and said, "I didn't mean that, Mom. You're not so bad. I'm sorry." This crisis, too, had peaked and ended—just like that. But so much damage had been done. I was wearing away. This unending cycle was chipping away at me. This was beyond me, and getting bigger, and I had no idea why.

"Okay, Ben. Thanks," I said. *I can't do this anymore*, I thought. We walked back home together, silently. But I knew, then, that I was out of answers. Ben had to go to Montana. They had to be able to fix him.

I called Adventures again, and found that they had a wilderness assessment trip starting on January 10, and that there was room for Ben in it. Yes, they would be happy to talk to Ben about it and answer any questions. Yes, it would be best if he chose to go and went willingly. Yes, they would provide an escort to get him there if I needed one.

The remaining question was this: would *Ben* be able to see that going on this trip might be best for him? Could I pull this off without forcing him to go? I thought about his social world, which was getting smaller and smaller. His old friends from youth group were all focused on their last year of high school, on their future in college. They were happy to see Ben in temple, but they had very little in common with him now. Lindsay had been his world—but now even she was getting tired of the changes in him, even frightened. In December, she went out to Arizona to look at a college there. She and Ben had a huge, painful fight when she came home, and they broke up. He was heartbroken and confused—but ripe, I hoped, for the change I was about to spring on him.

I wanted to present options, but they couldn't include going on the same way we had been. I found that there were halfway house residences in our state that specialized in handling cases like Ben's and that he was eligible for their programs. So he had a choice, and I hoped Montana would be the one he'd pick.

It wasn't as hard as I thought it would be. I sat Ben down at the kitchen counter late one morning, after he had rolled out of bed and gotten some cereal and rice milk to eat. He was unshaven, unshowered, his long, curly hair matted into his version of dreadlocks. They didn't look like any dreadlocks I had ever seen; I longed to take a pair of scissors and cut off every tangle, every greasy knot of hair. I missed his curls. I missed a lot of things about him. I missed his ambition. I missed his sense of humor. I missed his warmth.

"What's wrong, Mom?" he said. "You look bummed. What did I do this time?"

It's what you haven't *been doing, Ben. You haven't been working, you haven't been trying, you haven't been loving, you haven't been keeping promises, you haven't been learning from your mistakes.* I didn't say any of those things. What I said was this: "Ben, this isn't working."

"What isn't working?"

"Your living here under this roof."

He held his spoon in midair. Rice milk spilled onto the table. His brown eyes opened wider. "Mom, you can't say that. I'm your son."

I had prepared for this moment for so long that the rehearsed words just rolled out. "Ben, you have had every chance in the world to stick to the bargain we made when you moved back in here after you ran away. You've run out of chances. You have lost every job, and your promises mean nothing to me anymore because you haven't kept them."

He ate his spoonful of cereal, put the spoon down, and looked at me. "So?" he said.

"So," I said, "you can't live here anymore. You have two choices. I've found another place for you to live where they will be in charge of you and help you get back on your feet, or you can go to the program in Montana."

"What?"

"That is it, Ben. There is no third choice. You move to a halfway house or you agree to go to Adventures."

He sat still before me. He did not blink his eyes. Then he sighed. "What's the program in Montana again? I forgot."

I told him all that I knew. The twenty-six-day wilderness trip. I mentioned the other programs they had, but I had been advised to keep it simple. Don't lie to him, but don't overwhelm him with information. Don't tell him more than he needs to know.

While I was explaining, Ben finished his breakfast and listened. When I was done, he put his dishes in the sink and turned to me. "Can I call them and ask some more questions myself?" He looked sincere. More than that—he looked excited. He looked almost lit up, almost hopeful.

"Sure, Ben," I said. I gave him the number. He called right away and took the phone into the living room. After half an hour, he walked back into the kitchen.

"That sounds awesome, Mom!" he said. "I'd love to go. Here, Larry wants to talk to you." He handed me the phone.

He'd love to go. No halfway house. At least three weeks of vacation from him, just Ali and me. Some peace for us—and hopefully for Ben. Something for him to look forward to. Thank God. Now I just have to get him on that plane.

We had lots to do before he left. There was camping equipment to buy, packing to do, nonleather hiking boots to find (not easy). During that time, Ben seemed a lot more like his old self. For the first time in months, he had something positive to say whenever he was asked what was going on in his life. He was occasionally nervous about the trip, though, and I watched for signs that he might change his mind. I was determined to hold firm, even if he brought up the subject. The decision had been made. My hope was riding entirely, now, on this move. It was our last resort.

The morning of his flight, we drove to Bradley Airport in Hartford in silence, except for the prayers going on inside my head. *Just let him get on the plane, please. Let there be no last-minute scenes, no last-minute panic in the airport. Let him get there safely. Let them help him.*

Inside the airport, I remained on high alert. Any moment now, it was still possible that Ben might bolt. He was now visibly nervous. Every time he left me—to go to the men's room or to buy a cup of coffee—I had to resist the urge to follow him. He didn't say much, but I recognized the frightened look in his eyes, the way he paced around the waiting area. I knew he was having last-minute doubts.

I didn't dare ask Ben how he was feeling about this. I checked my watch every few minutes and checked Ben's face even more often. Finally, they called his flight. Finally, he gave me a good-bye hug. Finally, he boarded the plane. Finally, I could breathe.

That night I got a call from Steve, who was part of the Adventures staff and leading the wilderness trip. But the news was good—this was just a courtesy call. "Ben has arrived safely, and he seems very excited about the wilderness course. He looks very happy. Don't worry. He's in good hands." He sounded kind. He sounded confident. He sounded like someone who would take no bullshit from Ben.

Ben was safe. I was free. "Thank you," I said.

"We'll be taking Ben for a haircut tomorrow, before the trip leaves."

A haircut! This really was going to be good.

Our home life relaxed into a new calm. The distance from Ben's daily mood swings was intoxicating. When Ali's friends slept over, we didn't have to worry about when he would walk through the door, and what he might say or do when he did. We marveled at how predictable our days were. Ali did her homework in the living room instead of hidden in the bedroom. We went to the mall. We felt normal again, although with Ben away our little family seemed awfully small—and almost strangely still. I felt happier than I had felt in a long time, but I also felt guilty. *Why don't I miss him?*

One evening I was driving Ali home from her rehearsal for a school production of the musical *Anything Goes*. Ali had finally found a few niches in Trumbull High, and this was one of them. We were alone in the car.

"How was rehearsal?" I asked. Maybe I'd get an answer of more than one word. You never know.

"Fine," she said. *Oh well.* Then she looked over at me and said, "Mom?"

"Yes, honey?"

"Do you think they can make him better?"

I knew exactly what she meant, but I asked anyway. "You mean Ben?"

"Yeah," she said. "I mean, when he comes home, will I be able to talk to him again, the way I used to? Will he stop being so weird?"

Oh, how I wish I had the answer to that. But those are my hopes, too—exactly my hopes. "You miss him, don't you?" I said.

Ali stared ahead until the light turned green. "Well," she said. "Yes and no. I mean, it's so nice now. I don't miss the screaming and the arguing and the way he smells so bad all the time. And I like that he's probably having a good time, since he loves hiking and nature and all that. But I miss him the way he used to be, before he got so strange. I miss talking to him, back when he used to listen to me." Ali's voice started to crack. She was trying not to cry.

I remember that, I thought. *I'd almost forgotten. They'd had secret jokes, secret games they played. They had been friends. Her friends used to think Ben was cute. Some even had crushes on him. I miss that, too. Oh, how I miss that.*

I pulled the car into the garage and turned off the ignition. We sat there for a moment, waiting for the garage doors to reach the ground. I hadn't thought about Ali's missing Ben, at least not so soon.

I'd thought that the absence of chaos would override any other emotions for a while. Sometimes, it's only when someone is gone from sight that we can see the whole picture. While Ben was swinging from one extreme to the other, it was hard to focus on anything except the current crisis, whatever it was. Now we were both free to remember other, better, moments. Now we could both dare to hope.

Ali was, as usual, twirling her hair around one finger. Her almond brown eyes held unspilled tears. "Ali," I said, "I don't know the answer to your question. I don't know if they can bring Ben back to the way he used to be. All I know is that they do wonderful work there, and have a lot of success stories. So—maybe. Maybe. It will take time, though. Ben may have to stay there until he figures things out. But I think there's a chance. I think there's a good chance." I prayed that I was right.

"Okay, Mom," she said. "I want him to be my brother again."

"Me too, honey." *Me too.*

Other people were also hoping for a turnaround in Ben. My brothers, their wives, and my four nephews were wondering how this had happened. Ben's friends from happier days often asked me how he was. They all missed him, too. I was not the only one waiting for a miracle to happen in Montana.

A few days later, my fragile vision of Ben's new start in life was smashed by a dose of reality. Jessica, the Adventures staff psychologist, called to fill me in on what had been happening. "Well," she began, "you sure have an interesting son."

Oh, how I used to love to hear that phrase. Now, I hate it. I know what "interesting" means now. It means trouble.

Jessica told me what had happened on the trip so far. "When we picked Ben up at the airport, he was initially very talkative and cheerful. Right away, though, he tried to manipulate the staff into letting him bring barred materials along—music, books, candles, cigarettes. When we said no, he became childish and petulant and threatened not to participate at all. Then he tried to sneak cigarettes along."

"I'm sorry," I said. I didn't know what else to say.

"Oh, don't be sorry. This is what we do. We've seen this all before." I relaxed. "Still," she went on, "Ben's behaviors have been a bit more extreme than usual."

"What do you mean?"

"When he debates the rules, he takes it too far. He doesn't let it go. He keeps trying to explain his side by coming up with analogies, as if the staff is just too stupid to get his point. Then, if he doesn't get his way, he tries other things to make the point."

"Such as . . . ?"

"On the third day of the course, he announced that he was ready to go home. He said that he had already gotten the point, even if it might take the others longer to get it. When we told him that he couldn't do that, he tried to leave. He also began a hunger strike."

"What?"

"I kid you not. He refused to eat, drink, or move until the staff let him go home. And he compared himself to Gandhi and Siddhartha. He said his cause was justified; he just would not listen to reason."

"Oh no."

"I'm afraid so. He didn't eat or drink for twenty-seven hours, although he did help with chores during the strike. We think he became cooperative because he thought the ploy was going to work. He also seemed to like the attention."

This sounded familiar. Too familiar. I just couldn't believe he had pulled this in such a new situation. This was supposed to be his fresh start. "So what happened?"

"Well," Jessica said, "when no one paid attention to his fast, he lay down on the ground in the middle of the path and refused to move. The whole group, even the other kids, was annoyed with him by now."

"How old is the rest of the group?" I said.

"They're all between sixteen and eighteen. They just don't understand why Ben is being so weird. He is shutting them all out, not just the staff."

I felt my fantasies shatter like glass. This one crack in my hope was spreading out of control. *This was supposed to be different*, I thought. *New place. New people. No past history. Clear structure. No pot. No distractions.* But Ben's reactions had not changed.

This was going to be a harder job than I'd hoped. *What is wrong with him? Why are the other kids getting it, and not Ben?*

Still, he was thousands of miles away, with people I'd chosen to trust. When I hung up the phone, he would still be in their hands. "What happened next?" I asked.

Jessica said, "Steve told Ben he couldn't let the group down like that. So he picked Ben up and carried him on his back for three-quarters of a mile."

I tried to picture that. *This Steve must be an angel. A strong male mentor, just what Ben needs.*

Jessica continued the story: "And then, Ben broke down in tears. He got off Steve's back and cried and cried. Then he agreed to continue with the hike. He said he would go with the group and participate in the program, at least to midpoint. Then, he said, he might want to fast again, because he still wanted to go home."

But that was the last thing I wanted. "And did he keep his promise?" I asked.

"He did. Actually, he had a pretty good week after that breakdown. He was more accepting of the program with each day, although he still moved very slowly and was always the last to finish tasks and pack up his stuff. To justify his laziness, he tends to analyze and spout philosophy. It's like he won't look at the present. He has to be outside himself and the situation, always away from reality."

I had noticed this at home. Ben had developed the habit of walking slowly and thinking fast—but not about what was happening in the moment. He always seemed distant. He watched and manipulated. I had thought it was a symptom of marijuana use. Now that he was clean, I didn't know how to explain it. That was even scarier.

Jessica went on: "Ben also has periods of depression and sadness, when he cries a lot. Then there are times when he flies off the handle. At those times, there's just no reasoning with him. Later on, after he calms down, yes—but until then we can't reach him. He's single-minded about going home, too."

"But you won't let that happen, right?"

Jessica laughed. "No, we've got it under control. Don't worry. Ben really needs to finish this, or whatever confidence he has will disappear. We're going to see him through this. We see so much potential in him, but it's very hard to find out who he is underneath all his avoidance and philosophizing."

Don't give up; please don't give up. He needs more people who believe in him. I can't do it myself.

Jessica had gone to visit the group at the midpoint, and she brought letters for the group from their families. Before Ben read his, he told Jessica he was going back on his hunger strike. He compared himself again to Gandhi and said that he was protesting the wrongs against him.

"What happened?" I asked Jessica.

"It was the strangest thing," she said. "Ben was talking about Gandhi, and how he was being just like him. Then I looked at him and said, 'But Ben, Gandhi was fasting for the greater good of his people. You are fasting for your own selfish purposes. You're not trying to help anyone other than yourself.'"

Somehow, that got through to Ben. "He just looked at me, thought for a second, said, 'Oh—I guess you're right,' and then said 'I think I'll go have some lunch then.' And that was the end of that." Jessica went on to tell me that Ben had then gone off to read my letter to him, and had seemed strongly influenced by it. He promised to try to work on his laziness, defensiveness, and stubbornness.

And after that he did try harder. Still, the staff noticed a lot of holding back on Ben's part. He was going through the motions, but he didn't really buy into much of the teamwork or honesty lessons. He wrote in his journal that he "didn't need boundaries," and he only seemed to complete the assignments that he felt agreed with his own philosophies.

The trip ended with a breakthrough for Ben. After weeks of refusing to talk about William, he opened up to the group and told the story around the campfire. This seemed like an important step. Maybe. It was so hard to tell.

Now we had to figure out what to do next. It was time for parents to fly out to Montana for family meetings. For me, it was time to tell Ben that he wasn't ready to come home yet. We all agreed—the Adventures staff, Ben's therapist, Art, and I—that Ben needed more. Otherwise, the three weeks would have been a waste. Larry said, "We feel that Ben has made some progress so far, but my guess is that if he goes home now, you'll have a honeymoon with him for about two days, and then it will be as if he had never left." I knew he was right.

We decided that Ben could stay in Montana for a spring semester of sorts. He would join Adventures' residential program, called Cabin Life. While he was there, he would spend time on academics, too. He could even sign up for college as a correspondence student. They would help him study. If he worked hard, he could have six or even nine college credits under his belt by the time he would have graduated from his senior year of high school.

I couldn't think of a better way to spend his college fund than this. Maybe we'd even catch up financially. I told Ali about the decision, and she asked, "Do you think he'll start acting normal again?" She was smiling. "He won't be so weird? You mean, I might have a brother in college next year, like everyone else?"

What I wouldn't give to give her back her brother.

I wrote another letter to Ben, explaining why we all felt this was the best way to go. The WAC group drove up to Montana for the final three days: solo camping on the Adventures property. This would mean mastering practical survival tasks as well as using the solitude for reflection and discovery. Ben would be reading my letter and completing journal assignments to help with the process.

Before I left for the airport to catch the plane to Montana, I spoke with Jessica one more time. She said that Ben had received the letter and taken it with him on his solo. Each boy was visited by a staff member daily to make sure all was well; the word was that Ben had read my letter and seemed to accept it.

But you could never be sure with Ben. Jessica added, "He took the news almost too easily. It was—I don't know—almost calculating. He was too quiet about it."

Two days later, when I finally arrived at the Adventures site after a six-hour flight to Spokane, Washington, a three-hour overnight drive through the pitch-dark and unfamiliar Idaho/Montana roads, and a night at the Lakeside Motel, I found out why Ben had been so calm.

He had run away.

He must have been planning it from the moment he put my letter back in the envelope.

I arrived at Adventures at the appointed midmorning hour. There were several sets of parents, all of us there for "family conference weekend," but when I walked in I was ushered straight into the kitchen by Larry and his wife, Patricia. "Ah, your son," they said, and sighed.

Ben had been fine the night before, they told me. A staff member had checked on him, and watched as he'd climbed into his sleeping bag. But sometime during the next two hours, Ben had taken the plastic "stuff sacks" that usually hold the sleeping bags and put them on his feet to replace the shoes he was not allowed to have on the solo. In the cold and snowy Montana February, Ben had then taken off with stuff sacks on his feet and tried to hitchhike on the main road. The police had brought him back to Adventures at about 3 a.m., waking everyone up in the process.

"Where is he now?" I asked.

"He's doing chores right now, washing the windows in the lodge. We have to have a group meeting with him. He has to face his group and the staff. He has to face you. He's thinking about what he did. He seems very depressed but has been compliant with what we've asked him to do."

I was so angry. I had left Ali behind, three thousand miles away, and had spent all this time and money to come out and see Ben. Why couldn't he just do what he was supposed to, for once? "Please tell me," I said, "that this isn't the first time you've seen this." I desperately needed to know that my son wasn't a hopeless case.

"We've seen it before," said Larry, "but not quite this way—not with plastic bags for shoes. We have had kids run from the program, but often they come to their senses and come back. And, years later, we get an apology—and thanks for sticking it out with them."

I tried to picture this, to let the comfort soothe my shame.

We let Ben have time to cool off while I met with the other parents and the staff. There was a certain comradeship among us instantly—we had reached our respective wits' ends and sent our sons to this program—but I did notice that I was the only single parent. I felt inadequate. I was jealous.

How come they have people to talk it over with, to share the burden? Why do I have to do this alone—and pay for it alone? What is wrong with me?

We each had individual family appointments set for us later in the day; mine wasn't until midafternoon. I walked around the town, so sleepy in February but clearly meant to come alive in the summertime, and soon it was time to return to the Adventures property. This time, I could take in some of the scene. I was not as nervous as I'd been in the morning—after all, the shoe had already dropped.

The eighty-acre property was a five-minute drive from the town's center, past the railroad tracks, up some narrow ice-over-gravel roads, and past small trailers and cabins backed up by huge open spaces, countless evergreen trees, and mountains. Maneuvering past the gate and up the long private driveway to the Adventures property, I pulled into an empty space in front of the log home where Larry and Patricia lived with their three children and the teens in a Home Base program they also ran. The driveway and parking areas were full of snow and ice—unlike the East Coast, where we immediately plow, shovel, and spread salt to make walking easier.

They just seemed to cope with the ice here—and wear the proper shoes. Which I most definitely was not wearing. I made it to the front porch, but just barely. What passed for winter boots in Connecticut were not quite cutting it here, and I was sliding more than walking. Once safely on the porch, though, I could turn around and take a good look at the land. I took a deep, cold breath of the winter air. It felt clean and sharp. It smelled of snow and of wood smoke.

The front door opened, and a young man I had not seen before came out. "Hi," he said. "Are you Ben's mother?" He seemed so polite. There was no judgment in his voice. He looked me in the eyes, and his voice was warm.

"Yes," I said. *He must be from the Home Base program. Is this what Ben may act like, a few months from now?* It was almost too much to hope for. But first I had to face my son, and the stunt he had pulled last night.

"Come on in," the boy said. "I'll tell them you're here."

Right inside the door were about twenty pairs of boots of all sizes, lined up near scarves, hats, and gloves. I smelled the wood stove going at full blast. There were oversized comfortable couches and natural wood tables. It all fit perfectly—like a *Montana Life* magazine cover, if there was such a thing. Over in the corner, the family dog lay on a comforter that struck a familiar chord in my brain and then my heart.

I recognized it as the same pattern as the sheet I'd used to make a comforter for Ben back when he was two years old, for his first "big boy" bed. The other side of the comforter had been a solid sheet, with a rainbow I had appliquéd over the entire width of the blanket in long curves of color. I had stitched *Benjamin* in the corner. Ben had always loved that comforter. Now the sight of the pattern almost made me cry.

Suddenly I heard my son's voice. "Hi, Mom." Ben walked in through the kitchen. Larry and Patricia were right behind him.

"Ben." I held out my arms, and he walked into them and returned my hug.

"I missed you," he said.

"Me too, Ben." Now that he was here in my arms I realized how true that really was.

Suddenly he pulled back and looked at the comforter in the corner, and then at me. He smiled. *He smiled.* "Recognize that, Mom?"

I told him I did, and I smiled, too.

"Isn't that funny? I love that comforter you made me."

My little boy. My troubled young man. My darling son. You are inside there. You are in there.

An icy path lay between this cabin and the one where we were to hold our official family conference. Patricia told me I'd never make it in the shoes I had on. "Just grab any pair by the door that fits you," she said. "That's what we all do. It doesn't matter."

I did as I was told, and we walked outside and across the yard. This building was also made of logs, but seemed more institutional on the inside—folding chairs, metal tables, storage for camping gear. We opened a few chairs and sat in a circle: Jeff and Steve, who had led the WAC, Jessica, me, and Ben. Ben already looked defensive.

The evaluation meeting started out easily enough. At least all the behaviors and decisions were already out on the table—no surprises. We'd all have to present a united and unshakable front about the decision to transfer Ben over to the Cabin Life program instead of letting him come home. If we allowed a crack, he'd rip it open.

We were firm. We were loving. We were gentle. We reminded Ben that his decision to run away the night before had only convinced us all further that he needed to remain in Montana and work on the things he had only begun to grapple with.

As we spoke, Ben began looking trapped. I could see the wheels turning. His eyes darted around, then became focused as he chose his words. He defended his actions on the trip, said that he'd been merely sticking up for his rights all along. "And, Mom," he said, "I did so well on the WAC! I made so much progress! Don't I get any credit for that? You just want me to be perfect!"

I wanted so much to fight back, to out-argue him, to win. I wanted him to *want* to stay. But staying would have to be good enough—even if it was because he simply had no choice. *How do I begin to explain this?*

Then Jeff, thankfully, stepped in. "Ben, your decision to run away last night shows us that you really haven't made as much progress as you'd like to think you have. That was dangerous. You had us all scared. Plus, you lied to everyone. You let down the group. You had a commitment, and you didn't keep it."

"But—but—it's all because I wanted to go home!" Now Ben was shouting. Now Ben was standing up. "Mom—that's how much I wanted to go home! Home is the best place for me now—not here! I hate it here! And you don't even want me! My own mother!"

I kept my responses locked inside my head; instead, tears came streaming down my cheeks. That was the last thing I wanted to do. I didn't want the sadness. I didn't want the guilt. But those emotions were quickly overtaken by confusion and horror.

"You hate me!" Ben shouted "You think I'm a failure!"

"Ben," I said, "of course I don't think you're a failure. I just . . ."

"No! No!" he cried. "You think I'm a *failure*. I'm going to pick up this pen and write it all over myself!" Then he did. Ben picked up a Bic pen that was lying on the metal folding table and began to write on his arm: FAILURE. I AM A FAILURE—over and over again.

"Ben!" I said. I stood up to go to him, to make him stop. This was crazy. Crazy.

Jeff gestured for me to sit back down. "Randye," he said. "I think Ben is going to need a little time without you right now."

"No!" Ben said. "She *hates* me. My own mother!" Then he walked over to the window and started sobbing. He didn't just cry; he wailed, his entire body shuddering.

I felt powerless.

Jeff gently walked over to Ben and took the pen away from him. FAILURE was written all over Ben's arm.

I felt like one, too. I left the room, and let the staff do their work. *I'm not any good to my son right now*, I thought. *What* am *I good for? Why can't I make it go away? Why can't I love* him *back to normal?*

Afterward, Ben was calmer. He spoke to the staff; somehow they worked things out. By the following day he was resigned to staying in

Montana; he even seemed to be looking forward to the new program, now that he knew he couldn't talk his way out of it.

For the rest of the weekend, Ben was warm and loving. He proudly showed me some of the journal work he had completed on WAC and told me about his successes. Now I could see that he had gotten something out of the experience after all. He listened to me when I spoke about how his behaviors in the past two years had made me feel.

By the time I left, Ben was ready to own up to some of his past actions, and we shared a long farewell hug. I told him Ali and I would call every week, and that I was proud of him. "Work hard," I said, "and you'll be home before you know it, and you'll have some success to bring with you. I know you can do this, honey."

"Bye, Mom," he said. "I love you. Tell Ali that too, okay?" I knew he meant this. I could almost believe the "failure" incident had never happened. The picture of Ben, hysterical and writing all over his arms, seemed unreal. But it stayed near me; it terrified me. He had been so far removed from reason and so desperate. There was no pot in his system; this had been a clean, sober, and still out-of-control Ben.

I drove off, leaving him in good hands. Mine were not the right ones now. I was so grateful that they were willing to take on my son. And it seemed, to love him a little bit, too. On the three-hour drive back to Spokane, my heart felt lighter with each mile.

I treated myself to a night alone in Spokane. My flight was early the next morning, and I needed transition time, alone time. I checked into the Hilton, then treated myself to a movie. I watched *Angela's Ashes* alone in the dark theater, where the luxury of being completely anonymous, no chance of running into anyone I knew, allowed my mind to go blank. As I watched Frank McCourt's story unfold, I tried to absorb the recent events in my own family.

As I walked out of the theater toward my rented car, I stopped cold in the middle of the sidewalk. Something, some feeling, was overwhelming me. I stood there as strangers walked past, and let the emotions radiate.

And then I knew what it was. It was simply love. Pure, overpowering love. Trapped for so long between anger and relief, I'd almost forgotten how much I loved my son.

I'd almost forgotten.

The next morning on the airplane, halfway across the country, halfway between my troubled son in the West and my waiting daughter in the East, I felt the pull in both directions. I was in limbo. Physically I ached for Ali. I wished she could have been with us in Montana, to experience it all

CHAPTER GUIDEPOSTS

What Siblings May Feel When a Relative Develops Symptoms of Mental Illness

- Shame and embarrassment
- Social stigma of having a "strange" family member
- Anger, jealousy, and resentment—more attention paid to "ill" sibling
- Depression and guilt
- Living with household stress of coping with illness
- Mourning the loss of the brother or sister they knew, who has changed
- Pressure to succeed
- "Survival guilt"
- Fear of becoming sick themselves
- Forced to play unwanted roles, such as guardian

What to Do

- Education, even for young children
- Support groups
- Pay attention to needs and rights of the rest of the family—including the right to have fun
- Give them opportunities to talk about it, and listen without judgment
- Allow them to grieve
- Remind them they are not responsible
- Recognize their accomplishments

Dual Diagnosis

The combination of mental illness and substance abuse is called dual diagnosis, and it's very common. The prevailing thought seems to be that they are linked, biologically and physically. Integrated treatment is often recommended.

One of the problems with dual diagnosis is that it's hard to tell what causes the symptoms: the illness or the substance. When your relative becomes clean and sober, and symptoms still remain, that may be more evidence that the problem isn't "just" substance abuse.

rather than have to get the stories from me secondhand. To see her brother in person, to hug him herself.

How I hated that my little family was split apart by this situation. And all I could think about was the power of my love for my children. *So powerful that it almost hurts. I will never, I will never, give up on either of them. No matter what.*

A LEGAL ADULT

Mom mentioned something to me in the car today, that when you come back the three of us should take a road trip somewhere, I said no—just me and you should. Maybe if you get your license we can!!

—Ali's letter to Ben, April 2000

In my past year of self-centeredness I was never really appreciative of you for all you are, and I just want to share with you how meaningful you are to me. You are a beautiful, wonderful, loving, honest person; you are my sister who stuck with me and still saw my good sides through my bad sides; you were and are here for me and help me even when I reject it. I love you and thank you for being my sister.

—Ben's reply, April 2000

Ben remained out West for almost ten months. Even out there, even in the hands of competent and caring staff, with clearly defined structure and—most importantly—with no drugs or alcohol in his system, his progress never seemed to solidify. There was no predictability. Nothing seemed to stick—at least, not for long. Crisis still found its way to Ben. True connection to others still seemed to elude him. And I kept hoping that a lasting solution was just around the corner.

But there was always another crisis.

There was the day of Ben's eighteenth birthday, in April. For three months I had parented from afar. Sunday phone calls revealed remarkable progress in Ben, with only a few glitches. By the time I heard about any setbacks, they'd usually already been resolved by the staff. It was heaven. I was optimistic. But this time the phone call came in the middle of the week—not a good sign.

I was just about to try to find my way through the dirty dishes to the bottom of the kitchen sink when the phone rang. I turned off the water and wiped my hands on my jeans. "Hello?"

"Randye." It was Priscilla, a Cabin Life staff member. "I'm so glad you're home. We've got a problem here."

Problem. What? Broken leg, campfire burn, animal bite? Physical traumas flashed through my mind. But no.

"Ben has decided to leave the program."

I sat down at the table. I felt like I'd been punched in the stomach. *Oh no. Not again.* "Where is he? What happened?"

"Well," she said, "he hasn't gone anywhere yet, but today, right in the middle of a camping trip, he got up and announced that it was time to say good-bye to everyone. He was turning eighteen tomorrow and was not legally forced to be here. So he was leaving."

I could just picture it. Unfortunately. "Well—did he say where he was going?"

"Nope. He had no plan. He was just—leaving. Now, we don't know if he just wanted some attention or what, but the entire group of kids started letting him have it. They told him he couldn't let down the group like that. 'What about your commitment, Ben?' they kept saying."

Sounded right to me. *What* about *his commitment, his promises? What about all the hard work he had put in? Was it all gone? Was it all an act? Was this all for nothing?*

"Tell Ben that there will be *no* money coming to him from me, to support this decision. He'll be completely on his own for food, shelter, everything. But that I *will* continue to pay the bills for him to stay and finish at Cabin Life. Nothing else," I said.

"Just what we needed to hear from you," Priscilla said. "Thanks. We'll take care of it."

And they did. Priscilla called back to report that together they had all managed to talk Ben out of his flight plan. A united front had done it: the staff's rebuttals to Ben's justifications, the disappointment and anger of his peer group, the reality of my ultimatum, and time for Ben himself to think again and change his mind.

After this birthday crisis, Ben seemed to relax again. It was as though he'd had to explode into that rash announcement, into the drama of it all. The staff and the peer group helped him in the debriefing process, and other kids got to share how disappointed and angry they had been. Ben seemed sincerely sorry and apologized to everyone. The rest of the camping trip went well. After letting it all out, Ben had become helpful and cheerful once again.

Academically, Ben was having a hard time focusing on his school-work. He had asked for nine college credits—a much larger load than recommended. Ben had been convinced he'd have no trouble with it, even though he hadn't been in formal school for almost two years and had never really developed organizational skills and study habits. There was also the unanswered question as to whether or not he had a reading disability, as had been suggested at Fieldstone. Ben still refused to consider the idea. "I can do it, Mom," he'd say. "I just have to stop being so lazy. Don't worry. I can do it myself."

But he *wasn't* doing it himself, and I *was* worried. He was trying, but he was easily distracted and far behind in his work. Perhaps this was the real problem: a learning disability. Wouldn't that explain it all? Something had to. But even with a diagnosis, what then? How could we get Ben to accept help, to consider medication if necessary? I couldn't imagine it—but I desperately wanted to.

May came, and I prepared for another trip to Montana for family meetings. After the birthday crisis, Ben's phone calls once again sounded enthusiastic and proud; he seemed excited to show me how well he was doing. I couldn't wait to see him, to hold him. I crossed my fingers and boarded the plane. I hadn't seen my son for three months.

The visit turned out to be just another trip around the cycle of emo-tions and mood changes that were all too familiar.

On the positive side, there was pride and laughter. There was the joy of seeing Ben finally a part of something again. He showed off his (clean!—by regulations) sleeping area, and the study cabin. I got to see him participating in the simplest joys: kicking a Hacky Sack around with the rest of the group, playing basketball in the driveway. There were planned activities for the families, both with and without our children. We made candles; the boys cooked a meal for us (with a vegan version for Ben); we all got to know the staff and how they worked with the group. I could almost believe we were visiting our children at summer camp.

One evening we all—parents and children, with a staff leader—gathered around a campfire circle on their meeting benches. Each of us drew a card from a deck with a word on it, then shared why we thought we had drawn that particular card and what it meant to us. Ben's word was "responsibility." He smiled at me as if we had a secret joke between us: we had a history of arguing about that word and its meaning. Ben spoke honestly and eloquently to the group about what that word now meant to him. I felt closer to him than I had in over two years. He seemed like himself again.

But then there were the other moments: Ben storming out of the town's general store because there was no lip balm without beeswax (vegan concerns, again); Ben off by himself at odd moments; Ben completely unnerved by the family meeting we finally held.

In that meeting, I broke the news that Ben least wanted to hear: he was still not ready to come home. The staff had met with me to affirm the doubts I already had: Ben's improved behavior was still precarious, and we might lose all we had gained by his returning home too soon. They had recommended as Ben's next step a transitional program for young adults in nearby Idaho, called Waterfalls. Here Ben could take a gradual path to adulthood, with guided phases toward independent living. Here he would have more freedom, but not all at once; he would begin with supervised group living, but he would actually attend real classes at the local community college; if all went well, the second half of the program would house Ben in his own apartment near the school. This way, the transition to living back in Connecticut could be gradual and guided enough to give him confidence and experience. We had to finish the job of helping Ben get back to reality. I still hoped, I still believed, that was possible. He was doing so well, even with the crisis moments. Surely, a few months more and the solutions would stick. I thought all he needed was that extra time of supervised living, with the next phase of increased responsibility and accomplishment. To me, this seemed ideal; would it really be that different from Ben's peers, who were getting ready to go off to college in the fall? Even though my son's path had been a little—well—unusual, he could still catch up to them this way. There was even a two-week break between programs, so he would be able to come home for a summer break and be with his friends from high school. *If he has any left*, I thought.

Ben, of course, did not see it quite the same way. He was hurt and resentful when we told him the news. I'd assumed he would be disappointed at first, but I hoped he'd come around after considering the whole picture as we were seeing it. But no. Ben lashed out at us, desperate for us to change our minds. He said he'd been tricked. He claimed I didn't love him, that all I wanted was to get rid of him. My guilt, though not logical, was powerful nevertheless. I was saved only by the fact that I wasn't alone in this decision. The meeting was emotional and heartbreaking, but at least I had others on my side.

When Ben saw that his protests were going nowhere, he gathered his dignity and left the room to "think it over." When he returned, he announced that he would agree to the plan. He said, "I guess it could be good, actually. I mean, I miss my friends at home, but they're all going away to college anyway, right?"

Relief. Such relief. "Yes, Ben, they are. And this way you can see them all during the summer and you'll come home for holidays just like everyone else. You'll actually be away at college, too."

He looked out of the cabin's window, at his Cabin Life friends who were chopping wood, sweeping the porch, reading a book, talking with their parents. "Okay," Ben said. "I'll go. I think it's a good idea. As long as I can visit home in between."

Later that day, as parents were preparing to leave, Ben's mood shifted yet again. He called me a bad mother, questioned my love, my devotion, my caring. I looked helplessly at the staff, who sent me ahead to the main house alone in one car and followed with Ben in another.

This was a good move. It would have been difficult to keep my thoughts to myself if Ben had been in the car with me. *How can he tell me, one minute, how much he loves and appreciates how I've helped him turn his life around by sending him here, and then accuse me of being a horrible parent a moment later? It's like one minute has nothing to do with the next. Like there's no connection. No connection at all.*

By the time we all got out of the cars, though, Ben had calmed down and ran toward me with an apology and a huge hug. He said he had just been sad that I was leaving, and he was sorry to have taken it out on me. Another mood, another swing. I was both grateful and sorry to leave Ben behind as I drove off to catch my flight back to my peaceful home.

9

PSYCHIC VAMPIRES

When I heard that you're having more doubts and showing signs of whatever—it makes me just wish that things were different. It makes me wish you had finished school, and been here your senior year to drive me places—and you could come home at regular vacation times, like everyone else's brothers and sisters. It makes me wonder why you want to be so different from everyone, because you know you could be in the same position as other kids your age. You know it's not something that's the fault of anyone else, teachers, school, or anything.

I don't want to have a brother with no success, who doesn't know where he's going in life. I don't want to get a steady job before you, or make a family, or graduate school—I don't want my kids to have an uncle that doesn't know what he's doing in life. I don't think any of this will really make a difference, but please let me be one of the reasons you keep trying out there. Do your work and make it in life. I'll love you no matter what but please don't make any decisions you'll regret—or that will stop you from attaining your goals. I love you,

Your sister, Ali

—written to Ben in Idaho, September 2000

The phone call came from Idaho in late spring, just a few weeks before Ben's nineteenth birthday. This was the call that finally convinced me that my son needed a completely different kind of help. This was the conversation that forced me to face the possibility of severe mental illness in my child.

We'd gotten through Ben's two-week summer break seven months earlier, having spent it in the too-predictable pattern. Two weeks of reunions, of three people around our dinner table at last, of knitting Ben back into the fabric of our lives, while simultaneously watching out for signs of trouble, wondering how I would get Ben back on the plane to Montana if he refused to return.

We'd held a joyous welcome-home party for him, Ben caught up with doctor and dentist appointments, and he finally took the test for his long-coveted driver's license. After the first few days, though, Ben began slipping away from his best-behavior mode. The cracks were showing. I found myself counting the days until he went back, praying this fragile truce wouldn't fall apart.

Still, something was definitely *not* quite right. Despite a full schedule, Ben seemed directionless a lot of the time. To my chagrin, he was chain-smoking cigarettes again. *Pick your battles*, I reminded myself. But now, he'd often take his cigarettes out to the front or back yard, sit cross-legged on the grass, and *stare* while he smoked.

He's just communing with nature, I'd thought. *After all, he's been in Montana for months, spending a lot of time getting in touch with the outdoors. I can't expect him not to do that here.* But he often seemed to prefer this to actual conversation. Too often.

He was still very much "in his head," too, and at times this was scary. At the movies, he spent a lot of the time with the memo book he kept in his pants pocket, writing things down. It was as though he could not just be in the moment—he had to constantly step outside of it and observe.

He's always done that, though. Hasn't he?

One good day was rarely followed by another. Ben tried in vain to talk me out of my decision to send him back to Montana, where they would supervise the transition and escort him to Waterfalls in Idaho. He was struggling, I could see that—and I wanted him back on the plane there before everything unraveled for good. How desperately I'd wanted—*still* wanted—his problems to be fixable. *Just a few more months out West. Surely they can finish the job they started.*

And I—somehow—got him back on that plane and heaved a well-deserved sigh of relief. Ben got settled in Idaho at last in late summer, with the help of the transitional team from Adventures. He spent the next three rocky months at Waterfalls alternating between trying to please and stretching his limits. His participation swung wildly from initial promise to growing alarm, He tried hard at first, but nothing seemed to stick. He withdrew from his housemates, he rebelled against the rules, he shifted too swiftly from cooperation to anger. The staff and I tried to solve the mystery of Ben's inconsistencies, of his inability to learn anything lasting. Why was he still unable to finish the college courses he'd begun in Montana? Why wasn't he connecting with his housemates, even though he was sweet and courteous? Maybe it was that untreated learning disability, compounded by frustration. I sent them books about it. Maybe he was homesick. No. He'd just been home, and that hadn't helped either. Ben seemed incapable, somehow, of making any real connection with people.

"Randye, do you think Ben is, maybe, depressed?" the Waterfalls director, Doug, asked me late in September. "We can't come up with any other reasons for his behaviors. He sometimes sleeps so much—it's very hard to get him out of bed."

Well, that had been true for a long time.

"Also—he has taken to wearing only very dark clothing. Black, mostly. We can't get him to wear anything else. And he still keeps to himself—a lot. That's true even when he's with the group. He gets lost inside his own head sometimes. There's also the incessant note taking. It's as though he can't process anything, can't remember anything, unless he writes it down."

That, too, had been present for a while.

"And yet," Doug continued, "there are times when he comes out of it. But—*way* out of it. He stops the note taking. He talks again. He talks a mile a minute. He rattles on about how he finally gets it. He seems almost ecstatic. And the things he talks about get very weird. He talks about his own ability to read minds. He's always in love with his own logic, but now he says he can read the thoughts of people in the group. And I wonder, sometimes, if he thinks he hears voices."

Voices? "What kind of voices? Why do you think that?"

"I don't know," said Doug. "But he says he has answers that no one else has, and that he has his own secret ways of getting the information."

I went for my old favorite, reasonable explanation. "Is there any way he has gotten hold of some drugs?" I asked. I almost hoped it was true.

"Nope, we tested him and he came out clean. This is pure Ben. And the other guys are thinking it's really weird. Ben is going to be even more left out if he keeps this up, and there's not much we can do in the way of damage control. We just don't understand. Unless"—Doug hesitated a moment—"is there any possibility Ben is bipolar?"

The notion of bipolar illness had briefly crossed my mind before—but I'd pushed it away, especially since Ben was so resistant to *any* sort of diagnosis or treatment. I'd read that there could be an onset of mental illness starting with the late teens, but I knew so little—and Ben's therapists had steered me away from that idea so often.

I communicated with the Waterfalls staff constantly, as we tried in vain to figure out what was wrong, what was causing Ben to deteriorate so rapidly, to fail to respond to reason, rules, or consequences. He withdrew even further, and no consequence for disobeying rules seemed to get through to him—not even having his living quarters moved into the garage for not obeying house rules. Then, when they moved him to a tent outside for the same reason, Ben simply accepted it and decided it was just fine with him. This was not working, clearly. But I still kept hoping, kept trying to somehow make it right. If only I could find the key. If only.

He made no real friends in the program, but at the end of October he made a friend in town, named Steve. Unfortunately, Steve cemented this relationship by sharing a joint. As a result, Ben was kicked out of Waterfalls for breaking the most important rule: no drugs. Now Ben was "free." This thrilled him and terrified me. Gone was the safe cocoon of Waterfalls: the bed, the food, the classes, the staff. Where would Ben sleep? How would he eat? Who would help him? Could he land a job? Would he, could he, come to his senses?

He spent a few nights on his new friend's couch and made plans to enjoy this new independence. It wasn't long, though, before all those plans wore thin. Ben became hungry, lonely, and confused. He wanted me to rescue him, to send him money to come home and start again. *All that work, all for nothing. No.* I needed to finish the job these programs, Ben's supposed salvation, had started. I still believed that the lessons would eventually sink in, if only he would embrace them. I issued an ultimatum: "I will help you get back into Waterfalls, but I won't send you money to get home. You'll have to earn that yourself." I still hoped Ben would somehow sink low enough to learn to be responsible for his actions at last. But behind my strong stance I was frantic with worry.

So I dug in my heels, settled in, and waited for the last time for natural consequences to drive Ben back to his senses. Maybe, stripped bare of essentials, he'd finally take some responsibility for his own life, even if he did have a disability of some kind. Maybe this would, eventually, be for the best.

And so the next waiting period began. Another five months of waiting for Ben to miraculously come to his senses as he maneuvered through this new freedom and into early spring. Sometimes he called me every day; sometimes a few weeks went by before I heard from him. At first, he called to beg for money, or to tell me which new friend's couch he was now sleeping on. He reported looking for work, getting jobs, losing jobs within days. He called to tell me he loved me. He called to tell me he was hungry and it was all my fault. I held tight to my desperate belief that my tough love would help him in the long run, that this would all end soon with a difficult lesson well learned. Then the really weird calls began:

"Mom, I'm doing great! I spent all afternoon yesterday walking by the side of the highway and screaming. I feel so much better now. It's good to get your feelings out."

"I'm good, Mom, but I spent the night sitting on the roof and looking at the stars. They are awesome! Oh, and I sang to myself all night. It helps me concentrate."

"Steve kicked me out, Mom. His dad said I couldn't live there since I owe him so much money. But I think there's a homeless shelter that will take me in. Then I'll get a job while I'm living there and save some money and come home."

By March, he'd begun calling me every few days. I never knew what to expect, what he would say. Now he was on the phone again. "Hi, Mom. How are you?"

"I'm fine, honey. How are you?"

"I'm great, Mom."

"Great." That could mean anything. "That's good."

Silence. *Where do we go from here?* "Mom?"

"Yes?"

"Do you know what a psychic vampire is?"

I stood very still and closed my eyes to make this go away, like a child who doesn't want to see the milk she spilled. "A what?"

"A psychic vampire. 'Cause they have them here."

This was something I hadn't heard from him before. *What is he talking about?* Then: *What kind of drugs is he on?* Then: *Stay calm.* "No, Ben. What is a psychic vampire?"

"They steal all your energy. It's really scary. And there are psychic vampires here, I swear."

I had no idea what to say to that. I think I assured him that you could prevent these vampires from stealing your energy if you wanted to. *"Psychic vampires." What are the drugs doing to his brain?* If he was on some drug, he probably wouldn't remember this conversation anyway. But I certainly would. I added this conversation to the list of behaviors that were becoming stranger and more frequent.

I was back to thinking that this was just a problem of substance abuse, that Ben had to learn from natural consequences. To do that, he'd have to hit bottom. Good and hard.

And yet, another thought kept growing: the theory that Ben might be, after all, truly ill. What if he does finally hit bottom and is so impaired he doesn't even know it? What if this is not just a learning disability or a psychological problem? What if this isn't just about a drug? What if—*what if*—he *does* have some kind of mental illness? So many people had talked me out of that idea in the past. "No, I'm sure he just needs therapy. Sobriety. Structure. Discipline. To get closure with his father." On and on went the theories, on and on went my hopes that this was anything but a real mental illness. *Please let it not be true.*

If only I could have willed it to not be true, loved his symptoms away, I would have. But evidence had continued to pile up, even though I wanted to believe anyone who told me it didn't, couldn't, add up to something as serious as mental illness.

It was while Ben was in Montana that I'd finally begun to read books on mental illness, specifically depression and bipolar disorder. There were some symptoms that rang true, but I wasn't entirely convinced. There were so many unanswered questions, so many holes. Besides, I didn't *want* it to be true. And even if it were, the needed treatment would be so hard to administer and enforce. If this were an illness, then Ben would need medication in order to recover. And he refused it all. What would we do then? What *could* we do then?

Still—if medication could help this—maybe solve this—wouldn't it explain a lot? Wouldn't it be fixable then? Might Ben not open his eyes to how good it could be to feel better?

I'd started to ask more questions, and suddenly people who had dealt with these mental illnesses seemed to emerge in my everyday life. Some were young adults who had come out of the nightmare of misdiagnosis and/or denial and were now in integrated treatment with both medication and counseling as parts of the plan. They told me their stories.

"I put my parents through hell," one of them told me. "But now I'm back in school, and I can actually get the work done."

"After a few weeks on the meds," another confided, "the clouds parted. It was like, I thought, oh my God, *this* is what it feels like to be normal! *This* is what it feels like to be happy. I can't believe I let myself stay in the dark for so long."

This was a whole new area of possibility. A whole new area of fear, too—what would this mean, if Ben were truly ill? But we had tried everything else—many, many times. I was out of excuses; I was out of any other reasons for the past few years' events.

But—even if it's true—how in the world could we approach this with Ben?

How do you tell someone that something like this is true?

Will he ever, ever, believe it?

While Ben had been still safe at Waterfalls, I'd searched for a psychiatrist and learned that it's next to impossible to get an appointment with any highly recommended ones. They simply had no more room for any new patients. I'd called again. And again.

Finally, I found a doctor who would make some time. I'd heard he was a "good, solid psychiatrist." That would have to do. It was a start. I made an appointment for a consultation for later that month with Dr. Robert Zion.

Dr. Zion was a slight man, with a full head of gray hair and wire-rimmed glasses. He had a cool manner but a good reputation, and he seemed to know his stuff. After Art's laid-back manner and emphasis on gentle talk therapy, this man seemed more professional and more in line with the kind of expert help Ben would need, and the psychiatric knowledge that might help find the key to the chaos of the past few years.

Dr. Zion was part of a practice that also specialized in helping students with attention deficit issues. Just in case Ben's issues turned out to be mostly due to ADD after all, he'd be in the right place. This, however, was looking less and less likely. I met with Dr. Zion for consultations a few times, and by our second meeting Ben had been kicked out of Waterfalls. The stakes had gotten higher, the situation more urgent.

During the five months of waiting for Ben to wake up to the reality of his circumstances in Idaho after leaving Waterfalls, I'd continued to consult Dr. Zion and prepare for what might happen next, if Ben would somehow come to his senses and return home. It had been a long, uncertain waiting period. I felt impatient—and ineffective. I had to do something constructive. Anything. So I prepared for Ben to come home, whenever that would happen. I redid the upstairs sewing room into a bedroom for him. If and when he earned his way home, this would be where he would stay, upstairs with the rest of the family, under my supervision. No more isolation in the basement.

I painted the room a deep blue, brought all of Ben's furniture upstairs, and arranged everything he owned in this new space for what I hoped would be a new start. I threw out all the clothing that was ripped, stained, or too weird or suggestive (like the overalls with forty-inch-wide legs and the Bob Marley T-shirts). I put up posters Ben had bought in high school but had left rolled up on the floor.

CHAPTER GUIDEPOSTS

Facts about Substance Use and Schizophrenia

- Some research suggests a greater incidence of schizophrenia among teenagers who use marijuana before the age of twenty-one.*
- There is no evidence, however, that drugs actually cause schizophrenia.[†]
- For many patients with schizophrenia, though, even marijuana can trigger psychotic symptoms in an unpredictable way.[‡]

Additional "Positive" Schizophrenia Symptoms, Especially As the Illness Progresses

- Suspicious, superstitious
- Odd, peculiar behaviors
- Hypergraphia—writing everything down
- Sense of superiority
- Illusions; odd sensory experiences
- Delusions or false beliefs

Additional "Negative" Symptoms

- Flat (blunted) emotional responses
- Inability to relate to others (autism)
- Lack of motivation (avolition)[§]

Steps You Can Take

- Consult a psychiatrist on your own, even if your relative won't or can't come along.
- Do everything in your power to keep your child from substance use during the teen years.

---

*A report in the *British Medical Journal* showed that those who used cannabis in their teenage years had a 10 percent chance of developing psychosis by the age of twenty-six. The general public has a 3 percent risk. New Zealand *Herald*, March 24, 2005.

†E. Fuller Torrey, *Surviving Schizophrenia: A Manual for Families, Consumers, and Providers* (New York: HarperCollins, 2001), p. 106.

‡Torrey, *Surviving Schizophrenia*, p. 283.

§American Psychiatric Association, *Diagnostic and Statistical Manual of Mental Disorders*, 4th ed. (Washington, D.C.: American Psychiatric Association, 1994).

I loved doing this. It made me feel closer to Ben, having his things waiting for him in the bedroom right next to mine. It was my fantasy bedroom for Ben. It gave me comfort and also an illusion of control over something. I was making these decisions for him. By the time he got home they would be a done deal.

This was good, because during those five months, Ben's life had been out of my control. I found myself lingering often in his new room, touching his things, arranging his closet, dusting his books, trying to feel his presence.

Ben's nineteenth birthday was approaching, and he had made not one lasting, realistic move toward getting home to us. It was no longer enough to live my life between phone calls. My anxiety level always rose if too many days went by, or if the phone call itself was strange. More and more, this was the case. Now, I told Dr. Zion about Ben's latest call about the psychic vampires. Dr. Zion looked up from his legal pad and straight at me.

"Ms. Kaye," he said, "I don't think you are just dealing with addiction here, nor with just ADD. I think something else may be wrong—and if that's the case, Ben is never going to learn from hitting bottom. I really do think there may be some sort of mental illness going on."

So there it was. This confirmed my suspicions. "What do you think it is?" I asked.

"I can't tell with just the facts I have. But I'll tell you this: he needs to get home. He needs help. Can you get him home? Do you think he'd be willing to come back?"

Did I think he was willing to come back? What a question. "Dr. Zion, getting home is all Ben talks about. He'll jump at the chance."

"Well, figure out a plan and send for him. Get him home, and get him here to this office. Soon."

Get him home. He needs help. Badly. This I could do. Someone had finally given me permission to help my child come back.

BEN COMES HOME

Now I stood at the Bridgeport Amtrak train station, waiting for my son's train to arrive. I had not seen him for eight months, ever since his summer break in July, a thousand years ago. My brain and heart were on high alert. It reminded me all too well of the moment two years earlier when I'd driven to the Bridgeport bus depot to pick up the ex-husband I had lived without for twelve years. But this was different. This was my child.

A clean-cut man about my age was waiting for the train, too. He looked familiar. We heard the announcement that the train would be delayed and exchanged a look of mutual frustration. We began to talk and soon discovered that his daughter, who was coming in on the same train, had known Ben at Trumbull High. She, however, was coming home for spring break from her freshman year at George Washington University. Ben had boarded the train in D.C., on the last leg of his journey home from an Idaho homeless shelter. Same train—very different stories. Still, it was easy to explain if I left out the details.

"Well, Ben took a year off after completing his GED. He's been working on some college courses and traveling in the West to try and figure out what he wants to do next. He needed to grow up a little," I said.

"I know what you mean," the dad replied. "Sounds like something a lot of kids could use."

Ben's story sounded so good, so plausible, this way. If only his behavior hadn't gotten so strange. If only he hadn't called me to tell me about psychic vampires, to announce his special gifts, or to tell me that he'd screamed by the side of a highway for hours. If only he didn't have a mental illness.

But I could get Ben help. I was going to do that now.

At first, I'd actually seized gratefully at the potential diagnosis. *A mental illness. That could be why nothing seems to work. So—that means—it can be fixed, right? Correct treatment, including medication, and things will begin to make sense at last.*

The two weeks that had followed, leading to Ben's impending arrival on the train, were rough—confusing, frustrating, and frightening. After Dr. Zion's directive, I got to work on transferring Ben back to Connecticut, back into our home. There would have to be a contract. There would have to be an agreement, in writing. There would have to be an ironclad plan.

This time, treatment was nonnegotiable. Ben could not come home unless he agreed to see a psychiatrist (of my choosing) and therapist (he could help choose)—and he must agree to follow the instructions of the doctors. This was the big issue, because it meant that Ben would, most probably, have to agree to take meds if they were prescribed. It was the way—the only way—that the cycle could be broken.

Larry and Patricia had agreed to help Ben make the transition back home. They picked him up in Idaho and brought him back to Montana, to Adventures, for a few days. They gave him some chores to do, to keep him occupied while we all worked out the details. Ben, however, couldn't even focus long enough to do the chores or to stick to a decision. It took him two days to rake the leaves because he kept wandering away from the task, both physically and mentally. He agreed to sign the "house rules" agreement I'd faxed over; ten minutes later, he refused. He walked into town one morning where he met a man who offered him work pouring concrete; with the day's pay in his pocket, he ran away again. Back on the streets in Montana, he found a bed in another homeless shelter for a few nights.

Then Ben changed his mind once again. He called Larry and Patricia, sounding desperate. He said he was willing to do whatever was necessary to come home to Connecticut. He had finally made up his mind; so this time, he did exactly what was asked of him, one step after another. He apologized to Larry and Patricia. He contacted his ex-roommate in Idaho and promised to pay off his debt as soon as he got a job in Connecticut. He packed whatever stuff he still owned and shipped it home. He signed the agreement I'd drawn up, with Larry and Patricia serving as witnesses. They drove him, at last, to the train station and he began his journey back home.

I'd arranged for an Amtrak ticket for Ben, and held my breath each day until I heard that Ben was still on the train. At any stop, he could have gotten off the train and disappeared. But he'd called me from D.C. earlier that day and sounded so excited to be on his way home that I could almost think I'd imagined all those times he'd behaved so differently.

I imagined a warm homecoming, a rough start to treatment but eventual acceptance. Ben might be reluctant to start taking medication, but I'd give him no choice. And the meds would begin to work. The clouds over Ben's eyes would part. And he'd see. He'd see his life make sense again.

It was a lovely dream—and a necessary one.

So there I was, waiting alongside another parent with a different story, for this train to arrive in Connecticut. How long would it take, this time, for my fantasies of a reunited happy family to be shattered?

The train pulled into the station at last. The dad's daughter stepped out onto the platform—clean hair, shining eyes, pressed clothing, rolling luggage. My son was right behind her—matted hair, sleepy eyes, wrinkled T-shirt and ripped cargo pants, one overloaded duffle bag. But he saw me and grinned, and for just a moment his face lit up, too. Each child stepped into the arms of a loving parent, hungry for a hug from the person not held since too long ago.

My son was home.

10

DIAGNOSIS ROULETTE

I am most of my voices
Many different selves
I don't need to give in to what I fear
just give in to the fact that I'm afraid.

—Ben, c. 2001

The next two years began with the last shred of hope that Ben would return somehow to the normal path he'd strayed from, and ended with the certainty that his life would never be the same and neither would my family.

It ended with hope, too, but hope of a different sort. By March 2003, I would be shattered, shocked, heartbroken, and terrified—and also, amazingly, relieved and grateful—to find my son admitted to a psychiatric hospital. A psychiatric hospital! His stay there would be the first of five separate hospitalizations in that same year. Each one would chip away at my hopes, my safety, my family. By the time he was admitted for the fifth time, I knew we would never be the same again. Ben's life—all of our lives—would be redefined forever.

By then, though, at least I would know what we were dealing with. It hurt. There was grief. There was adjustment. There was sorrow. But none of that was as bad as the two years leading up to the diagnosis that was to come. The limits of my strength and resilience, and even my motherly love, were going to be stretched farther than I had ever imagined.

Ben came off that Amtrak train and back into our lives with symptoms I'd never seen before. On the rough and stupefying road ahead, I would learn that there was no possibility that Ben could be "fixed" by my actions alone. This was no mere rough patch.

121

In the two years to follow, he was to pass through the hands of four psychiatrists, several therapists, and several diagnoses and prescriptions. He would have some success: completion of three of the nine college credits he'd begun in Montana, a few more credits from the local community college, a Red Cross lifeguard certificate.

But Ben's success rate was small. He would try so hard at so many things—and fail so often. He would, in these two years, get hired and fired from ten jobs, with decreasing levels of success in between. He would gain a few friends and lose a few more. He would continue to blame others, usually me, whenever he failed.

He would try many ways to fool me into thinking he was taking his medication. His mood swings would continue. He would also retreat more and more into his own world, but come out of it by lashing out. He would call me crazy. A lot. And he would fight his treatment. He would always fight the treatment.

The first year was the year of searching: for the right psychiatrist, the right therapist, the correct diagnosis, medications that worked. It was a year of trial and of painful error. Which medications could help him? Which ones would he be willing to take? How bad were the side effects?

There was a progression of psychiatrists that year:

Dr. Robert Zion, who diagnosed Ben with ADD, anxiety, possibly depression, then obsessive-compulsive disorder (OCD), and finally bipolar disorder. Ben saw him for close to a year. Several different medications were tried.

Dr. John Marks, who first brought up the possibility of schizophrenia but, within one hour, decided that Ben did not have it. This assessment was based on Ben's answers to a series of questions, asked once during their only visit. His diagnosis? ADD and the frustration associated with it. Back to that. He prescribed medication accordingly.

Dr. Edward Tucker, whom Ben agreed to see only in order to be discharged from the emergency room on the first night I tried to have him admitted for psychiatric help.

Dr. Steven Taylor, who consulted with me about schizophrenia. Later on, Ben would become his patient.

The new therapists included Rob, who was cool. He liked Ben and thought his problems stemmed partially from the fact that Ben actually *was* psychic. They bonded—for a while.

Dr. Schneider was close to retirement. His theory was that Ben simply needed to live on his own. He believed Ben would learn only if he was away from me. He also thought Ben had a learning disability of some sort.

He had no opinion when I asked him about schizophrenia. Ben liked this doctor as long as he talked about independence; he tuned out any talk of learning disabilities.

And then there was NAMI, the National Alliance on Mental Illness. NAMI encouraged me to educate myself and showed me the way. NAMI put me in touch with other families who were dealing with mental illness. NAMI saved my life, eventually providing me with the opportunity to help others.

But before the parade of opinions, theories, and medications, there was the adjustment. Ben was home, and for the next few years I saw him do things and say things that continually redefined my concept of normal. My threshold of pain—the pain of watching my child fall apart—was raised each time he did something even stranger than the last.

Certainty of his serious illness grew. But what illness was it? And what could be done about it?

The first night Ben was home, I fell asleep to the sound of his conversation with his sister in the kitchen. I awoke the following morning with a feeling that was both strange and comforting—the knowledge that behind two closed bedroom doors next to mine were both of my sleeping children. This was the first time I'd experienced this since moving into this house, when Ben had chosen to sleep in the basement. I felt complete—and tried not to think about what tough decisions might lie ahead.

Ben had his first appointment with Dr. Zion, who diagnosed him with ADD, some depression, and generalized anxiety. He prescribed Xanax for Ben, on a temporary basis, just to get him to be calmer and more centered. He also started Ben on a time-release prescription for ADD.

Ben's first dosage was difficult. We got samples from Dr. Zion to tide us over until the prescriptions were filled, and Ben swallowed his first pills in the office. He looked at me right before putting the pills in his mouth. He looked resentful, and he looked scared. This was what he had fought me about for so long.

But he swallowed the pills. And that was how we began two years of medication roulette.

There were two major themes to the first year after Ben came home from Montana and Idaho. One was progress, moments of success that kept me going. The other was that he was, between such moments, behaving in ways that kept getting stranger. Odder. Unbelievably difficult to comprehend. Harder still to absorb.

The first change was that Ben's intentions, this time, really *were* good. He was truly trying to succeed this time. He tried to be agreeable at home.

He followed the rules. He attended at least one AA meeting per week, as we'd agreed. His drug tests came up clean every time. He also followed up on job interviews, got some work, paid off his Idaho debts.

Some of his academic plans were completed, too. With the help of a tutor, he finished one of the college courses he'd begun in Montana. He withdrew from the other two, but he passed Sociology 101 with a grade of B. He was now, officially, a college student. "Hey, Ben!" I told him. "If anyone asks, you can tell them you have a 3.0 grade point average in college! You're a B student!" Ben smiled. In spite of his protests, I could see how proud he was.

He took and passed a Red Cross lifesaving class—this despite the fact that he was suddenly afraid to touch people. He worked as a drama specialist in a summer day camp and lasted for the entire summer. He also found work in local restaurants and sometimes stayed employed for months. Not being let go after a day or a week was now a major success.

Ben's self-esteem also took a leap as he paid off his debts. He handed money to me from his paychecks and tips. By the middle of the summer, he had reimbursed me for the train ticket and his ex-roommate for back rent. He was "erasing his mistakes," he told me.

Ali began to trust in Ben again, and bit by bit I watched them inch their way back to a relationship. They joked with each other and tentatively had arguments about trivial things, like who ate the last potato chip. The trust that they could get through a disagreement like that, without a major tantrum on Ben's part, was a sign of the return of healthy sibling squabbling. I treasured it. Little annoyances were so welcome after the major blow-ups we'd survived in the past.

Things looked promising. Most of the success happened during the time Ben was taking some medication. But something was still getting in his way. Always. Lasting success eluded him. Why did nothing last? And the fact that he *was* trying to do good things made me want to cry—for him, for all three of us.

Some days were better than others. But overall, there was enough success to keep us going back for treatment. It seemed to be helping on some level, though Ben would not agree that his successes had any connection to his treatment.

But when the balance was off—especially at home, where Ben felt no pressure to perform—it was way off. Way off. And increasingly, frighteningly so.

These are the symptoms I saw. These are the moments that raised my shock level:

Within days of his arrival from out West, I noticed that Ben had become uncomfortable with affection. In fact, he seemed afraid. He refused to hug anyone, even to shake hands. He steered clear of bodily contact. If I did manage to put my arms around him, he'd stiffen and pull away. This was so out of character for him that I found it hard to believe at first. But it was undeniable. I could only hope that it would pass.

This fear of touch soon extended to inanimate objects like doors and silverware. I'd catch Ben testing these objects before touching them, the way we check a doorknob for static electricity in the wintertime. He told me that there is energy in all things and he wanted to make sure it wasn't bad energy. He also said he could read the energies in these objects, the way psychics could read auras around people.

Ben's talk of psychic vampires continued. He tried to convince me that they did truly exist and that they stole all your good energy if you weren't careful.

Some of these ideas, I hoped, were just picked up from whoever he'd befriended in Idaho. Maybe they'd been into metaphysics or some extreme form of Eastern thought. Or perhaps, even though he was now clean of any drug use (and randomly tested, as we'd agreed), there was some residue still affecting his thoughts.

But there was more. Often, out of the corner of my eye, I'd see him stop walking forward in order to take a few steps backward before continuing on his way. Once I asked him why he was doing that. "I just feel like it," he said. "It exercises my legs." Sometimes the backward steps came in sets of three. And these "threes" spilled over into other things. He started the washer by pushing the knob in not once, but three times. He closed the car door three times, if he thought I wouldn't notice.

Often he talked out loud to himself. Not just one sentence, like "Gosh, where did I put the car keys?" He could go on for several minutes at a time. "Ben, who are you talking to?" I asked the first time I heard this. "No one, Mom. I'm just thinking out loud."

And then there was the time he talked to the bush all night.

On the weekend of Ben's nineteenth birthday, I awoke to find him sitting on the front lawn. He saw me through the front window and came in the house. He was grinning. His eyes were bright—too bright. He was still awake from the night before.

"Mom! I had the *best* night!" he said. This enthusiasm was relatively rare, and it seemed too highly pitched. Even his voice was unnaturally high. "Oh, Mom, it was awesome! Guess what? I finally figured out how to be *happy*!"

I had no idea how to respond to this. It should have been a good thing, but it made me very unsure. "How did you do that?"

"I stayed up all night, Mom! And I was right next to that bush, and I actually communicated with it. I think God was telling me to be happy. God talks through nature, you know. And He told me the secret of happiness!"

Well. If only that were true. But then I asked Ben to explain it to me.

"Oh, Mom. I can't explain it to *you*. You have to find it out for yourself. But I'll try to write it in my poetry. This is going to help so many people!"

Oh my God. I tried to make my smile look real, be real. "Well, that's great, honey. I'm glad you had such a good night."

He stayed up all night, communing with a bush? God is talking to him? Was he talking to himself all night? Out loud? Did the neighbors see?

Ben yawned. "Well, I'm going to go to bed, Mom." He started for the stairs and then turned back to me. "Hey, are we going out for dinner for my birthday tonight? Chinese food?"

Ben slept for a while, but he talked for the rest of the day about the bush, about God, and about how he was going to help the world now that he understood so much. He talked all the way to the restaurant for his birthday dinner. Ali and I, in the front seat, could not get a word in. We first exchanged amused looks, then started to feel annoyed. By the time we were seated in the restaurant my head hurt from his nonstop monologue. I ended up promising Ben ten dollars if he would just talk about ordinary things during dinner. The weather. Anything. It was very hard for him, but he did it. He needed the money, and we needed the pretense of peace.

Then there was the night that Ben spoke to his car.

He was late coming home. He usually respected curfew, even though he complained about it, but this night he was way past it. I'd gone to bed at ten but slept restlessly because I hadn't heard Ben come in. Finally, at 2 a.m., I got up and waited for him in the kitchen, listening for the sound of the garage door. A few minutes later, I heard it.

Garage door opening, car driving in, garage door closing, car door opening and closing. I waited for Ben to walk into the house from the garage. And I waited.

He didn't come in. Three minutes passed. *What is he doing?* Then I heard sounds of conversation. Ben's voice. *Does he have a friend with him? A girl? What are they doing?* But I heard *only* Ben's voice.

With the lights still out, I crept toward the door that connected the kitchen to the garage. I listened through the door to Ben's one-sided conversation.

"I am not scared of you," he was saying. "See? I'm fine now. You are good. You have no control over me. I see that you are good. It is good energy. I am no longer afraid of you."

This went on for a full ten minutes. *Who is he talking to?* I heard him move then, and I tiptoed back to the kitchen table and turned on a light. Ben walked in and saw me. He started. "Mom!" he said. "What are you doing there? You scared me!"

"I was waiting for you, Ben. You're late."

He looked down at his scruffy sandals. "I know, Mom. I'm sorry. I was with some friends."

I have to ask. "So—who were you talking to, in the garage?" Who was he so scared of that he had to talk to them that way? And were they still sitting in his car?

He looked as though he'd been caught. "No one, Mom."

"Ben, I've been sitting here for at least ten minutes. You were talking. Who else is in the garage?"

"Mom, no one is in there. I told you. You can look if you want."

"Well, then, what was all that talking about?"

He locked eyes with me, then looked away. "I was talking to my car, okay?"

His car? I shuddered. "What? Why?"

"Mom," he said. His expression was condescending then, one of infinite patience. "Don't you believe in the energy of inanimate objects? I told you about this before."

He had. But talking to his car? *Afraid* of it? "But, Ben . . ."

"Mom, listen. I decided that there was no reason to be afraid of my car. I decided to take control. It's just mind over matter, right? So I confronted my car and told it that I wasn't afraid anymore. There's good energy, and that's what I'm going to choose to accept from it from now on. You're always telling me to express my feelings. So I took care of my problem. And now I'm back in control of my car, instead of the other way around."

I had nothing left to say. We went back to bed. The next morning, I faxed a description of these symptoms over to Dr. Zion. At our next appointment he changed Ben's diagnosis to include OCD, along with an episode of psychosis. New medications were prescribed. For a few months, these seemed to help.

Until mid-August. That was when, without telling anyone, Ben stopped taking his medication. And things began to fall apart, far apart, once again.

CHAPTER GUIDEPOSTS

And Still More Symptoms You Might See

- Sensitivity and irritability when touched by others
- Inability to express joy
- Inability to cry, or excessive crying
- Religious or other rituals
- Inappropriate laughter
- Forgetting things
- Losing possessions
- Unusual sensitivity to stimuli (noise, light, colors, textures)
- Refusal to touch persons or objects; wearing gloves, etc. (See "What are the symptoms of schizophrenia?" at www.nimh.nih .gov.)
- Giving inanimate objects human characteristics
- Shift from exaggerated feelings to lack of feeling (flat affect)
- Grandiose delusions such as receiving messages from God

MORE ROLLS OF THE DICE

We were trying treatments for everything, it seemed. Ben can't get out of bed on some days? Let's try antidepressants. Mood swings? Mood stabilizers. Every course of treatment required patience, time for the medications to take effect. *If* Ben was even swallowing them. I'd recently caught him "cheeking" his meds—pretending to take them by hiding them in his cheeks until my back was turned—and that had opened the gates for his complaints about the side effects he hated, his belief that he didn't need the treatment in the first place, and his desire to find another psychiatrist.

Meanwhile, he still found it hard to focus. He was absent-minded. He left lights on, doors unlocked or open all night. He left the cordless phone outside, or he drove away with it in his car. He also frequently "forgot" to take his medication.

I brought all this information with me to our next appointment with Dr. Zion, and Ben could no longer maintain the pretense he'd tried to maintain during appointments: calm but disconnected. He lost his temper. "Mom, you can't yell at me because I forgot to take my meds!" Ben said. "I don't need them anyway—I can do this myself. I can make myself focus!"

Dr. Zion put his pad and pen down on his lap and looked at Ben. "Ben, if you could make yourself focus, don't you think you'd be doing all the things you promised to?"

"I've just been lazy. It's not that I can't. I just didn't want to."

Dr. Zion was starting to look a little frustrated himself. "Ben, we're trying to help you. Once it's easier for you to focus, you'll be able to get to work on time, read a book, get along with your mom."

"Look, Dr. Zion," Ben interrupted. "I don't need these meds. My mom is crazy. She thinks I can't do it. Look, I'll prove it to you."

I started crying silently in my own corner. I crossed one arm around my chest and placed the fist of my other hand into my mouth. I didn't make a sound. I tried to be invisible.

Ben stared intently at the doctor. "See? I can make myself focus. I'm doing it right now!"

"But, Ben," said Dr. Zion, "you need to be able to do this consistently. It shouldn't be this hard. Besides, your behavior at home is simply not working. You aren't keeping the commitments you made to your mother."

Ben looked over at me. I nodded. "Look, it doesn't matter," said my son. "I'm moving out anyway. I'll be out of there in three days. My mother is the problem anyway. She has to change her attitude! She thinks I can't do anything!" He might as well have been writing "I AM A FAILURE" all over his arm again. Ben stormed out of the office.

I stayed to talk to Dr. Zion and to give Ben some time to cool off. "Supervise his medication more carefully," he said, "and we'll see what happens."

Ben asked to see a therapist—someone he could relate to better than Dr. Zion. We searched. That was when we found Rob, who met with Ben for close to six months. Rob was a cool guy, in Ben's eyes. He was hip enough to take Ben outside for a smoke, a walk, or even to a diner in order to bond with him during appointments.

Rob really liked Ben, too. He knew that Ben needed help and was not functioning well, but he was also willing to consider the possibility that Ben really *was* "a little bit psychic," that maybe a lot of these problems were due to the fact that he was so intelligent that, perhaps, he felt left out of the ordinary world.

That was a new theory. Ben rather liked the idea. But these supposed powers had a down side, too. The things Ben claimed to sense, to see, to hear, were not always good. Often, they were downright scary.

One Saturday morning in early September, Ben came into my bed-room and woke me up.

"Mom," he said. "I'm scared."

I rubbed my eyes and sat up. "Why, Ben? What's wrong? Did you hear a noise in the house?"

"No, Mom," he said. He sat down on the edge of my bed. "It's my friend Josh. He scares me." Josh was one of the two new friends Ben had made. I didn't like him very much, but by this time I was glad Ben had any friends at all.

"What about Josh, Ben?"

"I think he's *evil*, Mom. He's been putting fears into my head, astral projecting his thoughts to me. He's putting thoughts of death into my head."

Now I was really awake. "I don't understand, Ben. Is Josh here?"

"No, Mom. He's doing it from his house. He's sending me these evil thoughts. I'm *scared*." And then he started to cry and fell into my arms.

Oh my God. I held my child. I rocked my child. I was grateful for the chance to do the only thing I knew how to do for him. But I tried reason anyway. "Ben," I said. "Even if that were true, he can't do that to you if you don't *let* him."

"Really?" He pulled away and sniffed.

"Yes. I think you'd have to be *receptive* to his evil in order for him to give it to you. I've read about this. Just refuse his thoughts."

He looked puzzled. "I don't think that's true, Mom. Here. Put your hand on my heart."

I did. "Okay?"

"Can't you feel it, Mom? Can't you feel my fear?"

I paused, feeling his heartbeat under my hand. I spoke softly, calmly. "No, Ben, I don't feel any fear. I feel your heart beating. But I'll tell you what. Put your hand on *my* heart. Right here." He did. "Can you feel what's in my heart, Ben?"

"No, Mom, what?"

"Can you feel my love? My strength? You can't let in fear if you have love and strength." Sounded good to me. I thought it just might work. But it didn't.

"No!" he shouted, and stood up. "I don't want to, Mom. I don't *want* to! You don't understand how scary this is for me1 I've been up all night, working to not let Josh's evil get to me! I can't sleep!" He was truly scared, I could see that.

"Honey, listen to me. Remember early in the summer, when you were taking your meds every day?"

"Yeah."

"Well, when you were on your meds, you slept well. Every night. You got up and went to camp and you were never up all night."

"I don't want to talk about that, Mom. This isn't about my meds."

"Well, what are you going to do?" I said.

"I'm all right now. It's light outside." And it was. Early morning had come. Ben walked out of the room, and I followed him into the kitchen. I watched him take his meds, and checked his open mouth to make sure he'd swallowed them. Ben went outside to the backyard. "I'm gonna sort it out, Mom," he said.

I made myself a cup of coffee and watched him through the kitchen window. What would he do now?

Ben sat on the grass in his bathrobe. He was fairly still. It looked like prayer. Then he stood up, walked over to the bushes, and peed. He looked around as though he could feel me watching, so I went upstairs to take a shower. I wanted him to think he wasn't being observed—what would happen next? I was numb. This was like watching an Alfred Hitchcock movie. I had to do something normal.

I emerged from the shower, wrapped myself in my terrycloth robe, and stood hidden by the bathroom curtains to see if Ben was still in the backyard. He was, and he was—what? Shaking? Having a seizure? Crying? It was hard to tell. His back was to me.

No, not shaking. Singing. He was singing—loudly. In between verses, he was talking to himself. Still in his bathrobe, still in his bare feet, he walked around to the front yard, down the street to our neighbor's property. Then he turned around and started to walk back to our house. By that time, I was downstairs again, standing near the front door. I felt like a spy.

Ben spotted me and turned back around to walk away. This time he went out of my sight. I waited. An hour later, he came home. He walked in the front door. He looked calmer. He was smiling. "Thanks, Mom," he said. "I've sorted out my mind now. The meds really helped." Then he went upstairs to go to sleep.

I stood there, dumbfounded. I called Dr. Zion and Rob, and I left long messages about what I had just seen. If this was anxiety and OCD, it was going too far. I'd never read about symptoms like these. At other times that week, I found Ben walking oddly again. Afraid of touch. Crying.

Rob joined Dr. Zion in reassuring me that I'd just have to be patient, that treatment takes time. I didn't know if I could survive that long without doing something drastic. I wanted to just put Ben on a one-way airplane, destination unknown. Sometimes I hated being near him. He scared me.

He broke my heart. His behavior was confusing to Ali. Everyone was telling us to wait.

Was Ben swallowing the meds or just pretending to? Was he throwing them up after he took them? Had he *ever* taken them? If he *was* taking them, why weren't they doing any good? Was I doing something wrong? Was there something more I was supposed to know? *I feel so powerless. I can't help my own son.*

Dr. Zion changed Ben's profile to include what seemed, now, like episodes of delusional thinking. The new diagnosis was bipolar disorder. The medication was changed to a mood stabilizer. It seemed to work, for a while. It smoothed out Ben's moods but did nothing to help his irrational behaviors. Increasingly, I was unsure of the ability of Dr. Zion to diagnose my son. I wanted another opinion.

This second opinion came from Dr. John Marks. He specialized in working with young men, and he was only a few years out of medical school. He wore jeans. He came highly recommended. We set up a consultation and I drove a very reluctant Ben into New Haven to meet him.

We sat together in Dr. Marks's office at first. Once the initial background information was out of the way, Dr. Marks asked a series of questions I had never heard anyone ask Ben before, but which would become so familiar in the years ahead that I could rattle them off myself.

"Ben, do you ever hear voices in your head?"

"Do you ever see things that aren't really there?"

"Do you ever think that people on television are talking directly to you or about you?"

Ben's answers were all the same, essentially: "What? Of course not! Do you think I'm crazy?"

Dr. Marks spoke to Ben alone, then met with me. "I don't think Ben has bipolar disorder at all. He also doesn't show true signs of schizophrenia or of OCD."

"Really?"

"He seems like a good kid, very bright. He has good intentions, too, but he can't seem to figure out how to meet his goals."

Well, none of that was news to me. I knew all that. The question was: why *couldn't* he do any of those things? *Something* was wrong. What was it? "Okay, but why? He's on meds, but I'm never sure he's taking them unless I stand over him like an army sergeant."

"I know," said Dr. Marks. "The problem may be that he's being treated for the wrong condition. He may be suffering through side effects that aren't necessary, and those side effects are often the reason that people don't want to take meds."

So we're back to square one? Then what have we been doing all this time? "So what do you think he has?"

"It's hard to tell from just one visit. But he's not hearing any voices, and that rules out schizophrenia."

Schizophrenia? This was the first time I'd heard any mention of that diagnosis. I didn't know that much about it, but I knew I was glad Dr. Marks had ruled it out. The "test" he had used—a few basic, easily-lied-about questions, went right past my radar, guided by my desire to believe it couldn't be true. I didn't want my child to be hearing voices. That would be *way* too strange. It couldn't be that. It just couldn't.

Dr. Marks continued, "I think what Ben has is a very severe case of ADD."

Wait. We're back to that? But what if Ben was not telling the truth when he answered that question? So we were back to an old theory. But, oh, how I wished it were true. I asked, "What medication would help, do you think?"

Dr. Marks gave me a prescription for a new time-release medication that he said had worked well for many patients. For the time being, I let this second opinion sit in the back of my mind. Ben staunchly refused testing of any sort. But I kept the prescription. Just in case.

I had become increasingly disillusioned with Dr. Zion. His treatment didn't seem to be effective, and my patience was wearing thin. More importantly, his attitude toward Ben bothered me. He didn't seem to like Ben or bond with him in any way. I also felt that he was impatient with me, dreading rather than welcoming my input. He didn't feel any regard, much less empathy, for the struggles of my family. If *I* felt uncomfortable around him, how could I ever think that Ben wouldn't?

I wrote a letter to Dr. Zion, explaining that I had gone for another opinion and why. He did not answer my written concerns that Ben, who was still taking his prescribed mood stabilizer, was not responding to it.

So one night, I took matters into my own hands. Ben had been filling his free evenings with wandering. He walked aimlessly inside the house and outside in the neighborhood. He walked, just walked. He stared straight ahead or sang to himself. He couldn't focus enough energy to actually do anything, but he couldn't sit still either. "It's these meds, Mom," he told me. "They aren't helping me. I feel like a zombie."

Well, he was acting like one. This was almost worse than the times he'd try to engage me in a verbal battle. I couldn't take it anymore. This

CHAPTER GUIDEPOSTS

Why Is It So Hard to Diagnose Mental Illness Correctly?

Symptoms of the various mental illnesses often overlap, especially during non-acute stages of onset (prodromal) and residual, where some symptoms linger.

There is still no technology available for objective measures of diagnosis, such as lab tests.

Diagnosis is most often made by observing symptoms (clinical diagnosis) and noting response to medication.

was so scary that I called Dr. Zion's emergency number. When he called me back, I described Ben's symptoms to him.

"Look, Randye, you've got to be patient. Give the meds a chance to work. Are you sure he's taking them?"

Am I sure? How can I be sure? "I think so. I check his mouth. I don't allow him in the bathroom until some time has passed after he swallows the pills. But you don't understand. Ben's acting *very* strangely. He's aimless. He's lost in his own world. Are you sure your diagnosis is right?"

Now Dr. Zion lost patience with me—and he lost his temper. "Look, I have to see him again before I can see what's going on. Make another appointment, and I'll see you in the office. And if you don't like my diagnosis, feel free to get a second opinion and try something else!"

Well. I had already done that. I couldn't wait a week to see what might happen. In fact, I was now sure that Dr. Zion was completely on the wrong path. I had run out of patience, too. Maybe Ben really *did* have ADD. I knew this much for sure—I couldn't live in the house with this zombie who used to be my son. "Ben," I said, "let's try something else. I think you're right. This medication isn't working."

Anything had to be better than this.

FINDING NAMI

The pamphlet had been sitting on my desk for months, under a pile of psychiatrist bills and bank statements. I'd found it in a town hall waiting room—NAMI, the National Alliance on Mental Illness. On the front, it stated "When nobody understands . . . NAMI-CT does." *What's this? I've never heard of it. Well, I'll just take one in case I ever need it.* I hoped I never would, though.

Now I knew that I did.

Inside was an overview of NAMI, a "grassroots, self-help organization founded in 1979." Its mission was to provide:

- Support for families and friends of individuals with psychiatric disabilities
- Education and information about brain disorders and available mental health services, resources, and treatment
- Advocacy for improved services and more humane treatment

Why hadn't I heard about this before? No doctor, therapist, counselor, or psychiatrist had ever mentioned NAMI to me. I picked up the phone and called the number of the Trumbull affiliate. The woman who answered the phone talked to me for almost an hour. Just like that.

Barbara was the mother of five children, one of whom had been diagnosed with schizophrenia. She and her husband had guided this daughter, now in her thirties, through numerous hospitalizations, medications, and false hopes until—at last—she was properly diagnosed and began cooperating with her own treatment. The daughter was now doing well, living independently in her own apartment. She was not able to work yet but was putting in volunteer hours at the local library.

My God, I hope Ben's future will hold more than that, I thought. I had no idea then that, later on, I would be thrilled to have Ben functioning as well as Barbara's daughter was.

There was a support meeting coming up in a few days; I put the date in my calendar. It couldn't hurt to at least go and listen.

That Wednesday evening I drove to the local nursing home where the NAMI meeting was held. I sat in the car for a few minutes after turning off the engine. *Maybe I don't really need this,* I thought. *Maybe there's nothing really wrong with Ben. Maybe he's just slow to learn his life lessons. He can't have a mental illness. Can he?*

But it was getting cold in the car, and my excuses were getting cold, too. I knew I had to go inside and hear what was happening in there. Why was this any different from a ToughLove meeting, or from Al-Anon? I would take what I needed and learn what I was meant to learn.

There were about fifteen people in the meeting. Some were parents or other relatives of people with diagnosed mental illnesses, and two or three were "consumers"—short for consumers of mental health services—who were involved in their own recovery. The consumers' behavior ranged from quiet and withdrawn to open and warm. Some spoke with insight, even humor, about their own recoveries. I said little. I did say that I was there to learn more and see if something I learned might explain what was going on with my son. The group welcomed me and asked me for no more information than that.

The stories and problems I heard were beyond anything I had yet experienced. The families in the room that night were dealing with relatives in hospitals, day programs, and state-run housing. Some of their relatives were missing, some in prison. I listened, and I hoped I could somehow fix things in my family before they got to this point. Still, part of me wondered if, someday, I would know from experience what these families knew. It seemed so impossible. I couldn't imagine Ben in a psychiatric hospital. And yet, a few years before, I had felt exactly the same way about "troubled teen" programs.

That evening, I considered myself lucky that I'd never had to put Ben into the hospital. Only one week later, though, I would be asking for the secret from Barbara: how can I convince the hospital to admit my son? What does it take for them to see that he is not well?

I continued my search for help. I went to a different kind of NAMI meeting. This one was a "speaker meeting," where an expert makes a presentation and then answers questions. On this evening, the speaker was a psychiatric nurse named Maggie. She worked at the local West Hills Center for Behavioral Health. Maggie spoke about various illnesses: bipolar, depression, schizophrenia, and something called schizo-affective. She talked about the experience of the families of the patients. I listened; I took notes. For once, someone was addressing my needs, Ali's needs. Someone was giving voice to our struggle, our helplessness, as we watched Ben's odd behaviors.

I spoke about my son for the first time at that meeting. It was a beginning.

"I'm Randye, and my son has a mental illness." This was the first time I had ever said this out loud to strangers. I thought I would feel embarrassed, but the only expression I could read in the eyes of the group was one of pure empathy. And what I felt was relief—and resignation. "I'm not sure what it is, but I have a theory," I said. "How can I find a different psychiatrist, one who will actually respect my thoughts on my son's condition?"

I gathered information, just in case. Maggie gave me the name of another psychiatrist, and the phone number of the center. The NAMI group leader gave me a schedule of more meetings. I had begun, slowly, to accept that something was very wrong with Ben, and that it might not be entirely

---

CHAPTER GUIDEPOSTS

What Is NAMI?

NAMI is the National Alliance on Mental Illness, the nation's largest grassroots organization for people with mental illness and their families. Founded in 1979, NAMI now has affiliates in every state and in more than eleven hundred local communities across the country.

NAMI is dedicated to the eradication of mental illnesses and to the improvement of the quality of life for persons of all ages who are affected by mental illnesses.

NAMI members and friends work to fulfill our mission by providing support, education, and advocacy. Activities include:

- *NAMI educational programs* (Family-to-Family, Peer-to-Peer, NAMI Connection, Hearts and Minds, and more) provide critical education to help consumers and family members gain knowledge and skills for living successfully with mental illness.
- *Support groups* are provided through many of NAMI's state and local affiliates and offer invaluable connections with peers who understand the challenges and joys of living with mental illness.
- *StigmaBusters* responds to inaccurate and hurtful language and portrayals of mental illness in the media and promotes understanding and respect for those who live with mental illness.
- *In Our Own Voice* presents deeply personal and moving journeys of recovery by consumers living with mental illness.
- *NAMI's website* (www.nami.org) receives over 5.4 million visitors a year who turn to NAMI for information, referral, and education.
- *NAMI's helpline* (1-800-950-6264) is staffed by a dedicated team and serves over four thousand callers per month.

---

fixable. But in this room, I found doors I hadn't known were there. I was going to put up one hell of a fight.

After all, Maggie had also said, "Never give up hope."

THE EXPERIMENT

Ben couldn't stop talking. Seriously. He couldn't seem to stop. A rush of energy took the form of words and ideas that just kept streaming out of his mouth while I drove him to the theater where he was in the ensemble of a community theater production of *Man of La Mancha.*

Oh my God, what have I done? Is this my fault? I thought. All I had done was follow the advice of one psychiatrist over another. I also knew that many medications for ADD are not the kind of prescriptions that have to build up in order to be effective. They worked while they are in your system, and they wear off later that day. *What harm could it do to try it for one or two days? We can always stop. And I'll report the results to Dr. Zion, or maybe to Dr. Marks.*

Okay, I was desperate. I weaned Ben off his antidepressants and mood stabilizers and started him on Dr. Marks's prescription. For two days, the results had been remarkable. Ben had more energy than he'd had in months, and the light behind his eyes had come back on. Now, however, he'd crossed the line. Last weekend, the director and I hadn't been sure Ben could stay focused on the performance, or even if he could remain awake and aware despite how hard he was trying. At last night's brush-up rehearsal, he'd been remarkably focused, friendly, and alert. Now, I didn't know if he'd be able to stand still when the script called for it.

For a moment, Ben stopped his monologue. He stared at a car coming in the opposite direction. Then he looked at me. "Wow, Mom, that is so cool!" he said.

"What is, Ben?"

"Well, I was telling you that I think God is all around us, in nature, everywhere, right?"

"Yes, honey, I remember. I think that's true."

"Well, I *know* it's true now! Wanna know how?"

"Sure. How?" *Where is he going with this?*

"Well, see that car over there? At the *exact* moment I said that to you, he turned his headlights on!"

"And?"

"And, don't you see, that's a sign from God! The exact moment! It shows I'm right! See?"

Oh my God. What was I thinking, trying this myself? It had seemed like such a good idea at the time—or, to be honest, the only idea. We'd been through so many changes in diagnosis, and each conclusion came with a new prescription. After all that, a diagnosis of ADD seemed mild in comparison. We'd both agreed to try the new doctor's plan, but now it was backfiring. Ben was babbling about his special connection to God once again.

"Ben," I said. "Maybe you're right. There are a lot of people who believe in what they call the synchronicity of the universe. Other people call it coincidence. But, still, 'sign from God' is a little strong. Maybe it's true, but maybe it's not."

"Oh, I *know* it's true," he said. "Happens to me all the time."

We arrived at the theater entrance. "Well, I wouldn't tell a lot of people about that, okay?" I said. "You have to concentrate on the show."

"Oh. Okay, Mom."

I let Ben out of the car and watched him go backstage, then went inside to find the show's director, Kathryn. She was an old friend of mine and had known about Ben's situation when she cast him in the show. "Listen, Kath," I said. "I just want to warn you. Ben is on this new medication and he may not be able to stop talking. I'm so sorry. I don't know what you've got on your hands here. Want me to stick around, or take him home?"

"No," she said. "He'll be fine. Don't worry. We'll handle it."

Ben did make it through the show, though his performance had so much energy that he was in danger of upstaging the leads. No disasters, thankfully—and the next day he was much calmer. Ali said he was acting "more like a real brother." Where was the happy medium? Who knew the answer?

Two days later, I found Ben at the sink. He had his morning allotment of pills in his hand, under the running faucet. "I'm just washing the pills, Mom. I'm going to swallow them after I wash them. It's a cleansing thing."

Later that day, he went out on the front lawn and began to sing. Loudly. To the sky. Ali came to me and said, "Mom, he's doing it again. Why won't he stop? This is so *weird*."

Here we go again. I tried another approach. "Look, Ben," I said. "You're scaring Ali. Can you at least try to act normal in front of her?"

Ben looked at me suspiciously. His eyes were hard. "Well, Mom, define 'normal.'"

I tried. I recalled something I'd heard, years ago, on a radio talk show. "Well—just do normal things. Okay?" It would have to do.

That evening, Ben refused to go to his AA meeting. "I can't take any more people," he told me. His new cheerfulness was gone. So much for the second doctor, the second opinion. Over the next few days, we gradually reversed the medication process back to where it had been before. I waited for my next appointment with Dr. Zion, scheduled for later that week. It had only been a five-day experiment, but it was enough to convince me that neither doctor really had the right answer for Ben.

I'll never know whether or not my experiment was part of the reason that, a few days later, I found myself in the emergency room of City Hospital, praying that they would admit my son for psychiatric observation.

Did it really matter why he got there, why the police had to escort him there? He was going further and further down the rabbit hole and away from us. The shocks were coming too fast and furious to process.

All I could do was try to keep up—and figure it out later.

III

DEALING WITH
CATASTROPHIC EVENTS

REFLECTIONS

TIME: THE PRESENT

It's Ali's birthday. There are four of us now, celebrating over dinner: Ali, Ben, my husband Geoff, and me. Geoff and I have been living together for five years and the Ben he knows is relatively stable. Geoff wasn't around for the chaos, but he has witnessed firsthand some of the detours on the rocky road of recovery. He has seen Ben at his best, and he's seen Ben slip. Geoff also has taken one of my NAMI Family-to-Family courses, a step that cemented his place in my heart. Our relationship moved to solid ground when he accepted Ben's illness as part of the package.

It makes me sad, sometimes, that Geoff never knew Ben as a child, before he developed schizophrenia. The best I can do is show him the "old Ben" in pictures, videos, and stories, back when the light was in his eyes and the enthusiasm in his face was consistent. On the other hand, Geoff didn't have to witness the high-voltage tension, grief, and fighting in this family while the diagnosis was still unclear, and before I learned the skills to handle it. I don't know if he can really appreciate what a miracle it is to have a simple event like dinner in a restaurant, appearing to the rest of the world like any normal family. But I know. And Ali knows.

We both remember how painful it was to get through the steps toward accepting Ben as he now is. And we both know we came so close to losing him forever—to permanent hospitalization, to a life of homelessness, to suicide—who knows?

Now, tonight, here we are. Celebrating in a noisy Italian restaurant, with flowing conversation and laughter. All four of us. It feels so good. Ali opens her card from Ben. He has handwritten a message for her inside:

Ali—One of the benefits of being older is that I get to watch you grow up. I still remember playing birdie poop mountain with you when we were younger. I also remember being in Mom's car playing with the colored Swedish fish, when one was named Fredrich and the other Fredrica, and also saying "shall we go to the party" with funny accents.

And now we're so much older. I really enjoy hanging out with you and talking with you. I never told you this before but I think you are very good at making interesting conversation. Anyway, I love you a lot and I hope that every moment gets better for you.

Love, your brother, Ben

Ali's eyes fill with tears as she reads this. And she laughs, too. These are childhood memories she can only share with the one other person who was there, too—her big brother.

For this night, she has the brother back who remembers their child-hood games and talks about watching his little sister grow up. Tonight, Ben is her *big* brother once again. He is still here, and not just in her memories.

Thank goodness. Because there were times I feared they'd never have each other again. There were moments when Ali was afraid of the changes in Ben. And so, of course, was I.

11

ALMOST HOSPITALIZED

I need the god as manifested through the wind to help me understand and learn and know undeniable truth all the time. As in the background I hear "here it comes" and "ooh, you're a smart man" and "how old are you?" its weird people say so many things like that to me all the fucking time, and it is in their conversation.

I am one hundred and fifty billion percent sure I am not nor was Jesus. Those fears were fears that came from Montana, and here in Connecticut the only difference is that I am not controlled by this communal consciousness.

—Ben's notebook, December 2001

I stood at Ben's bedroom door, watching him shove clothes into his backpack. "I'm leaving," he said.

"And where do you think you're going?" This sounded like dialogue from a bad Lifetime TV movie.

"Anywhere! You think I'm crazy! I can't live here anymore!"

Well, I don't much want you living here either, I thought. Ben and I had argued by phone an hour earlier. I'd told him that I would be taking his car keys away as soon as I got home from my recording session. Bad move. By the time I got into the house, Ben had hidden the keys from me and was busy packing. All I had done was given him time to prepare for battle.

I started searching his room. Under the mattress. In his dresser drawers. In his coat pockets. "Where are the keys?" I said. "You can leave if you want to, but not in my car. You can take the bus to the nearest homeless shelter. Or you can walk."

"You would put your own son in a homeless shelter? What is wrong with you?"

"Why not, Ben? You put yourself there, in Idaho, didn't you?" I was yelling now, and I hated myself. This had to stop. Now *I* was getting out of hand, too. I left his room and went downstairs.

Ben was right behind me. "Well, you can't stop me. I'm taking the car and I'll take care of myself!"

Ali was seated at the kitchen table doing her homework. When she heard our argument coming, she rolled her eyes, gathered up her books, and went into the family room.

"Fine. Go. Get out of here," I said to Ben. I was so full of anger now that the fury had to go somewhere. I grabbed some paper towels and began frantically wiping the countertops. I emptied the dishwasher. I sorted the mail. Anything to stay in motion so I could stop screaming at him.

Ben followed close behind me—too close. He continued to defend himself—and the more I puttered and the quieter I became, the more he talked. And talked. And followed me. Into the living room, out the front door, into the garage, back into the kitchen.

I stopped short and turned around. I took a deep, ragged breath. "Ben, if I have to rip the battery out of that car, you are going nowhere in it. I would be a fool to let you drive it in your condition anyway. Forget it; you cannot drive that car—or any car." I grabbed every single set of keys from their hooks near the front door.

Ben glared at me. He started to grab for the keys I held, but stopped short. Even in his agitated state, physical fighting just wasn't in his nature. *Thank God for that.* He much preferred words; he launched into a mono-logue of accusations. Now he didn't even notice that I wasn't responding. He was inches behind me wherever I went, talking nonstop.

"Look, Mom. You're not being fair. You don't even *know* me any-more. You don't know how *tired* I am. You don't know your own *son!* I'm not fucking crazy! I am not crazy! You're the one with the dark side. You just hide it from the world. Everyone thinks you're so great because you're on the radio and everything but they don't know you have this *dark side.*"

Now I was near my piano and my eye fell on the portable cassette recorder I use for music rehearsals. With my back to Ben, I grabbed it and pushed "record." I didn't know why I was doing this; perhaps I was hop-ing this would all make sense later. I think I wanted, for the future, some evidence that I hadn't imagined this episode.

Ben was still talking, faster and faster. "Yeah, you," he said. "When my mom has actually pushed herself on her dark side so far as to actually consider doing bad things to people, that is *evil*. My mother likes to blame all of her problems on other people and she never admits it to anybody else. Because one thing that she does is whenever she gets angry she blames me, and she says 'Ben, why are you screaming at me?' So I get to sit here feeling *scapegoated* most of the time for my mom's dark side. And for your information, I was up all last night. I spent the whole night outside, by a fucking tree. I was praying to the earth. I wanted answers."

Ali was avoiding hearing this, holed up in the family room in the back of the house. Ben was still talking, still following me around the house and back to the kitchen, where I was turned away from him so he wouldn't see my expression of pure shock. I scrubbed the sink with one hand, held the tape recorder in front of me with the other. *What is he talking about?* I had no idea how to handle this. I couldn't look at Ben. He went on. "And I was scared, Mom. I was scared of the blinkee things. I was always able to figure it out before, because I'm just able to, you know? I have that ability. But I was scared. And so I asked the earth, 'Is this my mother?' and the minute I asked the earth this, I saw two shooting stars. See? I was right! It *was* you!"

My mouth went dry; my hands started to tremble. *"Blinkee things"? "I have that ability"?* What ability?

All the phone calls I'd made to Dr. Zion flashed through my mind. The information I'd given him describing odd symptoms, strange things Ben said, had been received with detachment, with annoyance. Like I was bothering him. Like I was overreacting. "If you don't like it, get a second opinion," he'd said. Well, I had. And now it was time for a third. And a fourth. For whatever it would take to stop my son from talking like this crazy person.

I need to get him to the hospital. Something was really, really wrong. And whatever I'd been doing, whatever fingers I'd been putting in the dike, was not stopping the flood. I was scared.

This is it, then. I picked up the phone and dialed 911.

"What are you doing, Mom? Who are you calling?" said Ben.

Please ring. RING. It rang. Somebody picked up. "Trumbull Police Department."

Thank God. I gave my name and address. And for the first time, I uttered the words: "I think my son is having a psychotic episode. I—"

Ben grabbed the phone from me and slammed it back down. "You can't send me away! You can't lock me up in an insane asylum!"

I said, "No one is trying to—"

Ben interrupted me. "I'm going to fucking kill you!"

I froze. Ben did, too. Immediately he took the words back. "No, I'm lying. I didn't mean it!"

The phone rang; I picked it up. The police had called back. Ben kept talking. "I'm trying to express my feelings. I'm different. I'm not crazy! I'm not going to kill her."

The tape recorder was still going.

I spoke to the police as Ben babbled in the background. "What's going on there?" asked the officer.

"It's my son," I said. "He's bipolar. He needs to go to the hospital, I think."

"What's he saying?"

"Well, he's the one who hung up the phone before. He said he was going to kill me, but he took it right back. He doesn't know what he's saying."

The officer's voice took on a very different tone. "Does he have any weapons?"

Oh, no, what have I done? "No, no. He doesn't have any weapons. He would never hurt me. He just said that."

"We'll be right there."

"Okay," I said, and hung up the phone.

Ben stopped talking and looked at me. Ali came out of the family room. "What happened? Who was that?" she asked.

Ben burst into tears. "Mom called the police," he cried. "Ali! Mom called the police!" Then he ran into the bathroom.

Ali looked at me, her eyebrows raised in question. I nodded. "Of course you can go to him."

Ali followed Ben into the bathroom. Through the open door I could see him turn around and collapse into her arms. His little sister held him tight. "Ali," Ben said. "Mom thinks I'm crazy."

"No, she doesn't," said Ali. "We just want to help you."

"What am I going to do?" said Ben, and he buried his head in her shoulder. His body shook with sobs.

Maybe this is over for now. The dam of real emotion has finally burst. He's always calmer after this—until the next time.

"Ben," said Ali. "Let's go in the family room, okay?" Ben sniffed and nodded. Neither of them looked at me as I stepped aside to let them pass. They sat down on the couch to wait. Ben had stopped crying and was talking quietly to his sister. I couldn't hear what he was saying, but I'd already heard enough for one night. I left them alone and went to answer the door. The police had arrived.

Two officers came inside, pads and pens in hand. Officer Weir, a petite young woman, went to talk with Ben. Officer Jones, a sturdy man of about thirty with a baby face and closely cropped red hair, stayed with me. "What happened, ma'am?" he asked.

I told the story as clearly as I could, emphasizing that my son had been on medication for bipolar disorder and that we had recently changed the dosage. "He didn't really know what he was saying, I'm sure of that," I said.

Officer Jones looked up from his notepad. "I'm sorry, but we're going to have to arrest your son, ma'am."

Arrest him? That's not why I called you. He needs to go to the hospital! "What? Why?" I said.

"Well, he made a threat against you. He threatened to kill you. Isn't that what you told us?" He explained that he had no choice in this situation. There had been a threat of domestic violence, and they were obligated by law to bring Ben into the station.

"But, I told you, he's not *well*. He isn't really responsible for what he's saying. He took it back the minute he said it."

"I know you say that, ma'am, and if your son were under the age of sixteen we could take your word for it. However, he is legally an adult, and it's your word against his. The law is designed to protect possible victims of domestic violence, who often defend their family members after things have calmed down."

"But—"

Officer Jones looked at me with sympathy. "I'm sure you're telling the truth, ma'am, but you have to understand our position. If we don't arrest him, and something happens at a future date, we are liable. We have to take him with us."

I imagined Ben being led away in handcuffs. He would be so scared. And he would never forgive me. *Oh God, why did I tell them? Ben, I'm so sorry.*

Arrest was not what I wanted. What I wanted was for Ben to get help. He needed a hospital, not a jail. He needed to see a doctor who would take this seriously, hear the underlying cry for help. "Officer," I said, "can't you take him to the emergency room instead?"

"I wish we could, but we have no proof that the threat against you was as harmless as you say. You say your son has bipolar disorder, but he's in the other room telling Officer Weir that there's nothing wrong with him. We can't legally take your word over his, since you are no longer responsible for him. It's protocol, ma'am."

Was this it, then? Was Ben going to jail—in his condition—despite my protests? And then I remembered: the tape recorder. I had the entire incident on tape.

"Listen, sir," I said. "I'm telling you that my son is unbalanced, and when he made that threat he was confused and desperate. I'm also telling you that he needs to go to the hospital. He is not making sense, and it's getting worse. I have the proof right here."

I rewound the tape and played back Ben's ramblings before the phone call to 911, and the way the "threat" had come out of his mouth. Even I was surprised at how heightened Ben's voice sounded while talking about the "blinkee things" and "praying to the earth." The threatening line came out all in one breath: "going to fucking kill you, no, I'm lying, I didn't mean it, I'm trying to express my feelings, I'm different, I'm not crazy, I'm not going to kill her." The sentences ran together without the pause between them that I thought I'd heard. We hadn't frozen at all.

Officer Jones reached over and turned off the tape. "I think we can make an exception in this case," he said. "Just let me call my supervisor."

The sergeant arrived about ten minutes later. He listened to the tape and said, "Let's get this kid to City Hospital." They called for an ambulance. Since Ben had been quietly cooperative with Officer Weir and had agreed to the trip to the hospital "to confer with a different doctor about the medications" he had been taking, there was no need to bring him into the hospital in handcuffs. I was grateful for that much. I called Dr. Zion's emergency number, told him what had happened, and asked him to alert the ER that Ben was coming in and should be held for observation.

Officer Weir rode with Ben in the back of the ambulance. The police report states that he was very calm on the way there and thanked her for understanding him. He also told her "that he was going to pray to the earth and to God, and that he was only lying when he said he was going to kill his mother."

At the hospital, Ben went quietly inside with the admitting nurse. A few hours later, at 1 a.m., a nurse allowed me into the room to see him. I sat with Ben for another hour while we waited for the doctor. Ben was generally quiet and sullen, but every so often he spoke to me.

"Mom, you know I have a special gift. I can see wavy lines coming out of certain objects. Everything has an energy. I can see it. Most people can't."

"Mom, I'm tired. I want to go home and go to sleep."

"Mom, why am I here in the hospital?"

At last, a young doctor came in to examine Ben. During the physical exam, he asked the same questions I had heard from Dr. Marks back in New Haven: "Do you ever see things that aren't really there? Are you seeing anything right now? Do you ever hear voices?"

Ben kept saying no. Once, he added: "Are there other people who really see imaginary things? They must be crazy." But Ben was distant, exhausted, and often seemed lost in his own world. The doctor finished writing on the chart and said to Ben, "Why don't you get some sleep, son? You look extremely tired. We'll keep you here until the morning, when the other doctors arrive. I'm only an intern, and I'd like them to talk with you, too."

Ben was too sleepy to argue. "Okay," he said, and he lay down on the cot and closed his eyes.

The intern walked out into the hall, and I followed him. "Why don't you go home and get some sleep, too?" he said. "We'll call you at around ten tomorrow. We'll know more then."

"What do you think is going on?" I asked.

"I can't say for sure," he said. "I've only started my rotations down here. But off the record, I'd have to say that this looks like schizophrenia to me. I'm not an expert; it's just that my brother-in-law has schizophrenia, and he acted the same way as your son."

Schizophrenia? Wait, wasn't that the thing that Dr. Marks had ruled out? This was the second time the possibility had come up, though, and I'd learned a lot since the first time. I'd suspected it when I was reading about it, but it took this intern's perspective to confirm what no psychiatrist had suggested, what I had not wanted to believe before. *Schizophrenia.* It was all starting to make sense. Horrible, terrible sense. *But what does it mean? What happens to people with schizophrenia? And what will it take to get a correct, official diagnosis?*

Dr. Zion, who had called to alert the hospital but had left no other clear instructions, was not the one to help. If I'd suspected this before, I was absolutely certain of it now: Dr. Zion had to go. It was time for a new psychiatrist.

I had to be at work at the radio station in two and a half hours. I went into the treatment room, kissed my sleeping son, and went back home for whatever sleep I could get. It would have to do. I made it through our morning radio show on automatic pilot. I was also in a state of heightened alert. *Please admit Ben to the psychiatric floor. He needs to be observed. He needs so much more help than I can give him. Please.*

At 10 a.m., I got the call from a hospital nurse. "You can come and pick up your son," she said.

"What? No. You can't. He has to be admitted," I said.

"I'm sorry," said the nurse. "He had a good night's sleep, and he keeps telling us that he's fine now. He seems all right. We can't keep him here against his will. He's over eighteen, and we don't have an order for involuntary commitment from his psychiatrist."

There was no way out. I reluctantly picked Ben up from the hospital, to start the cycle again.

In the light of day, the possibility that Ben might have schizophrenia seemed more remote. I didn't *want* him to have schizophrenia. I had more experience with depression, bipolar disorder, OCD. I knew people with these illnesses, people who were managing their recovery. Some public figures had written books about their battles and triumphs with these conditions. But schizophrenia? I didn't know anybody with schizophrenia.

We wouldn't see Dr. Zion anymore. But now where should we turn? I found the names of two more psychiatrists; Ben refused to see them, or Dr. Zion. The only person he liked was a therapist named Dr. Schneider, whose prescription was to let Ben go, let him live on his own, let him fail until he came around.

Things got worse after that. In addition to the mood swings, Ben continued to become more and more isolated. He turned away from people and toward the written word. He couldn't go to a restaurant or a movie without his pens and paper, a spiral notebook or scraps from his pocket.

CHAPTER GUIDEPOSTS

"Acting to protect our relatives with mental illness is the highest form of caring for them, even if it involves force or involuntary commitment."*

If the psychiatrist you're using isn't working with you or for you, fire him or her. Search for the right help.

If the police hear evidence of possible domestic violence, they may legally have to make an arrest. Be prepared for that. Jail is not a good place for someone with a mental illness. Opt for hospitalization if you can.

---

*NAMI Family-to-Family Education Program crisis file.

He wrote things down during conversations. He wrote during television shows. He could not stop writing. He was retreating into what he called his poetry. When he showed it to me, all I could see were symbols and scribbling.

And this was *with* medication—medication Ben was no longer willing to take, medication that wasn't working anyway. Then Ben announced that he wanted to stop taking the meds altogether. He wanted to go with Dr. Schneider's plan. "Just let me do it my way, Mom."

How many times would we try it Ben's way? Would he ever learn to be responsible for his own life, ever accept the reality of his illness?

The only thing I knew for sure was this: whatever we'd been doing was not working. Not at all. I saw nothing ahead but the same struggles, the same confusion, the same pendulum swinging wildly from promises to disaster. There had to be a way to break the pattern.

MOVING DAY

> I feel like everybody is piecing together this huge puzzle and I was born with it already solved. I guess that's a post-life thing. But with me it's always been about diving deeper. Delving and diving in gray water depths instead of trying to pull that water up to your level where its shade is altered.
>
> —Ben, April 2002

It was moving day. For fifteen months, ever since Ben's almost-admittance into City Hospital and my suddenly confirmed suspicion that he might have schizophrenia, I was out of ideas and exhausted from the fight. Ben clung to his belief that he would manage his life perfectly if only I would give him a chance to live alone. He would take care of himself once I stopped trying to control him, he told me. After the hundredth dead end, after the millionth argument, I gave up. *Fine. Let's try that.*

The thing about schizophrenia is that it can sneak up on you. Some people have a sudden onset, a psychotic episode seemingly out of nowhere. Ben's case, however, was fairly typical of the gradual onset type. Pretty normal childhood, but behavioral changes beginning in mid-to-late-teens that are so gradual that it's hard to figure out what exactly is happening. The hell of being in the dark, grasping at straw after straw.

It happens slowly, this profile of schizophrenia. It emerges bit by bit, until you find that your loved one and you have been pushed over the edge. And you don't know how you got there. Then all of a sudden you have a Child with a Mental Illness.

The biggest obstacle is the one I'd been trying to break through for years: a major symptom of mental illness, and schizophrenia in particular, is the lack of insight that anything is wrong. Ben thought he was fine. So why, then, accept treatment?

But we had tried. Oh, how we'd tried. Well—*I* had tried. Anything and everything, it seemed to me. Fifteen months of the pendulum swing from no medication at all to various prescriptions for symptoms of schizophrenia. We'd tried it Ben's way: stopped seeing psychiatrists, stopped the medications, stayed only with therapy. Ben enrolled in college classes, found another job, made promises I still believe he meant to keep.

For the next six months, I watched and waited. It was more of the same. He dropped all of his classes except for Poetry 101, which he barely passed. He lost jobs soon after he landed them. He got four traffic tickets and missed the court dates. His car was filled with old food, papers, garbage, but never enough gas or oil. Eventually it died an oil-deprived death, and Ben abandoned it at a local gas station. He owed money all over town; he had bounced checks one after the other, some for as little as five dollars.

I checked every night to make sure the windows were closed, the garage door shut, the doors locked. Some nights Ben came home on time, other nights he was gone until the next morning. He had been "walking around the neighborhood," or hiking, or sitting in the backyard. Most of the time, he tried his best to be respectful, polite, and to take part in family dinners and events. But the effort always showed, even when he was doing his best. His eyes were somewhere else.

The pile of things lost from his life got bigger, his sense of pride and accomplishment got smaller, and his delusions got grander.

"It doesn't matter," he said. "I like solitude, anyway. Unless I can be with people who are as deep as I am, who delve into their consciousness like I do, I'd rather just write poetry."

But if friends called, he lit up and accepted any invitation. He waited at the door for them to pick him up, like a puppy waiting for his master to come home from work. He always flashed me a huge smile on his way out the door. He looked so glad to have a friend.

"See you later, Mom!" he'd call, and on those nights he always made it home before curfew. It was as if, when he had some pride in his life and not just in his thoughts, he wanted to do the right things. He didn't fight me.

But at other times, Ben continued to lash out at me, angry that I would have such a "low opinion of my own son" that I would "accuse" him of having a chemical imbalance. I was exhausted all the time.

This, then, was it. We'd set several measures of success, Ben and I. He had not met one of them. We were approaching crisis mode again. I could feel it. I hated it. But it was the only way I was going to get him back into treatment. This time, I'd found a new psychiatrist who was an expert on schizophrenia. This time I prayed I would get it right. I set an appointment for us both to see Dr. Steven Taylor, the medical director of the West Hills Center for Behavioral Health I'd heard about at the first NAMI meeting. No matter what it cost, this time I was going to the top.

Dr. Taylor was a balding man, short in stature, with a gentle manner that seemed to contain great wisdom within his quiet tones. He was around forty years old. He met with us both, then with Ben alone. He got Ben to sign a release stating that Dr. Taylor would be allowed to share some pertinent information with me, especially if Ben's life was in danger. This was a smart move, a way to include me in Ben's treatment even with the new, stringent privacy laws. *Finally, someone who knows what he's doing*, I thought.

Even with smart treatment, there's no magic formula for successful treatment of schizophrenia. I'd read about a medication called Clozaril, but Dr. Taylor wanted to try that only as a last resort. "There are so many other medications that could work," he said, "and I'd rather start with those. Clozaril requires blood work every week at first, to make sure your white blood cell count is all right. There's a rare side effect from Clozaril called agranulocytosis, which could be very dangerous. There are lots of other treatments to try first."

And so we did. For the next few months we tried Risperidone. We tried Geodon. Zyprexa. Abilify. Small dosages, ramping up. Weaning off one, while starting another.

And, all the while, I watched my son. I kept track of changes, good and bad. Side effects. Signs of life, signs of relapse. Hints of effectiveness. Hints of the young man I used to know, the young man I still hoped I might see again.

I watched helplessly and hopefully as Ben went through side effects that, with luck, might be only temporary: extreme sleepiness or lethargy, or at other times agitation and relentless pacing around the house. These side effects meant that, at least, he was taking the meds.

I also noticed, after a time, some signs of life. Real life. Little things, but as miraculous to me as the unexpected light of the sun after days of clouds and relentless rain.

In late May, he actually completed his poetry folder for school and organized it. On that day, too, he said "I love you" to me, and he looked like he meant it. He did not ask me for anything. He just said, "I love you, Mom."

This was two days after we'd had a fight so out of control that I'd brought out the tape recorder again. During this fight, which began with an attempt at planting the flowerboxes together to celebrate Mother's Day, Ben said that I was crazy for thinking he had "bipolar disorder or whatever you want to call it," and that my assumption that something was wrong with him could only mean that I was hiding from my own dark side. Now, two days, later, his eyes were calm and warm. His face was more expressive. And he said, "I love you."

He also said, "You know, Mom, I think the side effects from these meds may be due to the fact that I'm so bored now. My mind is quieter, and I'm just *bored*. So I want to sleep."

Judging from the poetry he had written just weeks before, I could see that a quieter mind might seem boring to him. After believing he can save the world with his poetry, thinking he has special gifts, can he ever be happy with ordinary life again? Even if medication can relieve him of his delusions, will he miss them?

After eight months of this cycle of promising-to-disappointing results from his treatment, I could see one truth: this was getting us nowhere. Ben was fighting this so hard, fighting *me* so hard, that the only thing I could picture in the future was more of the same. More frustration, more isolation, more arguments, more trial and much more error. I couldn't live like this anymore, as policeman and in-house psychiatrist. I couldn't take any more scenes. Ali was in her senior year, getting ready for college, and her social life was suffering because of Ben's unpredictability; she was becoming reluctant to allow her friends to come to our house because they might see Ben wandering in the yard or muttering to himself or—worst of all— caught in yet another heated, illogical argument with me.

By January, the idea of living on his own had begun to consume Ben's energy. He saw it as the only solution to his life. "Everyone *else* gets to live on their own, Mom. Even Ali will be out of here next September. If I could only live on my own, away from here, I could prove to you that I can do this. I just need a chance to prove it to you. This time I'll take my meds, and you'll see."

This was the sticking point I so desperately held onto: my supervision of his meds, such as it was. Ben said, "Mom, I *promise*. If you'll just give me the chance to do this myself, I'll take the meds. I'm only so stubborn about it because we don't get along right now. Don't you see that?"

I wished I believed him. He wanted so very much to prove it to me. Was there any chance he could rise to the occasion, out from under my wing, and take the reins of his own treatment? Was there any chance for the miracle of insight into the illness that had destroyed the life we'd imagined for him? I prayed for the unlikely outcome: that he would *get it.* Keep the commitment. Take the medication. Let it help him. Manage his life. Grow up.

But in the deepest trenches of my gut, I knew the more likely result: Ben might crash. Big time. Fall hard enough, deep enough to finally hit a bottom that was indefinable, unpredictable. What would happen there? I had no idea. All I knew was this: he had to go there in order to get the help he so clearly needed.

For fifteen months I had waited for the chance to get Ben some more consistent help, more thorough observation of his symptoms, monitoring of his recovery. That could only happen in a twenty-four-hour facility—a hospital setting, a psychiatric facility. Everyone kept telling me that their hands were tied. Ben wasn't "sick enough."

Not sick enough? What is "sick enough"? Threatening someone? Disturbing the peace? Causing a scene so embarrassing that he'd never want to show his face in Trumbull again? What does it take to get the kind of attention that might actually do some good?

If I couldn't make him well, did I have to let him get sicker to get better? So the two possible options, success and dismal failure, could at least get us out of the useless cycle we were in. We began the search for an apartment for Ben.

There was a plan, of course. There was a team behind the plan: Dr. Taylor, Rob, Dr. Schneider, Ben, and me. We spelled it all out clearly. Ben agreed to keep seeing Dr. Taylor, keep taking the meds, and continue to have clean drug tests. If he wanted to see a therapist in addition, that was up to him. I took Ben to visit two community agencies that would provide job coaching if he couldn't find a job on his own within two weeks.

After a long search to find a willing landlord, we found one who took a liking to Ben and allowed a month-to-month lease. The apartment was on the bottom floor of a small residence ten minutes from our house in Trumbull. Far, but not too far. From his new apartment, Ben could walk into town or catch the bus. Perfect.

The apartment itself was a find. The entire house had been a lovely Victorian single-family residence in its former life, and it had since been sliced into apartments. The space that was to become Ben's new home was the part of the house that had been the front parlor, dining room, and kitchen. His double front door was directly off of the wraparound porch. Inside, the ceilings were ten feet high, with elaborate moldings. There was an entryway, with the bathroom straight ahead, and one large room to the right that was used as a bedroom. To the left, another large room housed a fireplace and led into the eat-in kitchen. Windows were large and plentiful.

In the right hands, this could have become a decorator's dream. But it was clearly a place that had long housed temporary tenants. It had recently been fumigated, and there were roach corpses in the kitchen. It smelled of Indian food, courtesy of the previous occupants. The painted walls were dirty. Plenty of potential, but lots of TLC was needed.

And so, we moved him in. On that February Saturday, Ben was so excited to be starting this new chapter that his happiness outshone everything else. He took his meds willingly, and he worked hard along with me and Ali to move into his new home. The apartment was partially furnished, so all we had to move in was our old modular couch and Ben's personal things: his stereo, clothes, posters, bicycle, and the dishes we'd bought at Goodwill.

It took several trips to move Ben's things. To prepare for the final load, I emptied Ben's old camp trunk of its contents so that I could take it home and repack it. I opened the trunk and took out the books, papers, and Ben's typewriter.

Suddenly, Ben stopped unloading his duffle bag and stared at me. His typewriter was still in my hands. "Mom!" he said. "Stop that!"

"Stop what, Ben? I'm just unpacking a little."

"I saw you, Mom. I *saw* you put evil energy into my typewriter. That isn't nice. Stop that!"

I looked down at the machine in my hands. My heart twisted. We had been laughing together not one minute before. "Ben, what are you talking about?"

"I *saw* you, Mom. You can't deny it. I *saw* the waves going from your hands into my typewriter. I don't want your negative energy!"

When will this ever end? What the hell can I say to that? "I did not!" was all I could manage. Then I threw the typewriter across the room, onto his bed. "You stop it, Ben! Stop it! I did not do any such thing!" I walked out of his new home and waited by the car, watching his front door. Five minutes later, Ben came out. He walked over to me. I unlocked the car doors, and we both got in. Neither of us said a word.

We drove for about five minutes in continued silence, my hands like a vise on the steering wheel. Ben looked sullenly out of his window and then spoke. "Mom," he said. "I'm sorry. It's just that I saw you do something

I didn't like, and I wanted to point it out to you. You shouldn't do things like that because it will come back to you when you die and your life gets judged. I'm just trying to *save* you from being judged harshly later on. I'm trying to point out your *mistakes*. Why won't you listen to me?"

I had heard and seen so much in the past few years. I wanted none of it to be true. I desperately wanted to make it stop. *Make it stop.* I felt like I was living in a nightmare, sleepwalking through every little crisis. All I could do was move things along to the next chapter and turn the page— exactly what I did on that February day. I gently assured Ben that I would never put negative energy into his things; I let it go, and we completed the last trip of his move.

Like a mother dropping her firstborn off at college, I tried to hover long enough to be helpful while leaving in time to allow Ben to set things up for himself. Only thing was, this wasn't college. Ben was alone. No roommates, no dorm life. As I left him in his own place, a pale imitation of the proud moment it might have been under other, healthier circumstances, I drove away with a feeling of lightness. Relief. I could return to my own home, and whatever extreme behavior lay ahead would occur without my constant witness.

Another NAMI parent had told me that her son only began to get better when she gave up control. She stopped trying to fix him and, in her words, "gave it up to God." I guess that's what I was doing by closing the door on Ben's new false independence and driving away that day. I was giving it up to God, as best I could. But the typewriter incident told me that Ben had probably not consistently taken his medication for several days already. *Here we go, then.*

Two weeks later, Ali and I were able to spend three days in Manhattan, celebrating her eighteenth birthday with tickets to two Broadway shows and a trip to Elizabeth Arden. For the first time since Ben had returned to us from the West, I felt at ease about leaving our house for two nights.

As we left the salon and walked through the icy streets of Manhattan together, Ali checked out her new red highlights in a store window and said, "Mom, this is the best birthday present ever. I'll remember it for my whole life."

I felt so worldly, sharing Manhattan with my beautiful daughter. I felt so happy—and yet, underneath, was this sense of emptiness. Ben wasn't there to share it with us. His presence, as it currently was, would have ruined the trip, but I couldn't help but make this wish: *Next year, let us be a complete family again.*

CHAPTER GUIDEPOSTS

"*Agranulocytosis*: a dramatic decrease in the number of infection-fighting white blood cells. Agranulocytosis is a very rare side effect of antipsychotic drugs, most notably of clozapine (brand name Clozaril). Even in the case of clozapine, it is said to afflict only 1–2% of users, and the ill effects of this disease can be reversed if identified early, and the drug discontinued."*

Approaching Psychosis

Schizophrenia comes in three stages: onset (prodromal stage), acute period (active stage), and the aftermath (residual stage). Symptoms overlap, both negative and positive, but during the active stage, you may especially observe the positive symptoms, such as:

- *Hallucinations*: voices, visual apparitions, bizarre interpretations of taste, touch, and smell
- *Grossly Disorganized Behavior*: bizarre actions, following rituals, swearing and shouting
- *Delusions*: False beliefs
- Catatonic Rigidity or Excitement
- *Disorganized Speech*: incoherent, loose associations†

---

*NAMI Family-to-Family Education Program glossary.
†American Psychiatric Association, *Diagnostic and Statistical Manual of Mental Disorders*, 4th ed. (Washington, D.C.: American Psychiatric Association, 1994).

Sixteen days after that, I was in the emergency room of St. Mary's Hospital in Bridgeport. Ben was in the lock-down room, incoherent, waiting for an available bed. It had happened: he was finally sick enough. And it hurt like hell to see it.

12

FINALLY, SICK ENOUGH

God grant me the serenity
to accept the things I cannot change,
courage to change the things I can,
and wisdom to know the difference.

—The Serenity Prayer

Four weeks. That's all it took from moving day to Ben's first hospitalization for mental illness. Despite all his promises and plans, any shred of hope that being out from under the wing of my supervision would magically result in a new acceptance of responsibility for managing his life vanished. Ben fell off his recovery plan with remarkable speed; when he did, I was completely unprepared for the new symptoms that emerged. They were worse, far worse, than anything I'd seen in him before. All the time he'd been living at home, at least partially balanced by his medications, the illness underneath the treatment had been marching on. Intensifying. The crash that came soon after he moved out—the one I'd been both dreading and hoping for—was devastating. I still tell myself that it was also unavoidable.

The first sign came in late February 2003, a week after my trip with Ali into New York.

Ben was invited to our other celebration for her birthday—family dinner in a restaurant. I'd arranged to pick Ben up on the way to the restaurant where we were to meet my brother Russ and his family.

Earlier that week, I'd visited Ben, and he'd seemed sad and lost. Gone was the excitement of moving in. Gone were the hope and promises of that first day. His apartment was no neater than his room had been at home. He himself was no more focused, no more ambitious.

161

I saw him mutter under his breath. I heard him laugh out loud at nothing. Was he really hearing voices? Was he sharing private jokes with them? "Ben, what are you laughing about?" I'd finally asked.

"I'm just enjoying my own thoughts, Mom. I have a *right* to have *thoughts*."

What do you say to that? I felt powerless. I couldn't wait to get out of there. "Are you taking your meds, Ben?"

"Of course, Mom."

I looked at the pillbox. The compartments for the past few days were empty. *Had* he taken them? Was the new prescription for Abilify not working, then? Or had he thrown the pills out?

Whatever was going to happen would have to happen. However, I was not prepared for the sight that awaited me when I got out of the car to ring Ben's doorbell that evening. It was nearly six o'clock; I'd called Ben earlier that day to remind him about the dinner once again. I'd left the message on his answering machine, several times. I assumed he'd be ready. He always loved to celebrate Ali's birthday. He always looked forward to seeing his aunt and uncle and cousins. He always loved a free meal in a restaurant.

I drove up to Ben's home and honked the horn. No response. I got out and rang the doorbell. Again, nothing. I peeked in his bedroom window. Unmade bed, with no one in it. Good, at least he wasn't asleep. I went back to the front door and peeked through the windowpane as I rang the bell again.

There he was. Ben was just *standing* there in the middle of his entryway. He had on sweatpants but nothing else. He wasn't even looking toward the front door. Instead, he stood facing his living room, near a makeshift hall table we'd fashioned out of an ironing board. He was not moving. He was just—there.

He forgot, I thought. *How could he forget his sister's birthday?* Then I realized: *He just got up! It's almost 6 p.m., and he's just gotten out of bed. How can he be so lazy? I will never forgive him for disappointing her.* I pushed the doorbell again, five or six times, muttering under my breath.

At last he turned toward me slowly. Very slowly. Then he walked, as if in a trance, toward the front door and opened it.

I was so angry that I hardly noticed he was just staring at me. "Ben, come on! We're late!"

He stared some more. Finally, he said, "Late for what?" His eyes were out of focus. He seemed to look past me, even though he was staring right at me.

"It's Ali's birthday dinner. Don't you remember? Come on! They're all waiting for us."

Ten seconds passed. It felt like ten minutes. "Oh," he said. "I forgot."

This was not like him at all—not even in the worst shape I'd seen him in before. I turned toward the car, motioned to Ali to wait a second, and walked past my unresponsive son and into his kitchen. His pillbox was on his kitchen table, the last two days' worth of pills still in it. Either he had forgotten to take them or chosen not to, then forgot to trick me by throwing them away.

Stupid, stupid. I couldn't even begin to absorb this new information. I had another child waiting in the car, ready to celebrate her eighteenth birthday. I heard myself talk to him. "Forget it, Ben, you blew it. We'll just go to dinner without you. I'll tell Ali you don't feel well."

He did look as though he had the flu: groggy, slow, red-rimmed eyes. I wished that it were as simple as that: the flu. Anything but the reality before me, that Ben was a mess.

He was the furthest from reality that I had seen him so far. But still, probably not bad enough to be hospitalized. He was vacant, but that wasn't good enough to force an involuntary commitment. Not good enough. I knew the big question they would ask at the hospital: "Is he a danger to himself or to others?" *Not yet,* I thought. *But how far does he have to go? What do I do? How close do I stay?*

It was possible that, if I waited a while, Ben would emerge from his grogginess enough to come out with us and be at least partially present for his sister's birthday. But that would be enabling; that would ruin everyone else's plans. I turned away, relegated my fear to a corner of my mind, and drove to the restaurant for Ali's celebration. We would see what tomorrow would bring. That was all that I could do at that moment.

I waited until I was in bed that night to cry and pray that Ben would be safe. *But how safe can he be, without me to watch over him? What if he wanders through this new neighborhood and is hit by a car? Or is approached by a drug dealer? What if he forgets to eat? What if he leaves a cigarette burning, and it starts a fire? Oh, God. Oh, God.* With Ben ten miles away from me, instead of the nearly three thousand miles separating us when he was in Montana, I felt more helpless than ever.

The next day, Ben called me to apologize. He was coherent again. Himself again. Sweet. Responsive. Happy. I was relieved, and I was also disappointed. If he was going to crash, why postpone the agony? I wanted him in the hospital, yet I didn't. Probably he was taking his meds again, but why? *Maybe this time he got it. Maybe this time he frightened himself enough to see that the meds really do help him.*

That week he called to tell me proudly that he'd cleaned up his apartment and filled out a job application. He also called to wish Ali well on the day she and I traveled to Rhode Island for her student orientation at Roger Williams University. I held my breath. I waited for the other shoe to fall and hoped I was wrong. Three days later, the next wave of worsening symptoms appeared.

Ben didn't answer his phone or respond to his messages all that day. When I finally reached him, when he picked up the telephone at last, there was a huge lag in response time to everything I said. Long seconds went by before he either answered my questions or simply asked, "What did you say?" Ben spoke slowly, as if he were trying to keep everything under control.

Oh no. Pulse racing, I drove over to his apartment and found him sitting on his couch, writing in his spiral notebook. "Ben," I said. "What's going on? Are you okay?"

He didn't answer me.

"Ben? *Ben?*"

He looked up at me and nodded his head. He watched as I walked past him into the kitchen, which I could see was filthy again: dishes in the sink, overflowing garbage, and a couple of roaches crawling over the kitchen counter. I grabbed a paper towel and crushed the roaches with much more force than necessary. I was fueled by disgust, by fear. I stepped as far away from Ben's sink as I could and opened the doors underneath to grab the can of Raid. One more roach in there—I sprayed it. I sprayed everywhere. Ben sat on his couch, watching me wordlessly.

Then I noticed that the electric stove was still on. One of the burners was glowing, red-hot. "Ben, you left the stove on!" I said as I turned the knob to off. "How could you do that?"

Ben got up and followed me into the kitchen. He looked at me, raised his eyebrows, then shrugged his shoulders.

"Honey, you can't leave the stove on. That could be very dangerous." Ben shrugged his shoulders again. I realized then that he wasn't talking to me. It was as if he were giving me the silent treatment of a pouting child. "Hey," I said. "Talk to me. What's going on?"

But he didn't look angry. This wasn't a silence born of anger. He just wouldn't talk. Ben went over to his fridge, took the dry-erase message board from the door, and began to write with a marker. "I am going to go job hunting today," he wrote. He pointed to the message with his finger and looked at me.

What is this? Is this some sort of superstition? I had no idea what he was thinking; all I knew is that it was freaking me out. "Ben," I said, keeping my voice as even as I could. "It's too late to look for a job today. The day is gone. It's five o'clock."

He shrugged his shoulders, then wiped off the word "today" and wrote "tomorrow." He pointed to it again.

I took a good look at my son, taking inventory. Wrinkled, dirty clothes: perhaps the second or third day in a row he had worn them. Hair: filthy. Face: unshaven. Eyes: frighteningly vacant. "Ben," I said, as calmly as I could. "Stop this. Talk to me."

He wrote some more: "I can't."

"How are you going to get a job if you won't talk?"

He shrugged again.

"And you can't look for a job like that. You're a mess. Ben, you have no food, you have no money. You were supposed to have a job by now. What have you been doing?"

Ben pointed to the board again, and shrugged. Then I spotted his pillbox on the crowded kitchen table. Three more compartments still filled in with his pills: Sunday, Monday, Tuesday. That added up to five days now, I calculated, with no medication at all. I pushed past Ben to the fridge and looked in. The food he'd filled it with over a week ago was now in various stages of decay. Uncooked, untouched, and moldy. Had he even forgotten to eat?

Maybe this is it, I thought. *Is this bad enough for him to be admitted to the ER? What am I supposed to do now?*

I did the only thing I could think of: I treated him like a toddler. "Ben, I can see you don't want to talk to me. All right. I don't know why, and you don't want to tell me. But your place is a mess, and I can't keep my promise to give you food money if you don't keep your promise to clean up."

"NOT FAIR," he now scribbled.

"Maybe not," I said, "but that's what I've decided to do. And more important, Ben, you're not taking your meds. Have you taken them *at all* since you moved in?" He stared at me blankly. "You promised," I continued. "You aren't keeping up your end of the bargain. I'm afraid you just lost this apartment. Be ready to see Dr. Taylor on Thursday. Your appointment is at 2:15. Write it on your calendar."

He walked over to the calendar on the wall and wrote the appointment in for Thursday. If we made it that far. My plan was to walk out of there, drive around the corner, and call Dr. Taylor to find out how to get Ben to the emergency room as soon as possible.

"So I'm going home, and when you've decided you can talk to me again, give me a call and I'll come back. Meanwhile, I'll see you on Thursday. Be ready. Bye now." I walked past Ben to the front door. I looked calm, I hoped, but inside I was trembling.

I could somehow feel something shift inside my son, though he remained silent. As I turned the doorknob to leave, he took a breath and spoke. "Sorry, Mom. I was just playing a game."

Some game. I turned around and made myself smile at him. "Is the game over now?" I asked, much more calmly than I felt.

"Yeah," he said. "And sorry about the stove. I used it to light my cigarette. I couldn't find the matches."

I looked over at the fireplace mantel, where a pack of matches was clearly visible. Ben was speaking, but he still seemed to be in a fog. "Never mind, then," I said. "Let's get this place cleaned up. And while we're at it, we'll get *you* cleaned up, too. And take your meds. Now."

He removed one day's dosage from the box and swallowed the pills reluctantly. "Don't take the apartment away from me, Mom. I *did* clean it! I can't help it if it isn't up to your standards."

Count to ten. Talk to him like he's a child—anyone's child but your own. "Listen, honey, we agreed on exactly what we meant by a clean apartment. Let's look at the list and go through it." Then, together, we worked to make his home livable again. Ben made a definite, but clearly difficult, effort to be polite and personable. One hour later, his place was vacuumed, the fridge cleaned out, garbage emptied, and the dishes washed. Ben himself was in clean clothes, and clean-shaven. His stare was still often vacant, though, and his attention sporadic. I gave him some cash for food and left him sitting with his notebooks and pens.

"Bye, Mom," he said. "Thanks. I'm going job-hunting tomorrow, I promise." He sounded almost coherent again. Even as my heart rose at the sound of this normal conversation, it sank back at the realization that we'd probably only postponed the inevitable. Today's emergency had passed, taking with it this opportunity to hospitalize Ben. He still wasn't sick enough—yet.

Once in the car, I drove halfway around the block until Ben's home was out of sight. I pulled over, dialed Dr. Taylor's emergency number, and told him what had just happened. "I think Ben is close to having to be hospitalized. What do I do when it happens?" I still couldn't believe I was having this conversation. It didn't seem real.

Dr Taylor said, "Ben will probably go back to sleep now, after taking the medication, but check on him tomorrow and call me if he's not better. Otherwise, I'll be seeing you on Thursday, and we'll see how he is. I agree it's probably just a matter of time before he breaks down again, but we can't do much until he does." Getting Ben admitted to a hospital against his will would be hard, but a psychiatrist's order for a seventy-two-hour hold for observation would at least get the process started. Dr. Taylor got the paperwork ready, just in case. Then we'd have to take it from there.

It will take way more than seventy-two hours in a hospital to help Ben, I thought. But once he was admitted, we could take more steps. One thing I did not want: another overnight "observation" like the one we'd gone through at City Hospital. This time, I wanted Ben to *stay* in the hospital.

One week later, I got my wish. Ben had the breakdown that, at last, qualified him as *sick enough*. My son became like a zombie.

He'd managed to hold himself together for Thursday's appointment. Ben was very afraid of going to the hospital, and he put all his effort into convincing everyone he didn't need to go. He tried very hard to be friendly and cooperative in Dr. Taylor's office. I could see the strain of the effort; I couldn't help but admire it on some level nonetheless. "Keep an eye on him," Dr. Taylor had said to me, when Ben left the room. "He's trying too hard. Call me as soon as you need to." The following Tuesday, I needed to.

The phone rang early in the afternoon. It was Chris, a friend of Ben's about the same age, who had bipolar disorder. Chris was in recovery, willingly taking his medication, and holding down a job at a local supermarket. He was my hero—not only because he was such a good role model for Ben, but because he hadn't given up on Ben. He remained friends with him, could empathize with his struggles, and tried to convince him to actively accept treatment. He'd picked Ben up earlier that day to take him to the diner for lunch.

"Randye," Chris said. "Is that you?" His voice sounded unnaturally thin.

"Chris?" I said. "What's wrong?"

"It's about Ben. I'm so glad you're home. I didn't know what else to do. I'm so sorry to call you."

"What is it? What happened?"

"I don't know," he said. "We're at the diner, and he's just acting so *weird*. I've never seen him like this. I can't get him to be normal. I'm scared."

I took a deep breath. "What's he doing, exactly?"

"Well, he's just—*staring*. I'm trying to talk to him about a friend of ours, a guy who just overdosed. Ben's usually so, like, sympathetic about stuff like this, but I don't think he even hears me. He just keeps talking to himself. He's muttering under his breath, and when he's not doing that he's just listening to the Muzak instead of me. Sometimes he catches the eye of little kids in the diner and smiles at them, but then he *stares* at them. I'm trying to get him to talk to me, and sometimes he snaps out of it and realizes I'm here and tries to answer me. But he's acting so weird. What do I do?"

I imagined how Ben must look to the other diners, to his loyal friend Chris, to those little kids. Was he frightening them? Were they burying their faces in their parents' arms? I recalled, fleetingly, when his phone used to ring constantly with requests for Ben to babysit. He was the favorite choice. Kids had loved him, had responded to his warmth, his humor, his intelligence. Was that really only a few years ago?

I snapped back into the present, to the grim reality of Ben's current vacant state. "Can you get him into your car, Chris?" I said. "Can you take him back to his apartment and wait there for me?"

"I think so," he said. He sounded so young.

"Listen, I'm leaving now and I'll meet you at Ben's place. I'm going to call his psychiatrist, and we're going to try to get him hospitalized so they can stabilize his medication. Don't say anything to Ben, okay? Just get him home, and wait for me if you can. I'll take care of the rest."

"Okay," he said. Then, "Randye?"

"Yes?"

"Is Ben going to be all right? I've never seen him this bad."

"I know. I don't think he's had such a small amount of medication in his system for a long time, that's why. I promise you, you did the right thing. Now we can help him."

"Okay. I'll see you soon," he said.

"And, Chris?"

"Yeah?"

"You're a very good friend to Ben. And to me. Thank you for calling. You've really been a big help and I appreciate it."

I heard him say something to Ben but I couldn't make out the words. "Please hurry," he said to me.

I hung up, then called Dr. Taylor to tell him what was happening. "I think this is it. Can you call St. Mary's Hospital and tell them to expect Ben?" Now all I had to do was get him from his apartment, into my car or an ambulance, and into the emergency room. I didn't know *how* I would do that, but I knew that I had to. I got in my car and went to see what I would find at Ben's place.

When I parked my car in front of the house, both boys were there, as promised, in the living room. *Thank goodness.* At least I wouldn't have to call the police—not yet, anyway. When I walked inside, Chris looked at me helplessly and let out a huge sigh of relief.

"Can you stay a few more minutes, Chris?" I asked. He nodded. I went to work. "Hi, Ben," I said.

"Hi, Mom." He was smiling almost foolishly, staring too long at whatever his eyes landed on.

"Listen, sweetheart, Dr. Taylor wants to see you." At least that was true. I hadn't had to tell a lie yet.

Five seconds, ten seconds, went by. "That's okay," Ben said at last. "When?"

"This afternoon, honey, right now. Why don't you get in the car, and I'll take you to see him?"

Five seconds, ten seconds. "Nah, Mom. That's okay. I'll go another time. Thanks anyway."

Try again. "No, really, honey. We have to go right now. It's important."

Five, ten, fifteen seconds. "Okay, Mom. I can do that. Let's go. Can I take my backpack?"

"Sure," I said, and I watched him go into his bedroom to get it. Chris whispered to me, "One of our friends just died from an overdose. I was so upset. I tried to talk to Ben about it, but I didn't think he heard me. Then he finally looked at me and said the weirdest thing."

"What did he say?"

"He said, 'What do you mean, *dead?*' and then he looked at me like—I don't know—like he knew a secret that I didn't. Or like he thought I was kidding. It freaked me out, big-time. The expression in his eyes, it was like—suspicious."

Suspicious. I'd seen that look sometimes, too. I hated it. I gave Chris a hug, then pulled back and looked at him. "Listen, honey. I know you're scared. I am, too. Ben's acting crazy. But believe me, it's his *illness* talking. When we get his meds balanced, he'll be better. You'll see."

He nodded. "I guess. My mom says I did some stupid stuff before my meds worked right, too."

Ben was ready to go. Chris looked more than ready to go, too. "Thanks, Chris," I said. "Thanks so much. You are a great guy. We'll keep you posted, okay?"

"Yeah, thanks, man," said Ben. "Thanks for lunch."

"You're welcome," Chris said. We left the apartment together and got into our separate cars. I saw the relief on Chris's face and the worry in his eyes, right before he closed his car door.

On the way to the hospital, I tried to say as little as possible, to avoid saying the wrong thing. Would Ben stay in the car or try to get out? What was he thinking? The fifteen minutes to the hospital ticked away way too slowly. Ben was pretty quiet. He stared straight ahead for a while. Once he turned to me and said, "Don't look at me like that, Mom!"

"Like what, Ben?"

"Like you think I'm evil or something. I know what you're thinking."

I felt the tears again. *No, no, don't cry. No crying. Do it later. Just get him to the hospital.*

I wanted to convince Ben that I was thinking no such thing. Instead I just said, "Okay, Ben." But I reached behind me to the pocket behind his seat, where I now kept the cassette tape recorder. I pulled it into my lap while he was staring out the window and turned it on. Would I need evidence? *Well, just in case.*

As we got off at the exit for the hospital, Ben realized that we weren't heading toward Dr. Taylor's office. He was in a haze, but he still knew his roads and streets. "Where are we going? This isn't the way," he said.

"I know," I replied. "Dr. Taylor isn't in his office today. He's working at the hospital. He has to see you there. He'll meet us."

It worked. "Oh, okay," said Ben.

Half a mile to go. I tried to make some conversation. The tape recorder was still on. There were long pauses before many of Ben's answers. He often lost his way right in the middle of a sentence. "So, you and Chris went to the diner."

"Uh . . . yeah!" His voice was high-pitched. It sounded false.

"What did you eat there?"

"We didn't eat or drink anything."

"So—you two just sat there without anything to eat or drink? That was nice of them, to let you just sit there."

"No," Ben said. "I bought something. What I bought . . . what did I buy?" So confused.

"Gee, I don't know. What did you buy, Ben?"

His voice squeezed through his teeth in the haughty tone he took on when he was trying to test me. "What do I *usually* have at diners?"

"French fries and coffee," I guessed.

"Yeah. Just checking. That's what I had."

"I'm confused now, Ben, because you said you didn't eat anything."

"Yeah, but I had . . . things."

"You had things."

"Yeah." There it was, that unnaturally high pitch again. If I hadn't known better, I would have thought I was talking to someone on LSD or falling-down drunk. But he wasn't either of those things.

We pulled in front of the ER at last. "Okay. You come with me," I said.

"Sure." Ben was trying to sound oh so cooperative.

I walked my son into the ER, sat him down, and went to the front desk. "My son is having a psychotic break," I whispered to the receptionist. That was the first time I had ever used these words. "He needs to be admitted. Dr. Steven Taylor should have left a message from West Hills."

I kept turning around to check on Ben. He was looking around. He had brought his backpack with him. He might bolt at any minute. But where would he go? St. Mary's Hospital is right in the middle of a residential city neighborhood; getting lost quickly would be easy, and then what would I do? I'd waited so long for this opportunity to get him admitted for some real treatment, and I'd managed this far. Right now I had the element of newness, and surprise, working for me. Next time, would he come with me so willingly?

The receptionist took quick action, and within five minutes I was led into the financial office to register and give insurance information. Before leaving Ben, I whispered to the security guard, "Please keep an eye on my son. He's having a psychotic break"—those words again—"and he may try to run."

The guard assured me that he would. As I walked down the hall, I saw the nurse lead Ben into an intake room to record his vital signs. "What are you doing that for?" he was saying. The fog he was in was starting to clear, which meant that we didn't have much time. I looked back at the security guard, and he nodded back. He would take care of it.

Inside the financial office, the clerk looked at my name and recognized it from our radio show. "Are you *Randye Kaye*? From the morning show?" she squealed. This was such a departure from the part of my life I was living at the moment that it hardly seemed real. "Yes," I said. "So nice to meet you."

"Oh my God, I listen to your show all the time!" She filled out the paperwork, smiling all the while. She called to her coworkers to come over and say hi to me. The irony of this exchange—a reminder that there was another part of my life that still existed—almost brought me out of the numbness I was feeling. Still, I was aware that this process was taking a little longer than I'd hoped. Thank goodness I'd alerted Security.

Paperwork completed at last, I headed back out to the waiting room. Coming in the front door was Ben, accompanied by not one but *five* security guards. His hands were behind his back; his arms were held tight to his sides by the guards. "I don't want to go in there!" he was saying. "I have a right to go home!" He was protesting but was, at least, walking in with the guards, not being *carried* in by them. Still—five guards to my one Ben. I will remember that sight forever.

The guards took him through sliding double doors into the treatment area. The doors slid shut behind them. Ben was in. I was relieved and devastated at the same time. The head security guard came over to me. His face was kind, which made me cry. "Sorry you had to see that," he said. "Your son went outside to smoke a cigarette, and I followed him out. He tried to run, and when I held him back he struggled so much I had to call for the others."

"I'm sorry," I said. "He's just scared."

"Don't apologize," he said. "Happens all the time. I'm just glad we didn't have to use cuffs on him. He mostly protested with words." Yes, that would be Ben. The guard started to walk back to his desk and then turned back to me. "He seems like a good kid," he said.

And that's what really made me cry. Those kind words in the middle of a nightmare—that reminder that the boy being led into the ER was still my Ben, my son. I will always be grateful to that guard.

The important thing now was to *keep* Ben behind those closed sliding doors. Despite his incoherence, despite his attempt to run away, there was not enough evidence yet to admit him for long. The rules called for a concrete reason to keep him there until Dr. Taylor's orders came through. The admitting nurse had a list of questions to ask me. She began with "Has your son threatened to hurt himself? Any talk of suicide?"

"No," I admitted.

She went down the list. "Has he threatened you in any way?"

"No, not really." Another "no" checked off on the form.

"Is he a danger to himself or to others? Is he capable of taking care of himself?"

Oh, please, don't turn him away. Not now. Then I remembered the stove.

"Well, last time he was in his apartment, he left the stove on. He could have started a fire," I said.

That did it. The nurse checked off a "yes" at last. Ben had finally made it to "sick enough." He was a danger to himself. I was allowed to come into the treatment area, and then I saw Ben through the window of a small room right next to the nursing station. He was in the lock-down room, pacing. My son was in the lock-down room. *How did we ever get here? How did this happen to my baby?*

I waited by the small window in the door of the padded room until Ben looked up and caught my eye. I waved at him; he stopped to wave back, then continued pacing and mumbling. I turned away from the sight. *I have to stay focused,* I thought. *If I let this get to me, I'll never do what has to be done.* I drove the image out of my mind long enough to supply the necessary information to the staff: what medication Ben was on, how much the dosage was, his doctors' names, his medical history. Meanwhile, Ben was given a mild sedative. When it had started to take effect, he was led into a treatment cubicle where I could sit with him.

Ben lay down on the cot and looked at me. His eyes were clearer, but his exhaustion was evident. "Am I going to the hospital, Mom?" he said. There was no fear or suspicion in his voice this time. He merely sounded curious.

"Yes, honey. They want to balance your medication."

"Okay," he said, and he yawned. The fight had gone out of him. "I think I'll take a nap." Ben grew quiet then, in voice and in body. I could finally comfort him, hold his hand, reassure him that he was safe and would be taken care of. When he finally dozed off, I stroked his sleeping face and smoothed down his hair. It was so easy to parent this sleeping child.

After several hours, a bed opened up at West Hills Center for Behavioral Health. Ben could be admitted the following morning, after spending the night at the ER. I was glad that he'd be in the familiar building where he'd gone to see Dr. Taylor for his sessions. This time, though, he wouldn't be able to walk out again after his hour was up. This time, he would be an inpatient. Dr. Taylor's orders guaranteed us a stay of at least five days. I hoped it would be for longer.

With the plan in place at last, I was told I could go home. "We'll take it from here," the head nurse said. "There's a lot to the admission process. They'll call you when they need you, probably tomorrow."

"Thanks," I said. I kissed Ben on his forehead. "Bye, honey." I walked out, feeling much lighter than I had when I'd walked in hours before. I walked easily back into the rest of the world, where I was free to go anywhere I chose. Ben would not have that privilege for at least a few days. I

CHAPTER GUIDEPOSTS

The Crisis: What to Do

Be aware, before the crisis erupts, of any escalation of symptoms; a visit to the doctor may help avert a psychotic break. If it happens anyway:

- Remain calm.
- Alert professional help: your doctor, the hospital.
- Try to convince the ill person to go to the hospital voluntarily; explain that the hospital may be able to provide relief from symptoms.
- If necessary, call the police but instruct them not to brandish any weapon; explain that your relative is in need of psychiatric assessment and you have called them for help.
- Ask someone to stay with you until professional help is available.
- Don't threaten or criticize the ill person.
- Speak softly and in simple sentences.
- Don't stand over the ill person or block the doorway: allow him to feel somewhat in control.
- Don't shout to be heard; you may need to repeat yourself, calmly.*

To Learn More about the Mental Health System, Including Psychiatric Hospitals

- NAMI
- Christine Adamec, *How to Live with a Mentally Ill Person: A Handbook of Day-to-Day Strategies* (New York: Wiley, 1996)
- Pete Earley, *Crazy: A Father's Search through America's Mental Health Madness* (New York: Putnam, 2006)

---

*NAMI Family-to-Family Education Program crisis file

went home, knowing for the first time in months that nothing bad could happen to Ben while I was away from him.

That sense of relief outweighed the shock of a now completely undeniable truth: my son was in a psychiatric hospital. He did, truly, have this illness. I could never return to the stage of denial again. This was real.

HOSPITALIZATION NUMBER ONE

Q: How has your condition affected your life?
Ben's A: I don't have a disease.
Q: Discuss denial, anger, bargaining, depression, and accep-
tance. Which stage applies to you right now and why?
Ben's A: Acceptance because I am in a state of internal har-
mony.

—Wellness worksheet from hospital group, April 2003

Thirty-five days. For thirty-five days Ben was an inpatient at West Hills
that first time. It wasn't long enough, not by a long shot. Still, the amount
of work it took to get permission from our medical insurance provider was
exhausting. There has to be a "good reason."

When I got home from the ER that first morning, I called a NAMI
mentor to tell her what had happened. "Enjoy the vacation," she said.

That, in fact, was what it felt like. Ben was in the hands of experts, and
I was not only allowed to stay away from him, I was asked to, at least for the
first couple of days. This time, my independence was free of guilt. I wasn't
abandoning Ben; I had done him a favor—hadn't I? He was in a place where
they would help him. Besides, he had sealed his own fate by refusing to take
his meds. Now, maybe, he would take some responsibility. The hospital was
no longer a faraway possibility; it was a measurable consequence of having
stopped his treatment. Maybe he would learn now. Maybe.

I was open to friends and family about where he was; I had learned
long ago that schizophrenia, like other mental illnesses, was just that: an
illness. There should be no shame in being hospitalized for any illness, and
so there was no need for secrecy. Still, once I was cleared for visitation, it
was a shock to see Ben there every time I was buzzed in through the door,
my blue visitor's pass stuck to my shirt.

West Hills is a beautiful facility on acres of parklike grounds in West-
port, Connecticut. The views from the windows in the inpatient unit are
of gardens, lawns, trees, and the other buildings of the complex: a school
for teens with behavioral problems, the other inpatient units, the offices.
Occasionally a deer wanders across the grounds. There's a central hub
where the nurses' station stands; two long hallways as spokes; and several
rooms in the areas between and along the hallways—kitchen, game room
and TV area, meeting rooms, patients' rooms, and a lounge at the end of
one hallway with comfortable armchairs and picture windows. The facility
is clean, the staff friendly and competent.

Those two hallways became a track for Ben and me during many of our visits. He couldn't sit still for long. We walked up one hall and back, then up the other and back again. Ben wore his hospital scrubs at first, then some of the clothing I brought for him.

Everything had to be checked by the front desk. No drawstrings, no razors, no shoelaces—the first time my packages went through inspection I felt like I was playing a part in a movie about psychiatric hospitals. But this was not a movie and Ben was not acting.

On our hallway walks, he constantly muttered to himself. They were the same words Chris had reported hearing in the diner: "That's good. Yeah, that's good." To himself. Over and over, after almost every sentence he'd say to me. *Who is he talking to? Are these voices? What is going on in his head?*

When he wasn't muttering, he was twitching. He often cricked his neck to one side or the other, or he would bring his chin forward in a turkey-gobbling way. That scared me more than the muttering. He looked so—so crazy. "Ben, do you know that you're kind of twitching?" I finally asked.

"No, I'm just stretching my neck," he replied—then, and every time after that if he caught me noticing the same tics.

I visited Ben at least four times a week, most of the time. Ali came with me about once a week. These visits were always so hard for her. It hurt to see Ben this way, and the truth was harder on her. She wasn't ready. She was in a different place. Ali's memories of Ben, and her hopes for his recovery, needed to be intact at that time. Every visit put a dent in those visions. She came to see Ben for his sake, but she could never stay for long. Her self-protection lay in keeping her eyes on her own immediate future—off to college in just a few months.

Since his backpack was locked away, Ben had asked for a notebook to write in. It was one of those black-and-white composition notebooks I remembered from elementary school, with a soft cover. Ben wrote in it constantly. I sneaked a peek inside once during the first week of his stay.

"Rachel will tell me how to get out of here," he wrote on one page. "Rachel is the only one I can trust." *Rachel? Who is Rachel?* I didn't know if she was a real person or an imagined voice. I wasn't sure if Ben could tell the difference at that point.

Ben was assigned a doctor for his hospital stay, Henry Russo, and a social worker, Peg Hartman. Dr. Russo assured me that Ben would stay for the full fifteen days allowed for the involuntary commitment ordered by Dr. Taylor, but that he could be released on his own volition anytime after that. After that, Ben could remain in the hospital only if he agreed to sign himself in; even then, he could sign himself back out as well. If I wanted him to remain in the hospital, I'd have to take legal action: petition to become his conservator, and then for the rights to involuntary commitment and, possibly, to medicate him against his will.

As the days passed, it was clear that Ben was not getting any better. Dr. Russo started Ben on Abilify again, beginning with a lower dosage. There was no change. Either the Abilify was having no effect yet, or Ben was still somehow managing to get away with only pretending to take it. The prescription was changed to Risperidone, but Ben suddenly refused to take any medication at all.

"No thanks, I'm fine," he insisted. His head twitched forward, and he muttered "That's good" to himself—or to the voices that might or might not be in his head.

Refusing medication was Ben's right as a patient. The staff could try to convince him to take it but could not force him to unless there was an emergency situation such as an attempt to escape, or possible harm to himself or someone else. Our hands were tied.

"He can't leave," I pleaded with Dr. Russo. "Can't I make sure he stays in here until he's getting better?"

The only way, he explained, was to get a court order for involuntary commitment. In order to get that, though, I would have to be granted the right to be Ben's conservator—of both his estate and his person. After that was granted, I could petition for Right to Involuntary Commitment and also Right to Medicate—which would only be in effect during this current hospital stay. If I got the ball rolling on this and a court date was set, the hospital was legally bound to keep him, at least until the court date. Even the medical insurance provider would not be allowed to dispute the length of Ben's stay, under those circumstances. As it was, the hospital had to justify Ben's stay to the insurance company every few days. There had to be a "good reason" to keep him in the hospital, such as a change in medication. This would buy us time—but it was a big step.

This was all explained to Ben on the Friday before his fifteen days would be up, in the hopes that he would commit himself voluntarily instead. Ben was merely counting the days, just biding his time until his release. Dr. Russo placed a legal form in front of him. "Ben, your mother is going to have to take steps to be in control of your life if you don't agree to stay here for a while longer. It would be so much easier for you if you just signed this and signed yourself in for a few more days."

Ben looked at the form. He read it and stared at the signature line. "I'm not signing anything," he said. "How do I know that this means what it says it means?"

Left with no other choice, I called the courthouse and arranged to go there on Monday morning—three days away. Later that day, I got a call from the hospital. It was Maura, the blond nurse who had always been kind to Ben and to me. "We had a little incident late this afternoon," she said, "and I wanted to tell you what to expect when you come to visit tomorrow."

Ben had tried to escape. He had simply decided he was leaving. He'd said, "I want to go home" and had asked for his backpack so he could leave. When they refused to let him into the office to get it, he'd become agitated, then gone toward the office. Things escalated as the staff tried to stop Ben from leaving, and he in turn became more insistent. It took five men to hold him back; he wanted to leave that badly.

Finally, they got Ben into the restraints room, so he could calm down. Maura said that at that point he'd been actively psychotic and had uttered statements that contradicted each other, such as "I'm going to take a shower—but I'm not going to take a shower!" He'd remained restless and ready to bolt, resisting efforts to convince him to return to his room, thrashing and protesting. Finally, they'd had to inject him with Haldol and Ativan—an antipsychotic and a tranquilizer. *Ben, in restraints. Emergency injections.* This just kept getting worse.

"How is he now?" I asked.

"He's asleep in his room. He'll probably sleep for quite some time. You can see him tomorrow."

"Did he say anything else?"

"Well," she said, "the amazing thing is how quickly the injection took effect. Within minutes, Ben was more coherent. He calmed down and said, 'I'm tired. I think I'll go lie down and rest in my room.' And that's what he did."

Haldol is an older medication I'd learned about—not in wide use anymore as a first-line medication because of side effects resembling Parkinson's disease. Possibly irreversible side effects with long-term use, but still very effective for situations like this. It had helped Ben go from incoherent to coherent within minutes.

The next afternoon Ben slept through my visit. It was easier than our usual walks up and down the halls. On this visit I could be the nurturing parent: hold his hand as he slept, adjust his covers, observe his sweet sleeping face.

Ben stirred and opened his eyes. He saw me. "Hi, Mom. I love you," he said, and fell back to sleep. Fighting back tears, I watched him for a few more minutes. *Still in there*, I knew. But buried how deeply?

After that, Ben went back on his medication for a few days, then refused it again. His behaviors went up and down accordingly. One day he'd show glimpses of clarity, personality, humor, and even appreciation of his meds. The next, he'd be shivering, restless, and unresponsive. I submitted my petition to become Ben's conservator; the court date for the hearing was set for Thursday, April 4. We'd bought a little more time.

One week before the hearing, I sat with Ben in the game room during our visit. We were trying to play a card game of War. Ben concentrated on the cards, talking to me between moves. "You know, Mom," he said, "you forgot something."

This seemed like a fairly harmless conversation. "What did I forget, Ben?"

"*You* know."

Maybe not, I thought. "No, honey, I don't know. What did I forget?"

"You *know*. I'm not gonna tell you since you know already."

I clearly wasn't going to win this round. "Okay, Ben. I'm sorry I forgot."

The card game continued silently for a few minutes. Finally we called it quits and declared Ben the winner since he had the most cards at the time. I'd had my fill of War—and of this visit. I could feel the welcome wearing thin, could see Ben was getting tired.

"Mom," he said again, "you *forgot* something."

I sighed. "What did I forget, Ben?"

He looked straight into my eyes. "You forgot to take me home."

You forgot to take me home. This really got to me. I couldn't help it. *Oh, my heart, my aching heart. My little boy.* "Ben. Honey," I said, putting my hand on his. He flinched, but let it stay there. "I know you want to go home. We all want you to go home. That's why we're all working so hard to help you get better: so you *can* come home."

He looked down at our hands, then at me. "Mom. You forgot to take me home." Again. I couldn't listen anymore. I had no idea what else to say. This was killing me. I got up. "Well, honey, I'll see you tomorrow, okay? It's time for me to go."

"Okay, Mom," he said. "Just wait a minute, okay?"

"Okay, Ben."

He walked down the hall to his room. I waited at the nurses' station. Ben came out of his room a minute later with a paper bag in his hand. He walked over to us. "I'm ready to go, Mom," he said.

I looked at him and took the bag out of his hand to look inside. It held his hospital notebook, his toothbrush, and some clothes. He had packed to leave. I looked helplessly at Maura; she took the bag from me, gently, and turned toward Ben. "Ben," she said, "visiting hours are over. Your mom has to go home now. She'll see you tomorrow."

"Oh," said my son.

"Come on; let's go put these things away. You'll go home another time." Maura came out from behind the desk and started to guide Ben back to his room. She turned to me one more time. "Randye, it's okay. We'll take care of this. Go on home."

I nodded, asked another nurse to let me out, and walked five steps down the hall until I could no longer be seen. Then I leaned my back against the wall, slumped down to the floor, and cried.

As the court date approached, Ben became more desperate. He called me from the patients' phone to tell me he was planning to "just leave." By the time I arrived, he'd packed his things again. He was walking down the hall, solemnly shaking the hand of each person he passed. He told the staff that he was just going to "walk out the door and figure it out from there." After trying to talk with him, I gave up. The staff sent me home. They told me later that Ben had gotten insistent again and was back in restraints. The court date was two days away, and Ben was only making my side of the case that much stronger.

The day of the court hearing arrived; we all met in the small room West Hills had reserved for the procedure. Around the table sat the judge, Ben's lawyer, two independent psychiatrists, Dr. Russo, Ben's caseworker Peg, and me. There was an empty chair for Ben. We went over the proceedings before we sent for him; finally he was led into the room.

Ben sat next to me and we began. One by one, everyone presented their findings: gravely disabled.

Gravely disabled.

Gravely disabled.

Ben's knee was twitching, his foot tapping. He listened as each person spoke. He mumbled to himself, staring at the table. Suddenly he looked up and faced the judge.

His leg stopped twitching. "Excuse me. Your Honor?" he said.

The judge turned to Ben. "Yes, son?" he replied.

"Can't I have a minute to tell my side of the story?"

We all turned to look at the patient. "All right, Ben. Go ahead," the judge said.

Ben stood up. "Well, I just want to say that everyone here says I have schizophrenia and I want to say that I *don't* have it. There is nothing wrong with me. I have not taken any test that proves I have it. No one here can prove anything. They are just talking about things they say they see, and I want you to know that that is just their *opinion*. It's not fact. I don't even *have* schizophrenia. They're entitled to their opinion, but it's wrong. I want to go home."

I couldn't believe Ben had managed to get out that long, coherent paragraph. He'd put so much effort into it. I had seen him physically gather his energy, stop his twitching and shaking, and present his argument. It was, actually, very impressive. But now he was exhausted. He was spent. He sat down; his knee started going again.

The judge thanked Ben for his words. He looked at the paperwork for a minute, then said he wished he could let Ben have his way, but that he was going to rule in favor of granting conservatorship to me. This would be my position for at least one year, with an option to report to the court and renew it.

Thank God. I let out the huge breath I hadn't even realized I'd been holding in.

The other two decisions came quickly: yes to Right to Involuntary Commitment. Yes to Right to Medicate. Both of these rights would end as soon as Ben was discharged from the hospital, but they could return us on the road to recovery once again. Now Ben would *have* to take his medication. I thanked the judge, and everyone else. So, until the medical insurance company stopped allowing it, Ben was safe at West Hills. My respite had been extended for a while longer.

Dr. Russo prescribed Haldol for Ben this time, since his response to it had been so promising during his crisis. "If we can just get him stabilized on this, we can talk about other medications later. The important thing right now is to get Ben back to a point where he can *understand* his treatment and begin to become part of it. One advantage of Haldol is that it can be administered in a long-acting injection called a deconoate. Then you won't have to worry about his daily compliance once he's discharged, and he can try living in his apartment again. It's only a temporary move, but our best one for now."

"But what about the side effects?" I said. Haldol could come along with restlessness, relentless pacing, sleeplessness, muscle stiffness, or tremors.

"There are other medications he can take to counteract the side effects, and after he stabilizes we'll be moving him on to the newer medications anyway. The side effects only become irreversible after a long time on the Haldol. We won't let it get to that point."

So Haldol it was. Ben began to respond within a few days. My friend Cathy came to visit him and brought him some brand-new shirts and expensive shampoo. Ben's face lit up at the sight of these gifts, and he hugged Cathy, actually hugged her. He was charming, engaging, and sweet—for twenty whole minutes, until exhaustion set in. Still—a world of change since the hearing.

Some days were better than others, but gradually the improvements seemed to become more consistent. Ben earned some privileges back: he could go outside, with supervision, and smoke a cigarette. He could go on afternoon patient walks. He could smell the outside air again.

Ben was very proud of having earned these rights back. How small and simple his world had become. It seemed like an easier way to live for him, especially once his mind began to clear. Follow the rules, earn the privileges. Easier.

On April 15, Ben was released from the inpatient unit. Since no medication changes were necessary until later in his treatment plan, the insurance company said he had to leave. Besides, he had been at West Hills for thirty-five days, and the limit for coverage was forty-five days per year. After that, insurance would no longer cover the costs of psychiatric inpatient stays. We had ten days left; I hoped we would never need them.

Ben met with Peg and Dr. Russo and me, and he promised to stick with his discharge plan. He was to go back to his appointments with Dr. Taylor, who would administer the Haldol shots. He also would start an intensive outpatient program (IOP) the following day, and attend it from 10 a.m. until 3 p.m., five days a week.

"So, Ben," said Dr. Russo. "What have you learned from your stay here?"

Ben smiled—a real smile. "Meds, meds, meds," he replied.

Dr. Russo laughed. "I hope you mean that, Ben."

"I do. I think, maybe, they really do help me," he said. I'd heard him say that before. *This time, it sounds like he really believes it.*

So that day, when I left the unit, Ben came with me. We went out for dinner that evening to celebrate. Ben's joy at being out was contagious, and my hopes for his future seemed possible. Ali was away for spring break, in a rented condo in Myrtle Beach, South Carolina, with six of her best friends. She was growing up so fast now; I hoped Ben could have a chance to do the same.

He was back in the same hospital less than one month later.

CHAPTER GUIDEPOSTS

Conservatorship

"When people have a serious mental illness, and due to the illness are a danger to themselves or others, or are unable to provide for their own basic needs for food, clothing, and shelter, someone else may be given legal authority to meet the person's needs and to make certain decisions about the person's life and, sometimes, property. This legal structure is called a guardianship or conservatorship. The conservator/guardian may be a county employee or a family member; the decision is made at a court hearing.

"Only by means of a guardianship or conservatorship can someone be treated involuntarily for any length of time. To find out the specifics of how guardianships work in your state, contact your local NAMI or Public Guardian's office."*

Collecting Evidence

It helps to keep records of everything as your relative's illness develops. You will need this information in case of hospitalization or when applying for disability benefits:

- Level of functioning before the illness: school, jobs, life skills (keep a record of schools, employers, landlords, etc., and the dates of each experience)
- Symptoms: when they first appeared, for how long, dates of most extreme episodes
- Medications: what has been tried, in what dosages, and patient's reactions
- Treatment: doctors, psychiatrists, psychologists (names, addresses, phone numbers)
- Medical insurance coverage
- *Write it all down and keep it where you can find it.*

---

*Rebecca Woolis, *When Someone You Love Has a Mental Illness: A Handbook for Family, Friends, and Caregivers* (New York: Penguin, 2003).

HOSPITALIZATION NUMBER TWO

Slowly walking without a pace
Wandering wandering place to place
Search for niche and searching space
Just to find that inner grace
I lost before when I began to race.

—Ben, May 2003

This time, the police called me. They'd picked Ben up at the local mall that evening, after they'd received a call about an "unwanted person" who was acting strangely. "Just a little too friendly" was the complaint. *Unwanted person.* That was my son.

In the month since Ben's release, he'd celebrated his twenty-first birthday, attended the outpatient program with mixed results, and protested with increasing intensity every time he was scheduled to receive his next injection of Haldol. Although the medication was working to clear the symptoms of psychosis, its side effects were unbearable to Ben: nausea, muscle stiffness, insomnia, relentless agitation, tremors. Dr. Taylor prescribed more medications to help counteract these symptoms, but Ben was inconsistent about taking them. As soon as he felt better, he'd stop taking the pills. "I thought it was like Tylenol, Mom," he said once. "I felt okay now, so I stopped taking it."

The dosage of Haldol, administered by injection, required fine-tuning. As one shot wore off, the next had to be well timed to keep Ben's behaviors consistent. He was back in his apartment ("One more chance, that's it!" I'd said to him), but I was able to monitor his actions and symptoms, because I drove him to and from his outpatient program every day. On the day before Ben was picked up by the police, his symptoms had returned to such a degree that I tried to move his appointment for his next one up by a day. No one seemed to think it would matter if we waited until his scheduled time on Tuesday. By then, he had clearly decompensated. He slept through most of the group sessions at his day program; the superior stare was back in his eyes. It took a lot of creative manipulation to get him to agree to the injection this time. I finally walked out of Dr. Taylor's office in desperation, telling Ben to find his own ride home if he didn't cooperate.

I got as far as the receptionist's desk in the main lobby. Ben ran up behind me and said, "Okay, I'll take the stupid shot." We went back downstairs. One more small victory. Would we have to have this fight every single time?

Haldol deconoates don't have the immediate effects of the emergency shots. The effects are on a time-release schedule, so it's a more gradual process. As I drove Ben home, I tried to keep my growing anger inside, to remind myself that he would probably be easier to deal with by the next day. But after ten minutes on the highway, about halfway to Ben's apartment, I just could not bear to be with him one moment longer. On that ride, Ben was loud. Rude. Argumentative. Accusing me again: I was the one who was crazy. I was a bad mother for forcing him to go to the outpatient program. I was being unfair because I wanted control of what we were playing on the radio. Things were escalating, I didn't trust myself to refrain from losing my temper big-time. I could feel myself about to explode.

I swerved into the exit lane, my mouth clamped shut in a tight line, angry words fighting to get out. We drove into downtown Bridgeport and I headed toward the bus depot.

"What are you doing, Mom? We're not home yet."

I was so sick and tired. Tired of picking Ben up every morning and hearing how unfair I was, all the way to the outpatient program. I was tired of being Ben's chauffeur. I was tired of feeling I could do no right. I could not stand one more minute of verbal abuse from this child, no matter what the illness behind it. I didn't care. I had to set limits on what I was willing to take.

I pulled over to the bus depot and told my son to get out.

"Ben, you can take the bus home from here. You know the schedule. I think there's one leaving in twenty minutes. Here's your bus fare. I'll see you in the morning. Be ready." And I handed the coins to him.

He sat there in disbelief. "You can't do that!"

Just hang on. Don't lose your temper. It will only make things worse. He'll go home, we'll both cool off, and by tomorrow morning he'll be better. Tomorrow will be better. But today—he's better off if I don't kill him.

"Get out, Ben," I said. "The bus will be here soon."

With one last angry look at me, Ben grabbed his backpack, got out, slammed the car door, and headed for the depot. I watched him walk into the terminal, then drove off.

He'll be fine. I figured it would take Ben about an hour to get home, and another few hours to calm down. He might be too angry to call me, or too much in need of disconnecting from me. He had his dignity to repair—so I really didn't expect to hear from him. But by eight o'clock that evening, I called him. Just to make sure he'd gotten home.

No answer. I waited. At nine o'clock the phone rang. It was Ben, but he wasn't at home. He was at the Trumbull Mall.

"Ben, how did you get *there*?" I asked.

"Well, I took the right bus, but it went to the wrong place."

He sounded confused, disoriented. "Wait by our usual entrance," I said. "I'll be right there."

When I got to the mall, however, Ben was not waiting for me. I drove to all the entrances. I parked the car, got out and walked around the mall. No Ben. *Maybe he got a ride home from someone else?* I went back home and waited for the phone to ring.

When it finally rang, it was the police on the line. "Ms. Kaye? We have your son Benjamin here. Does he live with you?"

What did he do? What did I do by leaving him today? "Why?" I asked.

"We got a call about an unwanted person at the Ruby Tuesday restaurant at the mall. Your son was being what they called 'overly friendly.' He wasn't doing anything wrong, per se, but he wouldn't leave when they asked him to."

Ben had worked there in the early stages of his illness; he'd lasted for over three months before they'd let him go because of his inability to focus. "No," I said. "He doesn't live here, but I'll take responsibility for him tonight. Can you bring him here to me? Will he come with you?" I asked.

"He will," answered the officer. "He's in the back of the squad car now."

I knew it was too long between injections. Why didn't they listen to me?

Two policemen brought Ben into the house, and between the four of us we pieced together the story of how he'd spent his day: wandering around downtown for a few hours, talking to the city's homeless population, then catching the next bus to the mall. He had wandered there, too, talking to people. "I wanted to help as many people as I could," he told us. He had gone, in the end, to "find his old friends" at the restaurant. They, in turn, had called the police about the presence of an unwanted person.

Ben's symptoms were evident this time. There was no need to convince the police that he was ill. We all knew he needed to go back to the hospital. Ben even agreed to go voluntarily—that's how out of it he was.

We called for an ambulance, and Ben was escorted into the back. I followed in my car, and we soon arrived at St. Mary's Hospital. This was like a bad rerun, all too strangely familiar now. We went through the admission process again. This time, Ben's information was already in the computer. This time, I was not in shock; I was just numb. I'd been through this before. I stayed with Ben until I knew there was an available bed at West Hills. I went home, slept for two hours, and got up to go to work at the radio station.

Ben was hospitalized, this time, for twenty days. Even though he had admitted himself voluntarily at first, it wasn't long before he refused his medications again. Back were the notebooks filled with illegible scribbling; back came the twitching and the muttering. I stayed away from visiting him at first—he seemed paranoid, bizarre. I couldn't bear to sit opposite him in the lounge and have him look at me as if I were the enemy and he knew my secret plans. Even Ali sometimes got those looks from him.

We had to schedule another hearing in probate court to reapply for the Right to Medicate, but right before the hearing Ben suddenly chose to willingly take the meds. He *chose* to! We didn't know why, but we wanted to think it might be a good sign. Gradually, Ben's suspicious looks disappeared. He was reachable again. He was Ben again. Ali and I visited more frequently, but other visitors were rare this second time around. Psychiatric hospitalizations get old fast.

I used this twenty-day period to start another legal process I'd dreaded for a long time: declaring my son officially disabled. Much as it hurt—and it did—it was time to apply for disability benefits for my twenty-one-year-old. As much as I wanted Ben to get a job, to be able to work, I had to face the fact that he might not be able to handle that for quite some time—if ever. The time for wishing was over. I went to the Social Security office, now able to represent Ben as his conservator, and picked up a massive pile of forms to fill out.

Disability. Ben hated that word; I hated that word. But the truth was the truth; at least for the time being, Ben was disabled. Sooner or later, he would need government help. He'd need Medicaid, Medicare. This all seemed so out of place for a young man in his early twenties: So unfair. So wrong. *It is what it is,* I grimly reminded myself, and I began the process of documenting the downward spiral of Ben's hopes and plans. I gathered information to reassemble his history: jobs, school attempts, hospitalizations, medications. I got letters from his psychiatrists to support his diagnosis. Every piece of paperwork seemed to seal Ben's fate as someone who was irreversibly sick, who was truly disabled, who was—I kept pushing the word out of my mind, it wasn't fair to Ben—a failure, in the minds of so many.

There was also the issue of where Ben could go for help once he was stabilized. I set up meetings with local agencies to ask about possible job support. I visited residential programs that might help him—some private, some run by the state. I balked at costs, I crunched the numbers, I looked at my ever-dwindling savings. I collected brochures; I filled out more forms.

Where would Ben agree to go? Nowhere, as long as he still had his apartment or thought he could live with me. But I knew now that neither of these options would end well. Both were roads to more angry dependence, more emergency rooms. There absolutely had to be a backup plan—or several of them.

But nothing, no solution was possible until Ben was stabilized on the right medication. Until then, all I could do was research the options—and push aside the guilt I felt because I couldn't cure him myself. Not with my love, not with my rules, not with my hopes for him.

Ben made a friend on the unit, a painfully thin woman in her twenties named Sarah, who told me she was in for drug addiction and anxiety. Ben saw her as his personal project, and in trying to help her he began to work at his own recovery a little more, too.

I was almost grateful to Sarah for being so needy. At least she was helping Ben to see outside of himself, to keep his attention away from that damned notebook and his own inner stimuli. By trying to be a friend to Sarah, he was feeling better about himself. *Maybe, someday, this is something Ben could do: help others, once he is well.*

It was a much-needed glimmer of purpose for Ben's life. Would he ever accept his own illness to the point where he could inspire others because of the nightmare he had lived? I didn't know. I still don't know. But I can hope—and I hang on to that picture.

A few days before Ben was released, one of the nurses said something that helped me more than she will ever know. I had arrived for visiting hours and signed the guest book; we were waiting for Ben to come out of his room. "You know," she said, "I just love Ben. We all do."

She loves Ben? They love Ben? I hadn't heard anyone outside of family say this about my son for a long time. I couldn't remember the last time it was said about the Ben he was lately, instead of the Ben of the past. "Really?" I said.

She smiled at me. "Listen, I know this is hard for you. You're his mom. But I want you to know that Ben is such a *nice* young man. Even when he's psychotic, he is always polite. He treats all of the staff with respect. Not all the patients do that—in fact, a lot don't. Ben clearly has a high regard for women. You must have done a wonderful job of raising him. It shows."

I burst into tears. I'd never done that right in front of the staff. This kindness, this high regard for my son, went straight to the center of my soul. I hadn't known how much of a failure as a mother I had felt until this

CHAPTER GUIDEPOSTS

Emotional Reactions of Family Members, Stage II: Learning to Cope

- Anger: why can't he/she just "snap out of it?"
- Guilt: what did I do wrong? is this somehow my fault?
- Resentment: feeling fed up.
- Recognition: something tragic has occurred that will change our lives forever.
- Grief: we mourn the time before the illness struck, grieve for an uncertain future.*

For More Information about Social Security Disability Insurance (SSDI)

- Contact your local Social Security office.
- Go to the Social Security website: www.ssa.gov.
- Ask for help from others who have been there.

What Is Medicare?

Medicare is the federal program providing health insurance for people age sixty-five and older and for disabled people of all ages. Medicare Part A covers hospitalization and is a compulsory benefit. Medicare Part B covers outpatient services and is voluntary (www.medicare.gov).

What Is Supplemental Security Income (SSI)?

SSI is a federal income supplement program funded by general tax revenues (not Social Security taxes):

- It is designed to help aged, blind, and disabled people who have little or no income.
- It provides cash to meet basic needs for food, clothing, and shelter (www.ssa.gov/ssi).

What Is Medicaid?

Medicaid is a jointly funded, federal-state health insurance program for low-income and needy people. It covers children, the aged,

---

*Joyce Burland, NAMI Family-to-Family class 1 handout, "Predictable Stages of Emotional Reactions among Family Members."

blind, and/or disabled and other people who are eligible to receive fed-
erally assisted income-maintenance payments.

Thirty-two states and the District of Columbia provide Medicaid
eligibility to people eligible for SSI benefits. In these states, the SSI application is also the Medicaid application. Medicaid eligibility starts the
same month as SSI eligibility (www.socialsecurity.gov/disabilityresearch/
wi/medicaid.htm).

nurse pointed out that I wasn't. "Thank you so much," I said. "You have
no idea what that means to me."

"Well," she said, "you've earned it. He's a wonderful guy. We're all
rooting for him to get better."

I lived on that remark for months. Sometimes I still do.

13

FROZEN: HOSPITALIZATION
NUMBER THREE

B en was frozen. Three days after his release from the second hospital-ization, I'd gone to pick him up for his day program. I'd let myself in when he didn't come to the door and saw him standing in his living room, naked from the waist up. He was facing the fireplace, his back to me, but I could see him in the mirror above the mantel. He was not moving. At all.

Frozen, like a statue. Ben's hands were folded together in the middle of his stomach, elbows bent at his sides. His eyes stared up toward the ceil-ing. He didn't blink. He didn't move his face. He looked as though he were in a trance.

"Ben? Are you all right?"

I could see him trying to speak. It took what felt like a very long time before he could move his lips. Finally he said, "I'm fine. I'm good."

Why won't he move? Maybe Sarah came over to visit him. She and Ben had been released on the same day. *Maybe she went right back to using drugs and managed to get Ben to join her.* "Ben, listen to me. Did you take any drugs? Did you smoke anything?"

I waited. "No, Mom."

It wasn't the first time I'd wished for an easy answer. Maybe Ben was lying, but I didn't think so. I didn't know what to think; this zombie-like behavior, though, was the most terrifying symptom I'd seen yet. He didn't talk much. It seemed too hard for him. But when he did, he said things like "I'm floating." Or "Sunshine." Disjointed words, short phrases. I searched my mind for what to do, and for what might have happened in the three days since his release.

Ben had been discharged on June 3, stabilized once again on Haldol—but this time his discharge plan called for a dosage twice the size he'd been prescribed the last time. What would this do to the severity of his side effects?

191

For the next two days, driving Ben to and from his program, I had seen that Ben was restless and agitated in body, even though his mind seemed pretty clear.

"Are you taking the side-effect medications, honey?" I'd asked.

"I don't like them. They make we feel worse than the Haldol does." Unfortunately, side-effect medications can cause side effects of their own. Yesterday, I'd made him swallow his morning dosage in front of me, but I couldn't be sure he was keeping them in his system. If his dosage of Haldol had been doubled, could this just be a severely inflated side effect?

So maybe that's it. But now what do I do? Get him in the car. Get him back to the hospital.

Our forty-five days of insurance were up, though. We'd surpassed the limit on allowable days in a psychiatric hospital for the year, as far as our insurance company was concerned. The next step was supposed to be charity care or a state hospital, but I decided I didn't care. He was going back to West Hills, where they knew him, even if I had to borrow the money. "Listen, Ben, you have to come with me now."

Ben turned slowly toward me, and I took his hand. There was no time to react emotionally. I just had to get him out of there and get him some help.

Gently, quietly, patiently. I got Ben to put on a shirt, found his ragged Birkenstocks in the corner, and helped him slip his feet into them. He took one step, another step; hesitantly, as if he couldn't remember how to walk. Out the door, down the stairs, pausing on each step. "It's summer," he said on the second step, as he paused to breathe in the sunshine.

"Yes, Ben." Each time he stopped, I was afraid I'd never get him to move again, that he'd be frozen forever on his front porch. *Come on, come on.*

At last, we made it to the car. I helped Ben bend his body to get in and fastened his seat belt around him. Around to the driver's side, barely breathing, numb. *Keep moving. Just get him to the hospital. He'll be all right.*

Finally, we were on our way to West Hills again—but no one knew we were coming. Forget the emergency room this time. Forget medical insurance limits. *Screw procedure*, I thought. *There is no way I'm taking him to a strange hospital where they don't know his case.*

The ride was unbearably long and unrelentingly surreal. This wasn't the way the morning was supposed to go. I'd been in a rush, with a tightly scheduled day carefully planned. I'd left the radio station right after the show ended at nine, and I was due at a recording studio by ten to narrate a medical training film for a client. The studio was near Ben's day program at West Hills, so I'd planned to drop him off a few minutes before the first group session and then hightail it over to my booking. So much for plans. I called my client to explain that I had a family emergency, then tried to reach Dr. Taylor.

All the while, I kept one eye on Ben. I felt like I was in a split-screen movie scene. On one side of the car was Ben, mostly silent and moving in extreme slow motion. On my side was a terrified mother navigating morning highway traffic, while keeping an eye on her son and making frantic phone calls. I got one voice mailbox after another at West Hills. Finally, I reached a human being—the front desk receptionist.

"Please leave messages for Dr. Taylor, for the outpatient program, and the inpatient unit. Tell them I'm bringing in my son, and he needs to be hospitalized *right now*. He's practically comatose. I'll be there in twenty minutes and will head straight for the intake desk. *Please*. Tell Dr. Taylor we'll meet him there."

My desperate pleas were punctuated by the occasional word or phrase from Ben: "Voice." "Eh." "Hi." That was all he could manage to say. *Oh, God.* We finally pulled into the West Hills driveway, and I helped Ben up to the front door. Two of the inpatient unit nurses were outside smoking cigarettes and saw us coming. "Ben!" said one. "Oh my God, what happened?"

"I don't know," I said. "I just found him like this when I picked him up."

Ben stood next to me, frozen again. The nurse said, "I'll go inside and tell them that you're here."

Inside the door, Ben tried to sit on one of the waiting room chairs. His aim was off and he almost sat on the armrest. "Honey," I said, "move over a bit. You're about to sit on the arm."

Ben moved a few inches and landed correctly. "It's called the *seat*, Mom," he said.

He'd managed a full sentence in order to correct me. I almost had to smile. *Stubborn to the end.*

We waited for about an hour in the tiny waiting area. I sat next to Ben, just watching. He was awake, but I couldn't tell how aware he was. This still did not seem real. Ben's eyes had rolled up almost into his head. His stare landed on the TV screen mounted in the upper corner of the room across from us. "Philip," he said.

Philip? Who's Philip? He said "Voice" in the car. Is that the name of the voice?

"Philip," Ben said again.

"Yes, Ben," I replied.

"Philip," once more.

Then I looked up at the TV. The brand name was below the screen. It said "Phillips." Well, at least one thing was making sense. He was simply reading a word.

"Thirsty," said my son. I got a paper cup, filled it with water, handed it to him and helped him drink. When he was done, he lowered his arm, and I took the empty cup from him.

His hand stayed frozen in the shape of the cup. I gently unfolded his fingers and helped him put his hand back into his lap. *Surreal.*

Dr. Taylor came into the room at last and examined Ben. "Do you know if he took any drugs?" he asked me.

"I don't think so. He's been clean and sober for over a year, and proud of it. But there was this girl he made friends with during his last stay, and I think she may have come over to visit him. Maybe she brought something with her?" *At least it would explain this.*

"We can't know how to treat this until we get urine and blood samples," said Dr. Taylor. This was not easy to accomplish. Ben could barely move; whatever energy he could muster was channeled into meek protest. Dr. Taylor stayed with us until a very reluctant Ben finally produced a urine sample in the men's room. Then he said that they would take Ben into the unit for the weekend. "We'll get the blood sample," he said, "and get to the bottom of this."

"What if he's clean?" I said. "What if this isn't drugs?"

"It could be just side effects from the larger dosage of Haldol. If Ben hasn't taken his other medications, that would explain it. But we have to rule out drug use first. If he's clean, then we'll give him an injection of the side-effect drugs. That should help almost immediately."

They led Ben into the familiar cocoon of the inpatient ward. I watched the door close behind them and felt the panic drain out of me—the panic, the numbness, and my calm front. This cleared the way, leaving room for the emotions I'd kept locked up all morning. Enter maternal shock and fear. I put my hands up over my face and leaned against the admitting room wall. Once again, I sank to the floor and cried.

There wasn't much time for emotion, however. I had become almost efficient when it came to my own tears. After a few minutes I blew my nose, wiped my eyes, and stood up again. I thanked the nurses, got back into my car, and drove on to my booking. Put on a happy voice. I was getting better and better at compartmentalizing my life.

Later that day, Dr. Taylor called with the results of the drug tests: clean. "We'll keep Ben in over the weekend for observation. We gave him an injection of Cogentin, and he's responding already. Let him sleep it off."

The very next morning, Ben himself called me from the patients' phone. "Boy, Mom, that was scary," he said.

No kidding. But he had spoken a full sentence. He sounded normal again, as if the day before had happened only in my terrified imagination. "Ben, you sound so much *better*," I said.

"I know," he replied. "Mom, it was so weird. I couldn't find my voice. I wanted to tell you something, but all I could say was 'voice,' because I couldn't make my voice work. I wanted to move, but I couldn't. I *never* want to go through that again."

Well, he's not the only one.

This time Ben's stay was five days. He was in West Hills for the weekend, plus a few extra days for reevaluation. I picked him up on Wednesday. This time the discharge plan included weaning him off Haldol, slowly, once a new medication trial was determined. But there was very little left to try.

The best remaining option was the one Dr. Taylor had saved as a last resort: a medication called Clozaril. Ben had refused to try this in the past, because of the weekly blood tests required to take it. In its early trials, Clozaril had been found to cause a dangerous decrease in white blood cell count in less than 1 percent of patients—a condition called agranulocytosis, which can be fatal. Therefore, blood tests have to be performed weekly at first, then less frequently as treatment continues. The blood cell count must be deemed healthy in order to renew the prescription. Clozaril, despite its possible drawbacks, has earned a reputation as the "gold standard" medication, one that is the *only* effective one for certain patients. It was time; we had tried everything else.

Ben is terrified of needles, and he hated the idea of blood tests; however, after the Haldol scare, he was finally willing to try the Clozaril. As with all such medications, dosages have to be very small at first, so we continued with the Haldol in the meantime, while we got the paperwork started for the new medication. But at least we had a new plan—and therefore, a new reason to hope.

Six days after Ben's third discharge from West Hills, Ali graduated from high school. He'd gotten out just in time to attend. I was thrilled to have this day: my daughter in a cap and gown, graduating with all her friends, and my son beside me on the bleachers cheering for his sister when her name was called. An oasis of normal.

CHAPTER GUIDEPOSTS

"Every person with schizophrenia or the family members should keep a list of drugs tried, dosage level (i.e., how many milligrams), and response. This can be extremely helpful and save weeks of trial-and-error medications in the future."*

First-Generation Antipsychotic Drugs

- *Only* class of medication for schizophrenia from 1950 to 1990
- Improve positive symptoms of psychosis, but not negative symptoms
- Low-potency drugs in this class (e.g., Thorazine) can be hugely sedating
- High-potency drugs (e.g., Haldol) can be administered in long-acting form
- Can produce severe and often lasting neurological side effects

Second-Generation (Atypical) Antipsychotic Drugs

- Introduced in the 1990s, starting with Clozaril
- Clozaril can have rare side effect of agranulocytosis
- Few or no neurological side effects
- Better relief of negative symptoms

*E. Fuller Torrey, *Surviving Schizophrenia: A Manual for Families, Consumers, and Providers* (New York: HarperCollins, 2001), 215.

We got five whole weeks of normal until hospitalization number four. There were ups and downs—I'd half expected that, since he was still at the mercy of the time-release schedule of his Haldol injections—but I was unprepared for the sight of my son being led to the ambulance, in handcuffs, on the evening of July 18. So was Ali.

14

HOSPITALIZATIONS
FOUR AND FIVE

Ideas:

- Anger management classes obligated for the angry man and woman (Mom!)
- Understanding animal classes
- Find a shaman to learn from and talk to shaman about having the government let Native Americans live off the land again
- Start my own country. In Africa
- New Holidays
- Open a school of my own

—Ben's hospital notebook, July 2003

Number Four. Five weeks had gone by since Ben's last release. That Friday, I'd invited some friends over for a brunch. This was a mini-reunion of women who knew Ben well—we'd met weekly, back when our kids were babies, for "playgroup." We'd been each other's lifelines back then, providing sanity, support, and a social life.

Ali had driven Ben to and from his day program, so I was unaware of his mood until he walked into the house with that unfocused stare that spelled "relapse." He was so out of it that he barely recognized any of the guests—women he'd known since he was one year old. He asked me if he could take a swim in our pool and then "hang out at home" for the day. "Of course, honey," I said. Besides, I needed to keep an eye on him.

The recovery plan this time had been different. Ben was spending only two days a week at the outpatient program and two weekdays at Bridge

House, a clubhouse for people with diagnosed brain disabilities. We'd visited Bridge House in the past, and Ben was finally willing to attend. Here I hoped he'd discover some sense of community, of purpose, and be inspired by mentors. Ben also looked into going back to community college. The fact that he was trying to accomplish so much was a miracle, but it wasn't a guarantee. Still waiting for clearance for the Clozaril treatment, still waiting to hear if he could receive disability benefits, we were in limbo. Ben's mental state had also been in flux, with the all-too-familiar ups and downs that came with time-release treatment.

Now, though, he'd fallen too far once again. Ben went in and out of focus that afternoon. I made sure he swallowed his side-effect medication, just in case that was the problem. I called Dr. Taylor, who called in a prescription for oral Haldol to bring Ben's levels back up until he could administer another injection. "If you can get him to rest, it should be in effect by the time he wakes up," he said.

Please, yes. I invited Ben to spend the night at home, in his old room. He smiled sweetly and nodded slowly in agreement. I picked up the new prescription at the drugstore and got Ben to swallow the Haldol pills. By this time, it was early evening. He went downstairs to sleep; Ali drove off to see a movie with a friend.

I started cleaning the kitchen from the reunion lunch, which seemed like days ago instead of hours. Ten minutes later Ben came upstairs from his room. "Hi, Mom," he said. He still looked lost.

"Ben—why aren't you asleep, honey?"

"I'm not tired, Mom." He started walking toward me, slowly.

"What's up, sweetie? You really need to sleep." I really wished he was asleep. *Come on, Ben. The Haldol needs time to work. We just have to make it until tomorrow morning. Sleep. Please.*

Ben walked up to me and took my face in his hands. He looked right into my eyes.

"I love you, Mom," he said.

"Thanks, honey. I love you, too."

"No, Mom. I *mean* it. I really love you." He was still holding my face in his hands. He was looking at me, but he didn't seem to see me. There was no connection.

"Honey, thanks," I said. "You can let go of my face now, though, okay?"

Ben kept looking into my eyes. Staring, actually. I was starting to feel nervous. "But, Mom," he said, "I want to put some good energy into you. I *love* you!"

This is my son. This is my Ben. He means well, I know it. But my heart was beating too fast anyway. I took my hands and placed them over Ben's. I gently, firmly, peeled his hands off of my face. "Thanks, honey, but you have to let go now. I'm feeling a little bit scared."

Ben took his hands away and backed off. "Oh, sorry, Mom." I could breathe again. *Thank God he's so good-natured. What do people do if their relative's delusions include thoughts of violence?* I prayed I would never have to find out.

Ben was telling me he was wide awake, but his eyelids were drooping. I led him back to bed and tucked him in. "Try to get some sleep now, Ben."

"Okay, Mom." Five minutes later, he was out. Dr. Taylor had said that once Ben was asleep, he'd most likely stay that way until the morning. I waited half an hour and checked on him again. He was still deep in sleep, snoring lightly. I went out to a theater rehearsal I was already late for, and I was back home less than two hours later.

I'd expected to find Ben still fast asleep, but he wasn't in his room at all. A few minutes later, I spotted him pacing outside in the backyard, mumbling to himself, gesturing in slow motion. He was wearing the backpack that contained all the spiral notebooks he filled with his illegible writings. There was no predicting where he'd go if I allowed myself to go to sleep; I couldn't wait until the morning to take action. Ben had to go back to the hospital, now. I called the police.

When the squad car pulled up five minutes later, Ben had moved around to the front porch. He was very confused but calm. The officers tried to get him to agree to go to the hospital with them. Ben kept refusing—ever so politely. "No, thanks. I'm good," he said. "Really, there's nothing wrong. I'm happy. Thanks anyway." Then he went back to his mumbling, rolling his cigarettes.

After forty-five minutes of this, one officer pulled me aside and said, "I'm sorry, but the only way we'll be able to bring him in right now, against his wishes, is by police order for emergency commitment. In order to do that, we have to call an ambulance. And we'll have to handcuff him. I'm sorry, but it's regulations. We'll be gentle with him."

Handcuffs? "There's no other way?" I said.

"I'm afraid not. Not if you want him on a seventy-two-hour hold."

I said yes. Five minutes later, Ben was led into the ambulance, hands cuffed behind his back. The officers placed him face-down on the cot for transport. I tried not to look. Even if this *was* the only way, the sight of it hurt way too much.

Ali drove up in her car at that very moment; she was just in time, sadly, to see her big brother through her front windshield being led to the ambulance. In handcuffs, escorted by police. She parked on the side of the road but remained in her car. I walked down the driveway and looked in her driver's side window. She was sobbing. I tapped on her window and she opened it. "It's okay, honey," I said. "It was the only way to get him admitted overnight. It's not what it looks like. He didn't do anything wrong."

"I don't care!" she said, and punched a number into her cell phone. "I have to call Ashley." When her best friend answered, Ali started telling her what was going on. Right now she needed her friends more than she needed her mother. For me, this was a double dose of letting go. "Okay, sweetheart," I said, swallowing my own tears. "I'll call you later from the hospital."

"Mom," she said, "I'm sorry; I just need to talk to Ash right now." I leaned into the car and hugged my daughter. As I walked away, I heard her say to Ashley, "I can't wait to go away to school." At that moment, I wished I could go away, too.

At the hospital, the same scene unfolded again: another sleepless night in the waiting room, another sedative for Ben, another wait for a treatment cubicle, another hunt for an available bed somewhere. This time, though, my insurance company wouldn't cover the cost of the stay. We were out of days—in fact, we were over the allotment. So now—would Ben be admitted into state care? I had no idea how this worked. As it turned out, there were no beds available at either local hospital, so West Hills agreed to accept him one more time. "We'll worry about the money later," Dr. Taylor told me.

This fourth stay was for another five days; Ben was stabilized once again. At last, the paperwork was finished for the Clozaril program to begin—starting with small amounts, increasing gradually. Ben took the first blood test to establish his base levels, and we added additional appointments for blood work and sessions with Dr. Taylor to the program that had been interrupted by this most recent episode. Slowly, Ben was weaned off Haldol. He began the Clozaril and reported new side effects: drooling at night, constant sleepiness. "That should go away in time," Dr. Taylor said.

Again, that precarious balance. It was difficult to tell which symptoms were due to the reduction in Haldol, which were side effects from Clozaril, which ones would go away when Ben reached his correct dosage. It was a period of watchful patience and new hope.

But it was only three more weeks until Hospitalization Number Five, the one that became the turning point for Ben's recovery. It happened on

CHAPTER GUIDEPOSTS

Basic Nature Counts

"While many people with mental illness act in unusual and unpredictable ways, they do not often strike out at someone. One of the best indicators of whether an individual has the potential to be violent is past history. If a person has never been violent, he or she is very unlikely to be so in the future."*

*Christine Adamec, *How to Live with a Mentally Ill Person: A Handbook of Day-to-Day Strategies* (New York: Wiley, 1996), 210.

August 14, 2003, on the day the power went out all over the Northeast. Ben came to swim, and he wound up back at the emergency room at St. Mary's Hospital, comforting a coughing elderly woman in between psychotic clouds.

Yes. He is still in there. Help him come back, through the splintered looking glass.

We're ready for Hospitalization Number Five.

Finally, Ben and I make it through the double doors, out of the waiting room and into the treatment area of the ER—well, at least into the hallway. Vital signs have been recorded, and we now wait to see the doctor. Ben has been placed on a gurney and is finally dozing, his long dark curls in tangles. I sit in the plastic chair next to him. A nurse named Bob is kind enough to hand me a pillow as he passes by. It's such an unexpected gesture, to have my exhaustion noticed and acknowledged without a word, that I feel my throat close with grief. It's never crisis that brings the tears, but the smallest act or word of kindness.

The lock-down room is across the hall from us. This time, it is thankfully not Ben who occupies it, but another man. He pounds on the door. Whenever the nurses or aides slip in or out, I catch a glimpse and can see that the man is naked from at least the waist up; his eyes are wild. I see the looks exchanged between the workers in scrubs, eyes rolling in exasperation and veiled contempt. And I think, now that I know better: in that lock-down room is someone's brother, father, spouse, friend. He is not the caged animal he seems to be. He is somebody's son.

IV

RECOVERY AND ACCEPTANCE

REFLECTIONS

TIME: THE PRESENT

When I was working on the first draft of this book, Ali walked over to my desk and read over my shoulder for a moment. She then turned to me and said, "Mom—you're calling this *recovery*?" At the time, Ben had just recently gotten out of the hospital again. I guess I see her point.

Ben's recovery began, in my eyes, on the day he finally began to take the medication that worked for him. These recovery scenes are in present tense in this section, for they seem like snapshots to me, moments in the process that illustrate our journey from the day Ben's medication regime started to be carefully supervised and reinforced—and not by me. The road has been neither smooth nor predictable; it has been far from easy for any of us. But it's better. We may feel many things, but we are no longer confused. We have met the monster, and its name is schizophrenia.

As Ben moved into recovery, we entered the stage of learning how to cope with the truth of his illness. These lessons are hard-earned and often painful. There are losses to grieve, decisions to make, old dreams to let go of. It takes a long time to get to acceptance and the reality that comes with it. It hurts too much. But sometimes you get those wonderfully normal days that hint that not all has been lost. The person you love is still alive, locked inside the symptoms of the illness but still peeking through its bars.

NAMI teaches that there are predictable stages for family members in the crisis/chaos stage (e.g., normalizing, hoping against all hope), while learning to cope (e.g., anger, recognition, grief), and in recovery. For the family who has already handled more crisis periods than they care to remember, recovery is the time for a new level of emotional responses: understanding, acceptance, and—when they're ready—advocacy. Each family member finds his or her own path to healing, to accepting the "new normal" after diagnosis. Ali majored in psychology in college; she is currently working as a care coordinator for a local nonprofit agency. I volunteer my time to teach Family-to-Family, train others to do so, and speak openly to groups and/or individuals about Ben's journey and ours. Others advocate by writing to their legislative representatives, or fight stigma by contacting members of the media. Some stuff envelopes for their local NAMI affiliate.

There are many ways to help, all of which can be interrupted at any time by a change in our ill relative's condition. If he or she goes back into crisis mode, then so do we. This is never easy, no matter how many times we go through it. But now we know how to handle the crisis and find our way back—if we're lucky. We learn, over and over again, to appreciate the good days, the ones that seem normal. They are precious in a way only those who have almost lost them can understand.

15

HE'S STILL IN THERE

In a dream I showed them the language
Listening to the man talk about this train
As they got bored until I let that carpet become
The train of which he spoke
We said "let's gather for a feast!"
"TO LIFE!! DREAMS!! LOVE!!"
yet they turned away in a crimson shame and in a frowning
    wink said simply
"It is you who's crazy . . . for we don't understand!"

—Ben, c. 2003

Ben is admitted to the hospital for the fifth time, in the early morning hours following the Northeast blackout. There's a search for an available bed within the state care system, because my private health insurance will no longer cover a psychiatric hospital stay for him—we've exceeded the allowed forty-five days for the year. There's supposed to be "parity" for those with mental illnesses, requiring the same coverage as for physical illnesses, but it's often a fight to get it recognized.

Besides, I know something else: if Ben goes into state care, he'll be eligible upon discharge for services he's previously been denied. I can finally get him into the system. I will no longer have to be his social worker and case manager as well as his parent. If we can just get him stabilized now, however long it takes, there will finally be some more people to help him in his recovery.

Because there's no room right now in the state mental facility, Ben is temporarily admitted to the psych unit right at St. Mary's Hospital. I breathe a sigh of relief as I hand him over to the nurses, along with a handwritten list of things they need to know, such as his medication dosages and history. I tell them that he's now taking 250 mg of Clozaril daily, and ready to go up to 300. Clozaril has to be introduced very slowly, as it can cause a decrease in white blood cell count (agranulocytosis) or heart problems (myocarditis), so this dosage information is vital.

It's now 2:30 in the morning, and I'm due at work at the radio station by 4 a.m. Time to be funny. In between newscasts and songs, the quick give and take of chat with my two male cohosts is the heart of the show. Our listeners know a lot about us; our lives are partially open books, our family stories a vital part of our humor. This will be a challenge today; I'm physically exhausted and emotionally numb. Once the show begins, though, I shift into automatic. The banter comes easily, almost by rote, as long as I push the events of the past twenty-four hours aside. I had to learn how to multitask my emotions years ago. Right now, having to be funny is a lifesaver.

I make it through the show, checking my cell phone every few minutes, then rush back to the hospital to see Ben. The nurse on duty on the psych unit says that he's been asleep ever since his arrival; he crashed soon after he swallowed his medication. I peek into his room and see that he's in a deep, motionless sleep. The nurse sends me home. "There's nothing you can do right now, dear. Let him rest."

I'm only too happy to leave. My eyelids are heavy, my muscles hurt, my heart aches. I need the break Ben's physical crash will give me. I look around, taking in the atmosphere of this seventh-floor hospital wing, source of my temporary reprieve. It's a far cry from the West Hills private facility; this seems so much more like a medical unit. It's clean but antiseptic. Its windows frame views of city buildings instead of forests and ponds. Still, I think Ben is in good hands. If he wakes with delusions, they'll be witnessed and evaluated by someone other than me. The nurses seem calmly efficient but also kind. Hopefully they know what they're doing. It's all so unfamiliar this time.

I leave the hospital, get in my car and begin to back up out of my space. I'm thinking about Ben and trying not to think about Ben. Then I feel my car make contact. My body is jarred. I hear the thud. I slam on the brakes.

Oh, no. Not now. I thought I had it all under control, going through the motions of leaving my son behind in a hospital bed, but forced calm has its limits. Lost in my own thoughts, I've backed into another car. I do not want to deal with this; it feels like a dream anyway. I am *so* tired.

The driver is a minister, the passengers his wife and mother-in-law. No one is hurt, luckily, but the side door of their Lexus is badly dented.

I've been in my forced state of calm for two days; now I break down and start sobbing. "I'm so sorry, I wasn't looking, my son is in the hospital, I should have been looking, oh I'm so sorry."

The wife gets out of the Lexus and pats me on the shoulder, glancing back at her husband. "It's all right, dear," she says to me. "We didn't have time to beep the horn. No one is hurt. It could have been worse." We go through more motions: we exchange information, I call my insurance company. Damage to their car is minor but still will require a claim. My car is undamaged, but my self-esteem plummets. I can't stop crying. I feel like a failure.

It could have been so much worse, yes, but still I'm kicking myself. I now feel stupid as well as heartbroken. After hours of being calm and

---

CHAPTER GUIDEPOSTS

Insurance Parity for Mental Illness

Growing public awareness of the prevalence of mental illness and the cost-effectiveness of treatment has resulted in unprecedented support for parity—fair and equivalent insurance coverage of mental health disorders. Without parity, millions of Americans who have a mental illness encounter different financial limits and cost-sharing requirements, limited coverage and access to providers, exclusions of conditions, limits on types and duration of treatment, and other provisions that result in inadequate care and poor health outcomes.

The majority of states now have some form of "parity" law, though these laws vary considerably in their provisions.

"An estimated 82 million Americans are covered by plans that are subject to federal law and do not benefit from state mental health parity laws" (www.nami.org).

About Relapse

"The process (of moving through the stages of emotional response) is ongoing—for most of us it has taken years. It is also cyclical; we will start it all over again every time our relative has a relapse, or suffers a setback."*

---

*Joyce Burland, Family-to-Family class 1 handout, "Predictable Stages of Emotional Reactions among Family Members."

sensible in the hospital, then joking on the radio, this minor accident has opened the gate to my tears. All of my doubt comes rushing back.

I can't do anything right. Why didn't I look where I was going? What is wrong with me? Ben is in the hospital again—and a new one this time. Will he be scared when he wakes up? Is this rock bottom, at last?

Oh, God, please let this be the low point. Let this be the worst of it.

CONTROL WHAT YOU CAN

String me a mystery
Weave me a dance
I'd do it myself but I reside in trance
Upon lack of recognition so I give you a call
For I'm too numb to even feel the sleeping withdrawal
Melt morning dreams into a canopy of reminisce
Where 'neath its shade I ponder

—Ben, hospital art class, 2003

A lesson I learn during Ben's fifth hospitalization: control what you can. Sometimes you have to cut your losses, just clean the slate in order to start again. My mantra, then and now: *it is what it is.*

I recognize now that I've stumbled onto a golden opportunity. Ben was so out of it during this hospital admission that I now have in my possession his beloved backpack and the complete contents of his pockets, including the keys to his apartment. I know, at last, that there can be no more "one last chance." He can never go back there. He needs supervision. He needs help. I call Ben's landlord, give the required thirty days' notice for vacating the apartment, and head out there to start packing up my son's try at independent life.

The sight that greets me as I unlock Ben's front door is not unexpected, but still it is a shock. It physically makes my heart hurt. I can feel it, heavy in my chest.

Bed unmade. Clothes tossed everywhere. Crumbs also everywhere— between the couch cushions, on the floor, the kitchen table, the coffee table, countertops. Cockroaches meander around the garbage cans, the fridge, and between the filthy pots, pans, and dishes piled chest-high in the kitchen sink.

Well, I've got to start somewhere, I tell myself. I head out to my car to bring in my truckload of plastic storage bins, garbage bags, and cleaning supplies. I recognize that, along with all the physical work I have ahead, there is also, finally, the chance to snoop. I can search for clues to Ben's condition and thoughts.

I begin in the kitchen, first spraying Raid everywhere. At least the roaches will stop moving. I open the fridge and am met with the stench of moldy cheese and the too-sweet fragrance of spoiled fruit. I begin to fill garbage bags, my sense of power and control increasing with each trip to the Dumpster outside. When I lift the lid of Ben's kitchen garbage can to add its contents to my collection, I see them at the bottom of the bag: the meds.

Ben's pills are in the garbage: Abilify, Clozaril, all the medication he has been insisting he's taken. Why he hasn't flushed them down the toilet is beyond me; he clearly made some attempt to fool me by removing them from the pillbox I'd arranged them in.

I pick the pills out of the garbage one by one, counting. Soon there is no doubt: Ben has not been taking anywhere near the dosage I reported to the hospital doctors. Ben has been given, at St. Mary's, what the hospital doctors assumed was a safely increased dosage of 300 mg per day of Clozaril. I now realize the information I gave them is totally incorrect, as the pills wound up in the garbage instead of in his system. It's now too late to begin his treatment again, safely, ramping up from a smaller dosage. This, I know, can be dangerous for Ben's heart. *What if he has a heart attack? Oh, God.*

But now I realize why Ben has been fast asleep for most of the past five days in the hospital. It's a reaction to the suddenly high dose of medication. I call the hospital to correct the information. I hope for the best. I hope this won't harm his health. I pray it isn't too late.

There is a ray of light behind this fear, though. *At least*, I think, *I know the meds were not necessarily ineffective. The reason he wasn't responding to them is that he wasn't taking them. They could still work.* I'm both very angry and very relieved. Better the truth of his noncompliance than the other option—nonresponse. Nonresponse to what many consider to be the "gold standard" for schizophrenia medications—the last stop, the last chance for a productive life outside of an institution.

Okay, I remind myself, *now we know where we are. Maybe, just maybe, he'll respond to the Clozaril now. Once he wakes up.*

It takes several days to clean out the apartment, to throw out clothes that are too ripped and stained to be worn again, to scour and pack the dishes and pots, sort through the paraphernalia of Ben's existence there: religious artifacts; scraps of paper with illegible writing on them; collections of Snapple caps, bird feathers, rocks. I try to read some of his endless spiral-notebook journals, but most of their contents are too messy and confusing to understand. I feel both a sense of shame at my endless snooping and a sense of being entitled to it. *He's sick, and I'm gathering clues to help him, right?*

Finally, all of Ben's worldly possessions in my car and ready for storage in my basement, I stop before I close and lock his front door for the last time. I regard the clean slate I have made of his life. I've left the apartment in scrupulously pristine condition, as if the landlord or the next tenant might take a moment to think good thoughts about my son and what a fine young man he must be.

He is a fine young man. But it's so hard, now, for many people to see it.

I go back to the hospital. Ben is still in the psych wing, awaiting a state-funded bed across the street in another facility. This time, he is awake when I arrive—but far from aware. Our visit is short. I hug him. He hugs me briefly and then goes back to staring at nothing that I can see.

The nurse on duty tells me that, the evening before, Ben was not in his bed at checking time. They finally found him in the men's room—dazed, confused, and incontinent. My false sense of confidence completely crumbles, as I imagine my son with either urine or feces all over his hospital gown—I don't dare ask which. The image is awful enough already.

Still, as horrifying as this is, it's not as bad as it was before, when I had no idea what was wrong with him. Living with the uncertainty, the ignorance, was even worse. At least now we have some idea of how to treat him.

He's got to get better, I tell myself. *Let this be the low point. Please, God, let this be the worst of it. Let the recovery begin at last.*

Now that Ben is really taking his meds, now that there's a nursing staff to make sure he doesn't throw them away, maybe we will get to have an actual conversation again—one where he both hears me and responds accordingly. It would be a not-so-small miracle. I know, I *know*, he is in there. Somewhere in there. The longing to see my son again is an overwhelming ache. I miss him so much, and I have for so long.

DO WHAT MUST BE DONE

My next recovery lesson is one of the most painful ones of all: in order for Ben to get the help he needs from the state, he has to be homeless. I have to *make* him homeless.

A bed opens up at the Connecticut state mental health facility across the street, after about a ten-day wait. Ben is transferred there, and now his life is in the hands of the government. He can have his own caseworker, social worker, psychiatrist, therapist—and none of these decisions will be attached to his mother. Maybe this is what he needs to make some different choices: a team of professionals not chosen by me. After all, he is a proud, stubborn young man. He needs to be separate from me and see the cause and effect of his actions for himself.

This facility is on the fifth floor of a brick building. Inside the unit, the walls are concrete. Old posters line the walls: "Eat Right for Good Health"; "Exercise Is a Good Habit." The TV room is lined with stackable plastic chairs. Meals come up on a dumbwaiter system from the building cafeteria. No snack kitchen, no cozy couches, as there were in the private facility Ben still remembers. But it is clean, and the staff seems caring—if overwhelmed.

The rules for visitors are stricter here. I have to leave my purse with the front desk. They call Ben over a loudspeaker instead of going in person to find him. His room is smaller, his bed narrower. He has a locker instead of a closet. This is his home for now—until he recovers enough to take the next step.

After a few days, Ben's temporary caseworker calls a family meeting. We sit together in the small meeting room furnished with more plastic chairs around a folding table, and she assures me that Ben is finally taking his medication. The staff is making sure he keeps the pills down after he swallows them. Slowly he has been improving, and they want to know what arrangements will be in place for Ben when he's ready for discharge. "Will he come home to your house?" his social worker asks.

I look down at my lap. I square my shoulders and look up to meet her gaze. "No," I say. "Ben doesn't live with me, and his apartment lease has terminated. He has no place to live." The words hurt me as soon as I utter them. *How can I do this to my son? How can I tell him he can't live at home anymore? What kind of mother am I?*

She doesn't flinch, though. "Well then, I guess we'll have to start looking for a bed in a residence somewhere, when Ben is ready to leave."

Ben looks at me, but I keep my attention on the social worker. I do not want to see whatever expression my son's eyes hold: anger, accusation, or—much worse—hurt. I couldn't bear it. But this is what I have to do. Otherwise we'll be right back to the same starting gate we've been at too many times before—and with the same dire results. "I think that's a great idea," I say to the social worker. "Ben needs to have his own life, and I'm sure he'll do better without me on his back." *Did I just see Ben settle into his seat? Could he perceive this as a good thing?*

He doesn't argue with me, at least, so it's a step. Ben leaves the room and the social worker talks with me privately. Her words give me unexpected comfort and validation. I will remember them always as a vote of confidence and a rare understanding of the guilt she probably sensed in me.

"I just want to congratulate you on your courage," she says. "I know that was very difficult to say, but it's the right choice. So many patients come through here in their midforties, with absolutely no idea how to manage their own life because Mommy has always been there to do it. Ben will learn to grow up. You did the right thing."

Tears spring to my eyes. Again. I did not expect this. "Thank you so, so much," I tell her.

Two days later I visit Ben. Ali comes with me; she's about to leave for college in Rhode Island, and we bring pictures of the campus to share with Ben. We all sit around the table in the eating room, high windows facing the city on one side and an all-glass partition on the other, which faces the staff desk.

Ben looks at all of Ali's college pictures and tells her how great it is, that it's so cool that she's going away. He seems much better today—coherent, making conversation, asking questions. Ali leaves to find the restroom, and Ben looks at me across the table. "Mom?" he says.

"Yes, Ben."

He plays with the campus map laid out in front of him. "How come Ali gets to go away to college before I do?"

Oh, honey. That's the trouble with reality: it can hurt so much when you come back to it. "She was able to finish the process it takes to get there, Ben," I say. "It was kind of a common path: finish high school, get good grades, apply to colleges, get accepted. Your path is different, that's all. If you want to go away to college someday, it will have to happen a different way."

"I guess," he says. "It still sucks."

I know. It must suck to have to be jealous of your little sister when she used to be jealous of you.

Ali walks back into the room. "Have fun at school, Ali," her big brother says.

She smiles. "Thanks, Ben. I'll write to you, okay?"

"Okay." Visiting hours are ending. I start gathering up our things. "Mom?" he says.

"Yes, honey?"

"I know I messed up at school this summer. It was too hard. But maybe I can go again in the fall and take one course or something."

I tell him I'll look into it. *He dropped out of high school, but he managed to get a GED. He has tried college classes before, with more failure than success. Still, he has earned a few credits. He could start again. Couldn't he?*

CHAPTER GUIDEPOSTS

"Frozen in Time"

Those who have spent many of their young adult years lost in the onset of a mental illness have not had the time or opportunity to experience and learn from the normal activities of that time of life: high school sweethearts, their first job, college, living away from home for the first time. Therefore, when they finally do begin to get their life on track, they may seem "frozen in time"—in the time before the illness took hold. They may seem to stay stuck there for a long time. Patience and lowered expectations are helpful attitudes for the family. Dreams for the loved one's life must be reexamined in light of the illness that has happened to him or her.

Living at Home versus Other Options: Ways to Make the Choice

It may be best for the mentally ill relative to live away from the family, especially if the atmosphere is so tense and angry that living together only seems to consistently make matters worse. Many families are neither prepared nor equipped to live with a mentally ill relative, especially if constant policing is required for medication adherence and other matters. In this case, it may be best to help your relative find other housing, where the supervision is not so personal. In more extreme cases, the choice is almost easier: psychotic episodes may put you or your children in danger.

No matter how much you want to help your family member, you also have an obligation to yourself and to the rest of your family. Discuss the matter with family members; get some ideas and support at NAMI; investigate treatment centers, halfway houses, group homes, crisis housing, clubhouses, or possibly live-in help, so you know what your options are.

SIBLING LOSS

Up until about five years ago, my brother Ben and I had a normal sibling relationship. We talked, we fought, and most importantly we joked around. I always looked up to him, because he was older and "cool." I was just his kid sister following in his footsteps—and now the situation has changed. Now I am the one who is excelling. It hurts me to realize I may never be able to connect with him again.

Every day, I'm faced with Ben and his problems. With his constant blank look, his eyes seem empty at times. My Mom says "baby steps" when he does something right and I guess every little bit helps. Now I too am part of the struggle to help my brother, and it's a major challenge in my life. I don't like to think about how he embarrasses me . . . because as long as I live, I will love him.

My brother has taught me a lot; I've learned that even when I have small failures, I can still move on. Knowing that it's hard for him to function on a daily basis makes me appreciate all I have. I have faith that maybe my brother will grow out of this stage and be able to succeed in his own way, too.

—Ali's college application essay, 2003

Sometimes you just can't stop the memories. Even for parents whose children are healthy, nostalgia often hits when you're surrounded by young families after your babies have grown up. Parents of children with mental illness have added questions: Could I have done anything differently? Were there signs I didn't see? Will my children ever recover the relationship they had when they were small?

I've just dropped Ali off at Roger Williams University in Rhode Island, to begin her freshman year. I'm used to feeling the void of being a single-parent family; her roommate, and almost everyone else around us during this orientation weekend, seemed to have two parents to help them get settled. We've gotten used to being a family of three, with no father in the picture. The loss I felt much more powerfully was the fact that Ben wasn't there, either; it was just the two of us, Ali and me. I wished Ben had been able to see his sister off to school. So many other brothers were around, carrying duffel bags up the stairs—the younger brothers looking envious; the older ones dispensing advice; all of them teasing, annoying, hugging their sisters. As much as I believed that Ben was where he needed to be in order to begin recovery, the feeling that something was missing kept creeping into the excitement of seeing Ali to the door of this new phase of her life.

I hurt for Ali; she says she's fine, that she's so excited about school she doesn't have time to dwell on the fact that our family seems so small right now. Ali *always* says she's fine; often she is, but I wonder what's really inside her outer serenity and quiet wisdom. Ali is the one who dispenses advice to her friends—and she's very good at it—but seldom asks for help herself.

Every once in a while, though, she breaks down. Sometimes she tells me how hard it has been for her to see her brother change so drastically, to behave so strangely, to be so unreachable. She has lost the big brother she once worshipped; Ben has become more like a little brother, needy and unpredictable. She misses the way they used to be together. I miss it, too.

Now Ali will be away from the tension of seeing Ben fall apart and picking up the pieces, again and again. I think she is hoping I can fix this, can make Ben better somehow while she's away at school. That makes two of us. This much I know: the fact that Ben will be living somewhere else—I don't know where yet, but *somewhere*—by the time she comes home again, will ease our tension and give him more responsibility for his own journey. It's the step we have to take, for Ben's recovery and for our own family sanity.

So—by the time I get home, I'll be in an empty nest. Both children have flown at once, in very different ways. In order to avoid (or postpone) the feeling of loss, I decide to mark the occasion with an overnight trip alone on my way home from Rhode Island—I take the ferry to a place I've never seen: Block Island. Good for contemplation, appreciation of nature, people-watching, and marking this milestone.

CHAPTER GUIDEPOSTS

Sibling Loss: Things That Help

- Provide information—keep learning, and make the information available.
- Acknowledge the feelings of the non-ill child—guilt, anger, loss.
- Let the sibling live his or her life.
- Don't expect the non-ill child to be a superchild.
- Be open to discussing the illness and its effects on everyone.
- Make support groups available.

Twenty-four hours of solitary contemplation is more than enough. I find myself watching families as I sit outside the snack bar, sipping coffee at a picnic table. All around me, it seems, are intact families, both parents at the helm, just starting out on their journey of raising small, adorable children. So full of promise at that stage. So full of possibility. I remember that feeling, back in the days when I believed that my love and care were all my children would need to succeed in life: *I will make this world wonderful for them. I'll protect them from harm. I'll raise my son and daughter so well that their future will be guaranteed.*

I'm jealous of these families; I can't help it.

I see a boy of about six playing with his little sister, teaching her how to pack a bucket with sand, helping her choose an ice cream from the vendor. My throat tightens with longing. How I miss my babies. How I miss the little vacations I took with them, when all they needed was each other to play with and me watching from the sidelines. How I miss the normal years.

16

BABY STEPS TO NORMAL:
REALISTIC EXPECTATIONS

It's the ninth of September, 2003, a few weeks after Ali started her freshman year at Roger Williams. Ben has decided to go back to college, too, for the fall semester. Three weeks ago he could barely remember the last sentence he uttered. Now he has signed up for three classes: algebra, composition, and ceramics.

Ben is probably the only current student at Riverside Community College to attend while still residing in a state mental facility. We've gotten special permission from the hospital for him to start classes before his discharge. The college has a wonderful program for students with disabilities, but Ben has insisted he doesn't qualify. He wants to seem—to *be*—normal.

"I am not disabled, Mom," he says.

We had a scare last week. Ben's heart started to race and he was rushed to the emergency room and then to a cardiologist. This was a side effect from his medication. There was no permanent damage, but there could be a risk to his heart if the Clozaril dosage is increased again. The doctor has therefore added a mood stabilizer called Depakote to the mix. This sometimes serves to enhance the effects of the antipsychotic without the increased risk.

There has been improvement in Ben. Slow but marked, and blessed, improvement, sufficient to inspire him to sign up for classes. He wants so much to get on with his life. He's often very sleepy—a side effect of sedation—but he is fighting for his quality of life. The "zombie Ben" has receded, and my heart opens to possibility again.

On the morning of his first day of classes, I go to the hospital to tell Ben it's time to leave for school. He is clean-shaven, dressed in freshly laundered clothes, and excited. His backpack is filled with brand-new spiral notebooks and the textbooks we bought last week in the campus

CHAPTER GUIDEPOSTS

The delicate balance of helping your relative through recovery is this: while lowering expectations to keep them realistic, it also helps to provide opportunities for challenge and accomplishment. Awareness, timing, empathy, and knowledge all work together in a dance to support progress while not demanding it, to cheer accomplishment but not to push it. This takes time, and often a few tries. Patience, understanding, and hope are invaluable tools.

bookstore. He has been waiting for me; we sign him out of the hospital for the morning.

The nurses and aides wish him well. "Have a good day at school, Ben," the head nurse says.

"Thanks!" he answers, and we head back into the outside world.

It takes ten minutes to get to the college; Ben is calm and happy during the drive. I let him out of the car at the front entrance. "Do you want me to walk you in?" I say.

"No, thanks, Mom, I'll take it from here." I watch my son walk into the front entrance of Riverside Community College. I think about how things can change, how shocked and angry I'd been when he'd dropped out of high school years before. Now I can only, as always, hope for the best. It is his life to live.

THE NINTH FLOOR

Ben is tired. He is always so, so tired. Sometimes he waits for me outside the front entrance to the building, hand-rolled cigarette in his mouth and backpack at his side. At other times, I have to park the car and go inside the lobby, where I find him fast asleep on one of the couches, snoring softly like he did when he was three. I pick him up twice a week and take him to school; he takes the bus home. He's trying, still, to attend his college classes.

Ben has now been housed in Transitional Living, also known as "the ninth floor," for three months. This unit is, essentially, a homeless shelter for those who have just been discharged from the psych floor. Medication is supervised, but other help is limited. Ben has been taking his prescribed medications, and though he is much improved, it's taking time for the side effects to calm down. The excessive salivation has stopped, and Ben's heart rate has returned to normal. One effect that remains, though, is the feeling of sedation—and the need for lots of sleep. Often Ben doesn't get in his necessary ten or twelve hours. On the ninth floor, though, the rules are clear: up and out by 8 a.m.

From eight in the morning to four in the afternoon, residents are encouraged to "do something productive" with their time: look for a job, go to school, attend an AA meeting. The doors to the unit are locked, but the lobby is open. Ben's "productive activity" is his class schedule at the college—if he can stay awake.

For three months, we've been waiting for a bed in a housing situation to open up so Ben can have a place to call home. Meanwhile, I've seen him at least three times a week. I drive him to and from school whenever I can, and he takes the bus when I can't. I bring him food and cigarettes; I take him out for lunch. I'm afraid to take him home for a visit because I'm not sure I could get him to leave again. I'm afraid I might have to call the police to escort him back to Transitional Living. I might have to change the locks. I don't want to live through that scene again. Ben has to see that the way out of here is to move forward toward his own living situation, not back to the same cycles that nearly destroyed our relationship. I have to keep rejecting him to get him to move ahead. This is killing me. The guilt tears me apart, no matter how many times I remind myself that it's the only way.

Some mornings I am resentful of this intrusion into my day, chauffeuring Ben to and from class. I don't want to be resentful; I want to be better than that. But on those days the sight of my son in his dirty cargo pants, snoring softly on the lobby couch, his bare feet with too-long toenails sticking out of his sandals, both makes my heart ache and sends my anger up several notches.

I'm angry at the so-called Transitional Program. *What kind of program is this? How can they just lock the doors and expect the residents to know how to be "productive"?*

Sometimes, too, I get angry at Ben—but then I kick myself. *How can I be resentful of Ben, when his life is so empty right now? I can get in my car, I can drive away. He has to stay here in order to find a way to his own independence, someday. And what courage he has trying to attend school under these circumstances! What courage! I must remember how hard this is for him. I must remember to be proud.*

The good news—the best news—is that the Clozaril seems to be working. Except for the exhaustion, which I hate. Ben must hate it even more. He always seems to be asleep, or to want to sleep. Sometimes, I know, he's gotten out of the car at school, wanting me to see that he's trying to succeed, but he never makes it to class. I know this because his algebra teacher is an acquaintance of mine who sneaks information to me. Ben started out getting As on the tests—the information he already knew from high school. I'm amazed that he can remember these things, but he does. Lately, though, he has not done so well and has missed a few classes. On those days, I found out, he goes straight to the bus terminal after I drive away; he takes the bus back to the mental health building so he can go back to sleep on the couch in the lobby.

But here is the miracle: Ben and I no longer fight. When he has had the rest he needs, he actually talks to me again—not at me, but to me. That seething resentment, that argument always waiting around the corner, the need to blame his life's twists on me—it's gone. We can talk again. Sometimes we even share a joke, and the punch line is not just in Ben's head—we both hear it. Compared to the unexplained bursts of laughter that used to come from Ben at odd times, making sense to no one else and followed by a defensive "I'm allowed to laugh, aren't I?" this common laughter is a miracle.

The thing about Clozaril that makes it still the gold standard of medications for schizophrenia—despite the high cost and need for blood work—is that it can work on the negative symptoms, the things that were taken away from the patient by the illness: emotions, connections, motivation. While other medications help remove positive (added) symptoms of hallucinations and bizarre behavior, the restoration of some of the qualities stolen by schizophrenia is what makes Ben come back to life.

This is the thing that brings tears to my eyes: Ben sometimes comes back to us. Gentle teasing of his sister, a sincere hug, a childhood memory we both share and treasure. I see my son at home in his eyes, sometimes, instead of the hollow look of schizophrenia called "blunt affect."

This, more than anything else, gives me hope. The nightmare road might just turn and fork in another direction. In the meantime, at least there are days when I see the son I used to know. He's still here.

Today is one of those days. Ben is waiting for me when I drive up. There's a big smile on his face. It is a real smile, an outward smile, a smile for me. Ben gets in the car with his backpack. "Hi, Mom," he says. "Wanna see what I got for you and Ali?"

What he got us? How? Ben has no money—it's not a good idea to have cash in Transitional Living. I bring him his cigarettes, his shaving cream, his snack foods.

"What is it, honey?"

"It's a Hanukkah present for you guys. I won it in bingo!" he says, and starts to unzip his backpack.

"Really?" I say. "They have prizes?"

"Yeah, someone donates them. And I won!" He takes a box out of his backpack. It's wrapped in an old T-shirt. "I picked it out just for you," he says. "It's not much, but I thought you'd like it."

"Thanks, honey." I uncover the box and see that it is a small red vase in a clear plastic box, probably bought at the Dollar Store. It's not gorgeous. But it's beautiful to me. *My son thought of us. He wanted us to have a gift. It's a good, generous sign.*

"I wanted to get you something better," he says.

"Honey, I love it," I reply. "You won it just for us. That is so sweet." I recall the time, not so long ago, when my anger was so strong that it felt like the only emotion I had left toward my son. This recovery period is difficult and painful, but no longer overshadowed by the confusion and conflict that ruled our relationship when his illness was developing.

Ben has come back to us for this day, which is the best gift of all. I am grateful.

LETTING GO

Letting go of control so that your child can recover isn't without its terrifying moments. There's always the part of me that wants to be there to protect Ben and Ali from every consequence of their choices. My head knows that children can only learn from their own experiences, but my heart wants to protect them from the process because—well, it just hurts so much. I wish I could prevent every pain.

Two weeks ago Ben was mugged. He had withdrawn some money from his savings account at the ATM. He wasn't supposed to take money out; he'd done it only because he wanted to lend it to a friend on the floor, who'd walked to the bank with him. They both were threatened by a man with a knife on the way home, who took the cash. Neither one was hurt; I am grateful, at least, for that. At the same time, I curse the fact that the Transitional Living Program is in such an awful neighborhood. When is Ben going to be placed somewhere?

And something else is not right this week. Ben's medication levels are down; he's been sleeping through some dosage times and has missed some required blood tests, too. How could this happen? How could the experts have let this happen?

I'm angry at this development; it has shaken my faith in the people who are supposed to know how to treat Ben. There's a silver lining in this, however: because of the slip-up, Ben now qualifies for more structured case management in addition to the Transitional Living staff. He'll now be assigned an outside caseworker from Assertive Community Treatment (ACT).

It took a medication crisis in order to be allowed to get this help. Why?

Maybe the ACT team can finally arrange a place for Ben to live. He's been living in this "transitional" situation for far too long. I've been patient with the government process, and so has Ben. The system is overloaded; they have to find the right match for a residence; excuses and reasons go on and on. Meanwhile, although he is responding medically to his treatment, Ben's pride and sense of self are continually wounded by his living situation.

If only he could get better at home, under my roof. But I know that he can't. He just can't. He will never grow up if he lives with me. Independence is his best chance, however long it takes, but the next step is frighteningly unsure.

Ben has lived in Transitional Living for this entire college semester; somehow, despite the exhaustion and inconsistency of the past four months, he's managed to complete one of the courses he started. He now has three more college credits, for a total of twelve earned at three different schools. Still, not bad for a high school dropout with schizophrenia. At least he keeps trying; at least he hasn't given up.

Ben still wants to work, too, but a job is even harder to find than housing. Part of his routine is to walk down to the diner on Boston Avenue with a friend from the floor and order a cheap lunch. They know him there and don't seem to mind that he seldom spends a lot of money. I know because I took Ben to this diner last week, and he didn't attract any strange looks. The cashier said "Hey, man" to him, and the waitress yelled, "Sweetie! Where have you been?" It is nice not to feel defensive about being with him. Ben is welcome here.

Today, Ben is visiting me at home. "Mom," he says. "Can you take me to the mall to buy some black khakis that fit me, and a white button-down shirt?"

"Sure," I say. These are not the kind of clothes Ben generally asks for—not by a long shot. "What are they for?"

"I got a job!" he says. He is beaming. He has wanted to surprise me with this.

"Really? Where, honey?"

The job is at the diner on Boston Avenue. They've decided to give him a chance. This hasn't happened in a long, long time. "When do you start?" I ask.

"Tomorrow," he says. "And you'll be really proud of me this time, Mom. I'm doing everything exactly the way they asked me to. I stopped by two days ago and got a copy of the menu so I could memorize it. I'm going to wear a tie. I'll put my hair back in a ponytail. I can't wait!"

CHAPTER GUIDEPOSTS

Assertive Community Treatment is a team treatment approach designed to provide comprehensive, community-based psychiatric treatment, rehabilitation, and support to persons with serious and persistent mental illness such as schizophrenia.

The ACT model of care evolved in the late 1960s out of the work of Arnold Marx, MD; Leonard Stein; and Mary Ann Test, PhD. ACT has been widely implemented in the United States, Canada, and England (www.actassociation.org/).

Dignity

"Every time our relatives 'get better' and show improvement, for them it means that they are moving back into a risk position. Being well signals that they may be required to participate in the real world, and this is a frightening prospect for the 'shaky self.' So, it's important for us to be very patient in wellness, as we are in illness."*

---

*Burland, "Empathetic Guidelines."

We buy the clothes; I find the aprons left over from his last try as a waiter, and Ben is all set for work the next day. He has studied the menu thoroughly; he is clean, neatly dressed, and very optimistic. He walks to work and arrives on time.

Unfortunately, he only lasts one afternoon. The next day he calls me. "I tried, Mom, I really did," he says, "but they said they couldn't keep me on. They said they really like me, but I just don't have enough experience. They need someone who can handle the lunch rush."

I try to imagine Ben, so newly into recovery, trying to keep a bunch of orders straight. I hoped he wouldn't fail at this, but I suspected he might. Still, it hurts. *He was so excited about this.* "Don't worry, honey," I say. "When you get a place to live, you can try again. Maybe you could try being a busboy to start."

"Nah, I'm okay, Mom," he says. "I'll be a waiter somewhere else." But he sounds like an eight-year-old who hasn't been invited to the birthday party. I wish, again, that his mind could make connections the way it used to. I doubt he realizes that it doesn't, but I sure do. I remember.

This time he really, really tried. That's what breaks my heart.

EARLY DETECTION:
A SUCCESS STORY

Ali has come back home from college. The semester that began with such high hopes and promise for the girl who "didn't need any help from anyone" has come crashing down around both of us. It was all too much. To lose your father at age three, to lose your older brother to schizophrenia a decade later—to have each of these men replaced by shadows of themselves—is a burden that has to be faced. She never wanted to confront it before. She never thought she had to. She was the "well one."

"I'm so sorry, Mom," she cries. "I'm sorry I couldn't even finish the semester. I'm sorry I let you down. I just couldn't handle it anymore; I really, really, tried." But there's more going on here than unexpressed pain. The symptoms Ali describes to me sound frighteningly like early signs of depression. She can't stop crying. She sometimes has trouble seeing the point of what she's doing, of getting out of bed.

I assure her that her mental health is much more important than her college classes right now, and I tell her she's made the right choice. It sounds like she's really in trouble, though, and I tell her it's time to stop trying to handle this all by herself. She *does* need help, and that's perfectly all right. For the first time in her life, Ali agrees to see a therapist. She wants to do whatever is necessary to redirect her life, even if medication is part of the treatment.

Oh, my poor girl. Not her, too. But I'm also relieved; I knew it was only a matter of time before her losses caught up with her. It's time for her to come out from behind her curtain of secrets, to face the losses she has pushed aside for so long. It's time to feel the pain. Then she can really begin to pick up the pieces, sadly but honestly. We have a long road ahead of us as she rediscovers herself.

Ali isn't the first college freshman to leave home with flags flying, only to return a few months later with emotional wounds instead. Some of her friends have come home, too; many others, she tells me, are suffering silently without reaching out for help. They feel ashamed.

The statistics about depression among high school and college students are staggering; many don't acknowledge it—or, worse, decide the only solution is suicide. I'm so glad that Ali has recognized her need for help; still, it hurts to see her disappointment. She'd had such high hopes.

"Honey," I say, "think of a jigsaw puzzle. You can look at the pretty picture on the box, but you can't put the real puzzle together until you open the box and spill all those little pieces out onto the table. Then you think you'll never get it together again. But you will. And you'll know you did it. But it will take time."

As it turns out, Ali is one of the lucky ones. Mild or situational depression can be treated with therapy and often a short period of mild medication that is not a lifelong prescription. Ali is able to accept what she needs to do, and she learns what she can handle. She comes out of it stronger and smarter. She does not become a statistic. Early detection has made all the difference.

CHAPTER GUIDEPOSTS

College Mental Health Statistics

One out of four young adults will experience a depressive episode by age twenty-four.

Nearly half of all college students report feeling so depressed at some time that they have trouble functioning.

If left untreated, depression can lead to suicide. Suicide is the third leading cause of death for those age fifteen to twenty-four and the second leading cause of death of college students (American Psychiatric Association, www.healthyminds.org).

"Mild" Depression

Dysthymic disorder, or dysthymia, is a type of depression that lasts for at least 2 years. Some people suffer from dysthymia for many years. Their depression is usually mild or moderate, rather than severe. Most people with dysthymia can't tell for sure when they first became depressed.

Symptoms of dysthymic disorder include a poor appetite or overeating, difficulty sleeping or sleeping too much, low energy, fatigue, and feelings of hopelessness. People with dysthymic disorder may have periods of normal mood that last up to 2 months. Family members and friends may not even know that their loved one is depressed. Even though this type of depression is mild, it may make it difficult for a person to function at home, school, or work.

Dysthymic disorder can be treated with an antidepressant medicine. This type of drug relieves depression. It may take a number of weeks, or even several months, before you and your doctor know whether an antidepressant is helping you. It is important for you to take the medicine exactly as your doctor tells you to. If the antidepressant helps you feel better, you may need to take this medicine for several years. You should continue to take the medicine until your doctor tells you to stop, even if you begin to feel better. If you stop taking the medicine, you may get depressed again. (www.familydoctor.org/online)

For more information on depression among college students, go to www.campusblues.com/nimh_dep.asp.

Early Detection

Whenever someone with serious mental illness has another episode, the long-term prognosis worsens, according to new research. Some scientists have gone so far as to argue that psychotic episodes are toxic to the brain. The idea here is that brain cells are altered or die during and immediately following an episode of psychosis.

In a landmark study conducted at the Hillside Hospital in Queens, New York, researchers found those schizophrenia patients that received treatment early and consistently had much better outcomes.*

*Xavier Amador, *I Am Not Sick, I Don't Need Help! How to Help Someone with Mental Illness Accept Treatment* (Peconic, NY: Vida Press, 2007), 23.

If only someone had been able to detect Ben's illness earlier. Could all the psychotic breaks have been avoided? Would he now be smarter, be better? Would he have less brain damage? Would we be able to hope for more—more than this required stay in a transitional shelter, waiting for a bed to open up?

It's probably true that earlier detection might have made a big difference for Ben, too, even though he has a different kind of illness. Research shows that brain damage can occur in the periods of psychosis that could have been prevented by early treatment. *Why did his diagnosis take so long? Why did no one catch it sooner?*

THE RIGHT WORDS AT THE RIGHT TIME

I love Ben's ACT team. They call me for information. They want to learn about Ben. They want to help him. They *like* him.

I sit in Helen's office one afternoon. The room is cluttered and tiny. There is a metal desk, behind which Helen sits; I'm in the one remaining chair, next to the overstuffed file cabinet. There are family photos on her desk, along with several piles of manila files and other papers.

Helen has been a social worker for more than twenty-five years, most of it in this office. She is a slim, attractive woman with red hair and a reassuring smile. She asks me for background information on Ben. I can't remember the last time anyone has actually *asked* me for Ben's history; I've always had to force it into their hands. I try to keep things brief. I cannot. There is too much to say. The next time I look at the clock, forty-five minutes have gone by. Helen has not chased me out of her office. This is amazing.

Then she asks me something no one else has, except my own therapist. "So," she says, "how are *you* doing with all of this?"

"Me?" I say, and I begin to cry.

Helen hands over the tissues and listens. After ten minutes, she asks another unusual question. "And how has your daughter handled all this? It must be hard on her."

I love this woman. We talk about Ali and her pain, too. At the end of our meeting, I blow my nose into the last of the tissues. Helen gets up from behind her desk and goes to open the door. Before she turns the doorknob, I ask one more question. "How do you do this?" I say. "You must have at least twenty-five cases at a time. How do you listen to these stories, straighten out the mess, time after time? Doesn't it get to you?"

Helen comes back and sits down on her desk. She folds her arms across her chest and looks away in thought for a minute. Then she leans toward me, meeting my eyes again. "It is hard. You're right. But you want to know why I do it? Do you want to know why I love my job?"

She loves her job? I can't remember ever hearing this. "Why?" I say.

"Because I love to see people get better."

She loves to see people get better. My heart leaps. "Really?" is all I can manage.

"Yes, I see it all the time. And Ben *will* get better. It will take time. It won't be easy, but it can happen. He's a good kid. You'll see."

I've lived on those words ever since. Helen saved my life that day, with two gifts: caring and hope. Some providers just know how to do it right.

CRISIS INTO OPPORTUNITY

Too often in the recovery process, it takes a crisis to ignite change. Sadly, the system is usually too overloaded for preventive action. For Ben, luckily, this crisis isn't tragic, and it results in finding housing for him at last.

It's a new year, and I begin it by escaping. Ali and I have just gone on a five-day cruise with my friend and her daughter. Five days with no cell phone access—absolute heaven. My home message machine doesn't seem to be working when I check it from Miami. What could happen to Ben in five days? Anyway, I'd sent e-mails and left phone messages so that Ben's ACT team would know I was out of town. I'd left emergency numbers, and no one used them. All must be well.

When I walk into the house, though, there are ten increasingly frantic messages waiting for me on our home machine, all from Ben's hospital caseworker. There was a crisis while I was gone. Ben was acting very strangely and a subsequent urine test showed traces of cocaine. Cocaine! He had never, ever, used that before.

Damn! Can't I even go on one vacation? And why didn't they call me if it was an emergency? And how in the world did he get ahold of cocaine?

After numerous phone calls—to Ben, the Transitional Living floor, the ACT team, the doctors—we piece together what must have happened. Ben, who still rolls his own cigarettes, was probably slipped a joint of to-bacco laced with crack cocaine. Great neighborhood. None of my messages had reached the ACT team, so they thought I had given up on Ben when I didn't return their calls.

We have to get Ben out of there! This nonsense has gone on long enough—waiting for a bed, being patient.

This crisis, as it turns out, is a sort of blessing in emergency disguise, because Ben now qualifies once again for more extreme treatment. The action escalates at last. Helen, his case manager at ACT, calls me. "We're going to milk this for all it's worth," she says. "I think I can get Ben listed now as a dual-diagnosis case—mental illness plus addiction. There are more beds available for patients that fit this description. I can probably get him placed by next week."

So you have to be really, doubly, in trouble to get help. So much for catching things before they get worse. No—wait until they get worse, and then the help is there. Something is very wrong with this picture.

Still, Helen is working with it, thankfully. "This will look a lot more convincing," she says, "if I can show a history of drug abuse. Has Ben ever had a problem with drugs before this?"

For once, I want him to seem *worse* than he really is. I tell her about Ben's history of pot use. "Perfect," she says.

One week later, Ben is accepted to a group residence. There is space available in Harrison House, a refurbished old home from the P. T. Barnum era in Bridgeport. There is twenty-four-hour staffing and a program to help Ben move forward when he's ready. The residents must attend meetings of Alcoholics Anonymous; all share a dual diagnosis.

Now all we have to do is get him to agree to go there. The problem with Harrison House is that the other residents are all middle-aged. We arrange a visit for Ben, and the guys make vegetarian lasagna for dinner that night in his honor. They all like him, but Ben wants to be with people his own age. We can hear the "No, thanks" coming now.

Another obstacle is that Ben has become *comfortable* where he is. After almost five months, he is afraid to move out. He doesn't want to face any other options. On the Transitional Living Floor, life is so simple. No decisions to make. Nothing to risk, no way to fail. He knows what to expect.

"If I can't move into my own apartment now," he says, "then I'll just stay here until I can." But it's time. Ben will die a slow, unmotivated emotional death here. It won't be long before he turns to drugs—and not by accident this time.

But Helen—she knows her stuff. She also knows Ben. She calls me the day before we meet with Ben to coordinate our strategy. I tell her, "I've been looking into another place for Ben, called Parents House. It would cost me another hundred dollars a day, but the other residents are Ben's age. He might be more willing to go there. Should that be our third choice?"

"We'd better keep this simple," Helen replies. "Three choices will be too confusing for Ben. Let's keep this very easy. Follow my lead, and I'll play bad cop if I have to."

The next afternoon we meet with Ben. He is distracted, very curious about Helen's new Palm Pilot. I see how she talks to him: with complete respect. She answers his questions about her Palm Pilot with intelligence and humor, and Ben relaxes. In that same vein, Helen explains to him that he has only two choices. "Ben," she says, "the way the system works is very clear. A lot of people are waiting for a place to live, and we've found you one. Unfortunately, there are so few openings that you only get offered a placement once. If you refuse this bed, you have to leave Transitional Living anyway. Then you'll have to go to a homeless shelter."

Ben looks at her. I wait silently, steeling myself for a fight. "But what if I hate it there?" Ben says. "What if I want to move somewhere else?"

"Once you're in Harrison House," she says, "we can work out the next steps. But we have to start you out there. After that, we can move you into another place if you find one."

"But right now, if I don't say yes, I'm going to a homeless shelter?" he says.

"I'm afraid so," says Helen.

Here it comes, I think. *The arguments.*

The tantrum. Instead, Ben looks at Helen. "Well," he says, "I guess I'd better go to Harrison House then. Beats a homeless shelter, right?"

CHAPTER GUIDEPOSTS

Families and Providers Working as a Team: Tips for the Family

- Be courteous.
- Provide information.
- Be respectful of their time.
- Ask how you can be involved in a supportive way.
- Request meetings, with or without your relative present, when you feel the need.
- Expect to be treated respectfully and with consideration.
- Keep in mind the frustrations and constraints professionals face.*

---

*Rebecca Woolis, *When Someone You Love Has a Mental Illness: A Handbook for Family, Friends, and Caregivers* (New York: Tarcher, 1992), 186–87.

Just like that. The amazing Helen. When Ben goes out of the room to have a cigarette, Helen and I smile at each other. "Wow," I say. "That went so well."

"Yep," she says. "And wait until you see him a year from now. He'll be doing so much better, this will seem like nothing."

I love this woman. I want to believe her so much that I do. I need other people who have faith in Ben, too. I need to have hope confirmed. There were so many solutions we tried on the way to the bottom of the hole dug slowly by schizophrenia.

A PLACE TO CALL HOME

The car is, once more, packed with my son's possessions. Ben has been living in an institutional room for six months. Six months in a temporary space that he could not make his own. One small locker, one bedside dresser. I drive to the Mental Health Center for what I hope will be the last time; I park the car, go upstairs to the ninth floor. Ben is waiting for me, excited. All of his hospital possessions are packed into plastic bags. He's ready to move into his new life.

"Did you bring my stereo, Mom? I really miss my stereo."

"Of course, honey."

I have the stereo; I have some of his favorite books; I have his CD collection. I also packed the rainbow comforter I made for him when he was a toddler—the one he always puts on his bed in a new place, the one he says makes a new place seem like home. I have the clothes that I think will still fit him, will accommodate his now meatier frame. Clozaril can contribute to weight gain, but Ben is one of the luckier ones. I've seen people gain sixty pounds or more. Ben has gained about twenty, I guess—all in his stomach—but it's not too bad. He says it doesn't bother him.

The staff and residents say good-bye, wishing him well. Ben shakes hands, promises to visit, walks out the door with me, and looks back only once.

We drive to Harrison House, about five minutes from the Mental Health Center where Ben has been living. HH is on the corner of two busy streets in a city neighborhood that is partly residential, partly commercial. We enter through the door off the side porch, which leads directly into the staff office. The residents usually use the kitchen door to come and go, but on this admission day we come in the official way.

The staff at HH welcomes Ben, and two of his new housemates come out to the car to help him with his stuff while I fill out the leftover paperwork.

This is my first chance to see Ben's new home and to meet the people who will become his new community. HH is designed to house eight: some are in single rooms, most share with roommates. Cameron, who runs the house, is a warm man with a kind and intelligent manner. He takes me on a tour.

The ceilings are ten feet high. The moldings are intricate, the windows on the ground floor nearly floor-to-ceiling. The furniture is basic, the kind my kids always wanted me to buy from the mall: couches and chairs made of planks of wood with upholstered cushions on top. It looks out of place in the old-fashioned and once-elegant building, but it is clean and functional. There's a fireplace in the living room, but its opening is covered up with plywood on which the residents have painted the picture of a tree. The focal point of the room, the television, is set in the bay window alcove.

We climb the stairs, divided into two flights by a landing, to see Ben's room. The hall smells faintly of urine. We unlock the door to the room he'll share with another resident. Twin beds, more lumber-inspired furniture. The room is large and Ben will have his own closet. There's room for him to have a small television if he wants to, and my old computer will fit nicely on the desk. The bathroom is out in the hall; he'll share that with the other guys. Not quite his own place, but a spacious palace compared to where he has been. It'll do nicely for now. He can have his own things around him. That's the good news.

The not-so-good news is that Ben has a roommate named Ted—and Ted is angry. Ted is used to having the room all to himself. He has set up a wall divider between their beds and is refusing to talk to Ben. Welcome home.

As we move him in, I get a look at Ben's other housemates. Some are smiling and friendly in a childlike way; others are sullen though polite. All are over the age of forty. Most look, on first glance, much less functional than Ben. Where will Ben find people his own age to relate to? Where will he find role models to help inspire him to move ahead from this place?

Suddenly I feel the knot in my stomach, and tears rise to my eyes. The reality of all this is sinking in. Ben's only option for now is Harrison House, and as much as I will myself to see its advantages, the vision of what "should be" keeps coming to mind. Roommates his own age. Raucous laughter. Frat parties. Guys slapping each other on the back. Pick-up games of basketball in the driveway. Girls dropping by.

Stop it, I tell myself. *Maybe someday. Maybe not*. But for now I have got to hope, while making the best of what's true for the moment. I force the tears back down and remind myself, and Ben, that it's a wonderful thing to have a bed to sleep in, chores to do, a reason to get out of bed. Ben will participate in the community here: he will cook on his assigned nights, attend groups, have company when he goes to AA or NA (Narcotics Anonymous) meetings. He will have a neighborhood. He can ride his bike to the library, to school. He can rent a DVD and watch it on his own TV. He can go to the kitchen and make himself a snack. He can play his video games.

I talk with Cameron while Ben finishes moving in, and I see glimpses already of his dynamic with his new roommate. Ben is trying very hard to be friendly, to win this guy over. Cameron explains that Ted has been used to bullying others into giving in to him. His last roommate, in fact, had always given in to him—brought him drinks from the kitchen, let him watch whatever he wanted on TV. I know my son, though, and Ted is in for a fight. Ben will not be pushed around. He will try to be helpful, but he won't be bullied.

"Well," says Cameron, "then Ted will have to adjust, won't he?" He smiles. "Probably be good for him. Don't worry, they'll work it out. We'll keep an eye on the situation."

Don't worry. Music to my soul, the very thought of it. I'll try. Yes, this will do for now. It will, in fact, be paradise. And then we can keep working on his recovery plan, all of us. This is where, I pray, Ben can get guidance

CHAPTER GUIDEPOSTS

What's the Difference?

Supported housing—Established by state-run programs, someone qualifying for supported housing will live independently in a community facility, either on the open market (such as an apartment), or in a non-profit or cooperative organization. Treatment is not associated with the living place, and there are usually not required group activities. The resident is not restricted as to how long he/she is allowed to stay, which provides stability and a sense of home.

Supportive housing—Cooperatives or group homes in the community. More structured than supported housing. There are generally scheduled group activities, and the management of the facility is in contact with treatment personnel for the residents. (www.schizophrenia.com/housing.html)

and a renewed sense of community. And I can be free, once again, just to be his mother. It's a start, a new start.

Ben comes back downstairs, and I hug him good-bye. "See you soon, sweetie. Have fun."

"Okay, Mom. Bye." Then he turns to Cameron. "Cameron," he says, "is there anything you need me to do for dinner?"

Cameron smiles. "No, that's okay, Ben. It's your first night; we're making something vegetarian for you. Look on the schedule, though—I think your turn to cook is on Wednesday."

"Good," says Ben. "I love to cook."

Yes. This is a step in the right direction. I wave good-bye and go out the door to my car, passing some of the guys who are smoking on the porch. "Bye, Ben's Mom!" says one. He is smiling at me sweetly.

"Bye," I say. "See you soon." It makes me think of the times I dropped Ben off at sleepover parties in second grade. I've said good-bye to Ben many times, but this time he's both far enough away to build independence and close enough in case he really needs me.

17

ORDINARY MIRACLES

When I look back at the years we spent in the dark about what was happening to Ben's brain, I often think of the cycle that always came back to escalating conflict. My home felt like a battlefield; I hated pulling into the driveway for fear of what Ben might be doing when I opened the door, what accusations would come out of his mouth next. It still feels like a gift to realize that Ben and I don't fight anymore. I no longer struggle with feelings of hatred for my own son that rise up, unwanted, like unexpected tears. Perhaps this is because his medication has brought him, at least partially, back to us; perhaps it's due to the fact that I've finally learned how to communicate with him. Maybe it's because I've learned the facts about his illness—especially the fact that it *is* an illness—and I no longer blame Ben for the illogical way he thinks, for his inability to plan realistically for his own future. Or is it because he doesn't live with me, and I don't have to be policeman and doctor and caseworker to him? The answer is yes—all of the above.

This is Ali's nineteenth birthday, and we're celebrating. One year ago, her birthday party was marred by the fact that I'd had to leave an incoherent Ben behind in his apartment. Today, he is with us. We're having a family dinner in a restaurant. No embarrassing moments at all. There is actual conversation. Laughter. Bickering.

"Ben," says his sister, "come on! You always take ten years to decide what you want!"

"Hey, stop bugging me, Al. I just want to be sure, that's all."

"Yeah, but everyone's waiting for you."

"Okay, okay, shut up, birthday girl!"—and he playfully pokes her on the shoulder.

Just like a normal family, I keep thinking. I love this bickering. Anyone watching us would think we were no different from anyone else.

I must remember this day and always know that it can happen. Thank you, whoever invented Clozaril. Thank you, ACT team, Harrison House, Narcotics Anonymous, Bridge House, NAMI. Please let days like this continue to be possible. Is it too much to hope for? Will I jinx this if I get too greedy and want more days like this?

Silly. But the thought is definitely there . . . just a little bit. I push it away and remind myself for the hundredth time to be grateful for the moment. I know all too well how suddenly things can change. The past taught me that lesson well. Now, though, I am happy—so happy—to be here, to seem normal, at this birthday dinner.

RESPECT THE CONSUMER

There's always more to learn about mental illness, always more to understand.

NAMI has other educational programs besides Family-to-Family. One is called Peer-to-Peer, and the concept is similar: it's an educational group experience, taught by a team of people who have been there, who *are* there. This program, however, is not for *relatives* of people with mental illness; it is taught by those who have a diagnosed mental illness and are managing their lives. Its leaders are trained to teach others in the same situation. The curriculum is similar: information, skills, issues about the major mental illnesses, with support and action built into the process. Peers teach others about the importance of taking their meds, taking care of themselves, managing their lives. I hope that someday Ben will be ready to take a Peer-to-Peer course. He's not ready yet, but he is still young. Often, realization and acceptance only come much later in the process. It helps to know that the help is there, when Ben is ready for it.

Another program is called Provider Education, and that's exactly what it is. Though the curriculum is similar to the other two programs, issues related to the providers' side of things are also addressed: confidentiality, case overload, new research findings. Provider Ed is unique in that the team that teaches it is composed not of two leaders, but of five. Five on the team, designed to give the providers a taste of what it feels like from the viewpoint of the people they are trying to help.

The team has two family members, two consumers, and one provider (a social worker, doctor, therapist, etc.) who is also either a consumer or family member. This way, by the end of the course, providers gain new insight into the experience of the person who is challenged by the illness, as well as the experience of family members whose lives have been changed by it. They learn how important it is to listen to the patients and to their families, and to understand the perspective from the other side.

I decide to take the training for Provider Ed as well; maybe I can do something to help change the system that has sometimes saved, sometimes failed my son. The training takes place over three days, in the same retreat where I first took my training for Family-to-Family: a former convent in Connecticut's Litchfield County, secluded in the country but only forty-five minutes from my home by car.

The experience this time is different, for I'm sitting side-by-side not only with people who have seen a loved one changed by mental illness, but also with people who are in the same position as Ben: diagnosed with the illness itself. They are managing their lives, though, and they are my peers.

Throughout the course of the three days, my respect for the consumers in the group grows without limit. I laugh with them. I listen to them. They listen to me. I *like* them.

I see what can happen when such peers come together. They share stories about their hospital stays. They smile at each other when beepers go off to signal "meds time." They compare tips about side effects and how to handle them. Most of all, they form a community for each other. I almost feel left out at our dinner table, when I am the only one without meds to take.

I wish Ben were here to see this, I think more than once. But I also know he isn't ready yet. He would like these people but wouldn't see himself as one of them. *Maybe next year. Maybe some year.*

Most of the consumers in our group are middle-aged; they tell me it took them a long time to accept their illness, and that Ben is still very young. They remind me not to give up hope, and most important, never to give up on Ben.

"He needs you," says Ralph, who has bipolar disorder and is also a husband, father, and Reiki master. "I don't know where I'd be without my family. I know so many people whose parents gave up on them; they're either missing, homeless, or in jail. Or they're dead."

"He's right," adds Liz, who also has bipolar disorder. Liz is a speaker for "In Our Own Voice," a NAMI speakers' program that goes to any group that requests it. It's a one-evening presentation by two consumers in recovery, who tell their stories from the dark days to rehabilitation. Liz is married, too; she met her husband ten years ago in a group residence just like Harrison House. Liz and her husband both manage their illnesses, and they help each other.

This makes me feel better. *Maybe, someday, Ben can still have a relationship, can still be in love, still make a home with someone. He doesn't have to stay where he is forever.*

There's only one young person in our group, a girl about Ben's age. Jessie has borderline personality disorder and has somehow accepted it already. She's been through hospital stays and various trials of medication and finally feels that she's found the right combination. She is still living at home but trying to stay in college at the same time. Jessie is beautiful, hard-working, enthusiastic, and often so tired that she falls asleep during our sessions. She just drops her head down onto the book and dozes. Still, when it's her time to read, she wakes up and knows exactly where we are. It is amazing. How does she do that?

In fact, this group is full of amazing people.

On Saturday night, we all play "Dictionary Fictionary," and the consumers beat the family members, hands down. They are so creative, so bright, so funny. Without the need to hide their illnesses, without the pressure to be something they are not, they are relaxed and inventive. Even though I've come to have empathy for Ben, pride in his courage, and hope for his future, I have not yet been able to feel *equal* with him. Like many parents but more so, I am always on the helping end, and it's hard to see him as a separate human being on a journey of his own.

Here, on this weekend, I relearn that I am no better than he is, no better than anyone else. Just, perhaps, luckier. I rediscover my respect for my son.

One afternoon there is a session during which we share three-to-five-minute versions of our stories, as we will when we go out as a team to teach. I've heard families tell their stories many times by now, but it's not that often I get to hear what it has been like for the consumers. We all listen to each other, and we pass the box of tissues to whoever seems to need it.

Liz leaves the room during the break, and when she comes back she is unusually quiet. Half an hour after we've resumed our session, she raises her hand and asks to speak.

"I just want you all to know where I was during the break," says Liz. "I've been in recovery for over a decade, but I never realized until this afternoon what my *mother* must have gone through while I was getting sick. I just never saw it through her eyes; I was too busy being angry with her. But after hearing you guys today, I got it. I just went to the pay phone to call

---

CHAPTER GUIDEPOSTS

NAMI Peer Education and Support

- NAMI educational programs (Family-to-Family, Peer-to-Peer, NAMI Connection, Hearts and Minds, Provider Ed, and more) provide critical education to help consumers and family members gain knowledge and skills for living successfully with mental illness.
- Support groups are provided through many of NAMI's state and local affiliates and offer invaluable connections with peers who understand the challenges and joys of living with mental illness.

NAMI Raising Awareness and Fighting Stigma

- NAMIWalks is a signature NAMI event that draws thousands of concerned citizens every year who walk together in over sixty communities across the nation to raise money and awareness about mental illness.
- StigmaBusters responds to inaccurate and hurtful language and portrayals of mental illness in the media and promotes understanding and respect for those who live with mental illness.
- In Our Own Voice presents deeply personal and moving journeys of recovery by consumers living with mental illness.

---

my mom and tell her how much I love her, and to thank her. So—thank *you*. Please keep loving your family members. We need you."

Liz sits down. One of our trainers starts the applause. We all join in. We are clapping for Liz, for her mother, for our ill relatives. We are also clapping for ourselves. We're applauding the gifts of time, patience, and the possibility of recovery—recovery from illness and the recovery of family ties.

I pray for Ben. I pray for everyone in that room.

18

THE DRUM CIRCLE

I pick Ben up at Harrison House early one evening in mid-May, 2004. He sits on the bench on the front porch—the official smoking site for the residents. He waits for me, his face alert and alive, his brand-new tribal drum sandwiched between his knees. We are going to do something fun together—it isn't a movie, a meal in the diner, or any of our usual activities. We are going to a drum circle together.

For Ben's twenty-second birthday in April, I bought him something from his wish list: this drum, two lessons, and the promise that we would attend at least one drum circle together. He's doing so well with his recovery that I was able to do this joyous thing, shopping for something frivolous for him. Maybe now he'll pound out rhythms on something besides the dashboard of my car.

Ben made me proud at the lessons. The drum teacher, Barry, is an old friend of mine who knows some of Ben's history. He was patient with Ben, while challenging him to improve. Ben was a quick study. He listened, focused—and he was polite, even charming. I still smile when I remember this. Will I ever take for granted the experiences that are extraordinary simply because they are ordinary?

Tonight we drive to a more rural part of Connecticut and gather in a meeting room with about twenty other people. The mix of ages, ethnicity, dress, and reasons for choosing drums as a passion are numerous and varied. Our group for the night ranges from a crisply dressed family of four with two preteen sons to a seventy-five-year-old woman in jeans and peasant top, her gray hair in a long braid down her back.

Barry leads us through various games and exercises; we all make music. This circle is a new experience for me and is strangely compelling. The drums take over, the rhythms themselves overcoming our self-consciousness. Ben

243

is good at this; it shows in the way he holds himself. His gaze is direct, his hands and brain move quickly. He teases me when he can imitate a rhythm more quickly than I can. I'm actually comfortable enough to compete with him. For once, I don't have to tread lightly around my son. He makes fun of me with a gently teasing smile, and then he helps me get the beats right.

Tonight, Ben is not fragile. Tonight, he is the way I always imagined a son of twenty-two to be: proud of himself. Grown past needing Mom to take care of him. Taking care of Mom, just a little bit.

Then it's time for a break; Ben retreats back into himself, just enough for me to see what an effort it was for him to concentrate so hard. He goes outside for a cigarette and some solitude, then comes back inside, renewed. He shares in the milk, cookies, and conversation.

One more hour of drumming and then we drive home. Conversation is easy. Ben seems happy. I'm praying that there will be more times like these.

In the past few weeks, there *have* been other times like this. We went to see his cousin Jacob in a classical concert at Wesleyan University. Jacob is three months older than Ben and is about to graduate and go on to law school. He's also a brilliant violinist. It's hard not to look at Jacob and think about where Ben might have been had he not had the bad fortune to be hit with schizophrenia. But these are wasted thoughts. *It is what it is,* I tell myself. *Comparisons are both unfair and pointless.* But sometimes I can't help it.

Ben loved that concert and had the good grace to compliment Jacob sincerely and proudly. He went back with us to Jacob's dorm apartment and socialized with the other students. When they asked him where he went to school, Ben said, "I'm going back to school soon. Right now I live in a house with some other guys and I'm doing volunteer work."

Good for you, Ben, I thought. *This can't be easy for you, and you're not wasting any time in envy or resentment. You found a way to describe your life with restraint but also in truth.*

And tonight has given me another taste of reassurance that Ben might have a future beyond his illness. *Enjoy this,* I remind myself. It's the same mantra I always repeated when the kids were babies, anytime I was reminded of the inevitable passage of time. Back then I held on to the things logic told me would end someday: the bear hugs, the sweet kisses, and the complete, trusting weight of a head resting on my shoulder. Today, I hold on to the moments that are evidence that Ben is still here, still capable of having fun, sharing love, building relationships.

For now, I want to trust that Ben will continue to recover. I *choose* to trust that, because it makes me happy. But there may be many more hard

CHAPTER GUIDEPOSTS

Please Keep in Mind:

- Your ill relative is still part of the family.
- Include him or her in all family celebrations if possible.
- Find ways to have fun together.
- Let him or her help with chores and other family tasks.
- Remember that your ill relative may not be able to express love the same way as before, but that he or she can still love.
- Keep your sense of humor as much as you can.
- Be alert for relapse signs, and act as quickly as possible.
- When things are stable, take the time to appreciate those moments.
- Do normal activities, but set and keep limits as to acceptable behavior and be prepared to enforce them.
- Remember that your ill relative may be stressed by excess noise and chaos.
- Family love matters. It matters a lot.

roads ahead. I've heard too many stories from other families struggling with mental illness to think that we are out of the woods forever.

Prepare for the worst, and hope for the best.

Tonight, though, I'm just happy. Happy that we made music together. Happy that no one in the room could tell that Ben is being treated for schizophrenia. It's been a wonderful evening. "Thanks so much, Mom," he says, when I drop him off at his house. "This was so much fun!" I'm extraordinarily grateful that he is still—again—capable of having fun, and with me along for company.

And now it's time for Ben to go inside the group home with his new drum—and take his meds.

COMMUNITY MATTERS

Spirit is wounded so the body is aching
healing's occurring and are you partaking?
For the ups are blooming
Desiring your hands to catch the tears for memory's sake
Shattering the mask fake

Truth meets the eyes hoping for some kind of recognition
And for the masquerade to end.
Bringing forth a new kind of freedom . . . unity.

—from Ben's poem in *Innervisions*, 2004

I've been asked to be the keynote speaker at the Family and Friends open house at Bridge House, where Ben has been thriving for three months. Last year, before his first hospitalization, Ben and I toured this clubhouse, "a psychosocial rehabilitation program for adults recovering from the prolonged effects of psychiatric illness." Back then, he insisted he didn't belong there. "Very nice, Mom," he'd said, "but I don't really need this. I'm not sick like those people. Thanks anyway." Now, though, he has embraced at least part of what its community has to offer.

If the foundation of Ben's recovery curve is his medical treatment, then the structure that rests on that foundation consists of many things: professional staff, Ben's own participation, certainly the love and involvement of his family and friends. But another important aspect is the community he has built around himself. Ben stays clean and sober with the help of meetings of Alcoholics Anonymous and Narcotics Anonymous; he attends meetings nearly every weeknight, by his own choice. He also takes the bus to Bridge House now, at least two days a week. Ben doesn't really want to be considered a part of the group here, since he doesn't agree that he has a mental illness. Still, he goes.

Bridge House is based on the Fountain House model in New York City. It's organized to support individuals living with the effects of mental illness. Daily activities include social, recreational, educational, and cultural events. When they're ready, members are helped with job placement, with returning to school, with learning to live independently. There are opportunities to volunteer within the clubhouse: at the front desk, in the kitchen, in the computer lab. Members are invited to be a part of this "community of people who are working together toward a common goal."

On the days Ben is not attending college classes, he comes here to Bridge House. On most days he helps out in the lunchroom, either cooking, clearing, or running the cash register; however, the staff has other, loftier ideas in mind for him. During his first week, Ben expressed an interest in writing some poetry for their literary collection called *Innervisions*. The staff saw potential in Ben and encouraged him to take on even more; they made him the editor of the spring issue. With this unexpected responsibility came a burst of pride; Ben took on the job with an enthusiasm for helping others that I hadn't seen since high school. He called me at work to ask permission to use the color copier, "because the club members deserve their artwork to be reproduced in color, Mom, don't you think?" Even if my employer hadn't been so generous in allowing us to use the copier, I'd have paid for it out of my own pocket. Seeing Ben want to help someone else, it would have been worth every penny.

With guidance from the Bridge House staff, Ben has produced the best *Innervisions* they've ever seen. Now he's talking about wanting to teach a poetry workshop there, so that more members can contribute poetry for future issues: small verses, like haikus. He wants more people to be represented. These things are signs of the Ben I know, the Ben I remember before his illness began to take over his personality, bit by bit, like untended weeds in the garden of his soul.

It feels like Ben is reemerging from the shadows; every day now he seems to come to life a little more. These positive signs, though, are merely clearings in a forest of symptoms that still linger: sleepiness, lack of clear ambition, inability to focus consistently enough for paid employment, an overinflated self-concept. But clearings they are, and inside them I see enough possibility to keep me going through the setbacks that are also part of this recovery process.

In the past few months, I've accumulated moments to keep in an imaginary treasure box in my heart: the time Ben asked for my help in getting his roommate a birthday present—we settled on gifts from the Dollar Store—and how excited he was to give them "because Ted doesn't have anyone to give him presents." The day he came with me to the library to find workbooks on literacy after he'd discovered another of his housemates couldn't read—Ben had already taught him five letters and wanted to teach him more. The morning he asked my advice about talking with still another housemate—"How can I reach him, Mom? He doesn't seem to listen to me."

Tonight I'll have the chance to share this pride, and hope, with a whole roomful of people at Bridge House who will know exactly how amazing these moments are, how well Ben is doing despite his illness.

The only trouble is that Ben will be in that room, too. This has never happened before. I've just finished teaching my third Family-to-Family series for NAMI, and I was thrilled to share Ben's progress in recovery with that group. They *got* it; they'd been there, might be there, or were there themselves. But now, with Ben present in the room where I will tell these stories, what will I say? He doesn't think he has an illness of any sort.

Now, seated in rows of folding chairs arranged in the snack bar for this occasion, are the friends and families of Bridge House members.

They've had a tour of the building and met the staff, and now it's time for the program to begin. Ben sits in a section off to my right side, reserved for the members and staff.

I look over my notes for my speech. From my chair on the makeshift platform I look out into the audience and spot some familiar faces from NAMI, St. Mary's Hospital, and West Hills Center for Behavioral Health, the private facility where Ben was hospitalized the first four times.

The executive director of Bridge House welcomes everyone, and the program begins. The mayor of Bridgeport says a few words about how happy he is to be there, and then it's my turn to speak. I'm introduced as "Morning Radio Personality Randye Kaye," and I walk to the podium to the sound of applause. The audience only knows me from my work on the radio. They do not know that I'm the mother of one of the Bridge House members.

I steal a glance at Ben and smile at him. He smiles back, but his eyes look unsure. He's afraid I will embarrass him.

A week ago, when I told him about tonight, he said, "But there's nothing *wrong* with me, Mom. You can't stand up there in front of all those people and talk about me like I'm sick." I wanted so much to brag about Ben for a change; I needed desperately to make it all right in his eyes, too. "Ben," I said, "I understand how uncomfortable it would make you feel if I talk about you in a way you think is unfair, or just plain wrong. But I'm so proud of what you've done with *Innervisions.* I want to tell everyone how far you've come in the past year." He finally agreed that it would be okay for me to speak—as long as I left out any reference to mental illness. How could I get the audience to see how far he'd come, though, if they didn't know how far he'd fallen?

I look down at my revised notes. I don't need to; I know the words by heart because they're *in* my heart. "I'm delighted to be here," I begin, "and though most of you know me from hearing my voice coming out of your radio, that is not who I am today. I'm here as a proud mother."

It feels so good to say those words: "proud mother." "One year ago," I continue, "my son Ben was a patient in West Hills. It was the third time he'd been admitted that year. Today, he's living in a home near here, attending college, volunteering here at Bridge House, and is the editor of the beautiful issue of *Innervisions* that you hold in your hands." I hold up my copy of the publication: twenty pages stapled together, with a member's artwork on the front cover—in full color. It is beautiful.

The room bursts into applause—not for me this time, but for Ben. I look over at him; he is beaming.

Now I say the words, carefully rehearsed, that I hope will satisfy Ben as well as myself. "Ben is in recovery. Now, he and I do not agree about what exactly he is recovering *from*, but the fact of the matter is that he's doing so much better than he was a year ago. Ben attributes this to the fact that he is now clean and sober, and has been for over a year."

More applause. I glance again at Ben. He smiles at me and nods.

"What I attribute this to doesn't matter right now. The most important thing that I can tell you is that I am so very proud to stand here before you as Ben's mother. I have felt this before: in elementary school when he got straight As, in my temple when he became a bar mitzvah, watching him receive the Johns Hopkins Award for gifted students. But I can tell you honestly that I have *never* been more proud of my son than I am right now. Because I know what it took for him to get here; I know where he has been, and I think many of you have been there, too."

CHAPTER GUIDEPOSTS

Narcotics Anonymous is an international, community-based association of recovering drug addicts with more than 43,900 weekly meetings in over 127 countries worldwide. Narcotics Anonymous sprang from the Alcoholics Anonymous program of the late 1940s, with meetings first emerging in the Los Angeles area in the early 1950s. The NA program started as a small U.S. movement that has grown into one of the world's oldest and largest organizations of its type (for more information, the website is www.na.org).

Fountain House is a professional self-help program, operated by men and women recovering from mental illness in collaboration with a professional staff. The program was first established in New York City in 1948, and there are now around four hundred centers internationally.

The emphasis at Fountain House is on relationships—member to member, and member to staff. Members engage with each other to regain their productivity and self-confidence, resume their lives, and reenter society. They also take part in promoting their rights, and in erasing the stigma that often separates them from their neighbors.

The innovative clubhouse model is today the basis for more than four hundred similar programs in thirty-two countries around the world, assisting some fifty thousand men and women. The Fountain House concept has been adopted in part by another one thousand programs in the United States and abroad. The original Fountain House is located on 47th Street in New York City (www.wikipedia.com).

Heads are nodding. One woman wipes her eyes. A man grabs his son's hand and squeezes it. I realize how true this is: I have never been more proud. "Ben, would you mind standing up?" I say.

He stands—to cheers—then actually *blushes*. This is one of the moments I will add to my treasure box. I end my speech with the poem that Ben just wrote me for Mother's Day. I can see and feel the impact of his words on the parents in the room. When I get to the last two verses, I find myself choking back unexpected tears. His words almost—*almost*—put the last few years into perspective.

Maybe there was a reason for all this, I think. *Maybe it's over. Maybe at least we've been through the hardest part.*

BEN'S MOTHER'S DAY POEM: MAY 2004

She waits	with cupped hands	to catch your tears	as you cry
She stands	unified	to defend	her smile
She's needed	by her children	who grow	as she watches
She's loved	by those around her	who aim to counteract	pestilence

Her smile can heal any pain
For as it begins the others wane
    She's well fed with the food of life
    Helping others conquer their strife
    And explore their path even when the road is rough
    —as has been mine as she well knows—
That's why me she chose to aid . . . even if I was afraid . . . to bloom

She's atop my mountain as I'm below
She pulls me up to help me grow
I'll let her help for now I know
That often some need help to glow

    And as I shine I think of her
      Being the railing in the stairwell
        To help me help myself up a mountain
          —and I love her for it—

        Thanks . . . Happy Mother's Day Mom,
          Love Ben

19

RELAPSE AND THE ROAD BACK

When mental illness hits your family, there is seldom a happy ending that lasts forever. You may find your way out of the tunnel and glimpse the light, only to have to go back in and find your way out again. You may progress through all the stages of acceptance, only to have to backtrack to the phase of dealing with crisis and trauma. But with any luck, you've left some bread crumbs from the last trip to help you find your way back out again.

This was the golden year. This was the year when I thought Ben might have found his way out of hell. And I guess he did, for a while. But there is, almost always, a relapse. Sometimes, it's because the medication has stopped working; often, it's because the consumer has stopped taking it.

This relapse hit hard because Ben had been doing so well. In this fall semester Ben and Ali were actually in the same college math class. They were enrolled in the same school for the first time since they'd been in the fifth and eighth grades. At first, he was helping her with her homework; he was a big brother again.

This was the year during which Ben participated completely in our family life: the Passover Seder, the birthdays, the holidays, trips to the movies. The year in which we began to make new memories, instead of relying on those from before his illness.

This was the year in which my children called each other on their cell phones, just to chat. This was the year in which they started to find each other again; I was no longer the translator and middleman.

This was the year in which Ben turned twenty-two. At our restaurant celebration, a couple at the next table came over to tell me how charming my son was. Ali's birthday card to him reflected on how much we'd all been through and how "unique" our family is. "Odder than most, smaller than most, better than most," she wrote.

Ben voted in an election that year. He spent a night or two in his old bed at home, managing his own medications and allowing me to supervise. He rode his bicycle one evening to attend Shabbat services at our temple, even though I couldn't be there. He was able to attend performances of every theater show I was in; unlike the years when he was away, in the hospital, or simply too unstable to sit through a play, he was part of the audience, sitting next to his sister. Friends began to call Ben on his new cell phone, and he got invited to spend time with them. His life was starting to—well, to come to life again.

This was the year when Ben became so comfortable at Harrison House that he often was mistaken for a staff member. One time in April, I walked in to find Ben helping to sort out everyone's laundry. "I don't know what we'd do without him," Cameron told me. "People who walk in here don't believe he's a resident. Are you *sure* he has schizophrenia?"

"Oh, yes, I'm sure," I replied. The staff of Harrison House had never seen Ben without benefit of his Clozaril. It was almost funny that they doubted his illness.

But now they are beginning to believe me. It is late fall, the golden year is coming to a close, and Ben's symptoms have resurfaced.

The relapse signs are unmistakable to me: the high-pitched voice, the too-happy attitude, the talk of the book he is writing. Ben has stopped attending classes regularly, and Ali tells me he has begun to act weird in class when he does go.

It is December, and Ben is visiting us at home for the afternoon. His symptoms have returned. He's out in the backyard, singing to himself and moving too slowly. I can hardly believe this. This can't be happening. The numbness sets in again, all too familiar. I am so—well, just so sad. Right now, it's as if this past year never happened. This is like waking up from a lovely dream that I want to recapture by going back to sleep. But I can't. You never can.

I call Ben inside and tell him we need to talk. "Okay, Mom," he says, and we sit on the stairs leading to the basement so we can close the door behind us.

Think, I tell myself. *How am I supposed to handle this?*

I recall the skills I learned and have now taught many times in NAMI's Family-to-Family classes: *"I" language. Reflective responses.* "Ben," I begin, "I'm uncomfortable with the things you're doing today."

"What things, Mom?" His eyes have the faraway, superior look that also spells *relapse* to me. *I hate this. I hate this!*

I take a breath. "I notice you're wandering around the yard like you used to, and some of the things you're saying don't make much sense."

"I'm looking at the trees, Mom. And I can't help it if you don't understand what I'm saying. It makes sense to me."

Stop being crazy! I want to scream. *Stop this behavior! Come back to normal!*

Reflective responses, "I" language . . . "Ben, I know that you're having a good time today. However, I get scared when you start to do the same things you used to do right before you went into the hospital."

"But I'm not responsible for your feelings, Mom."

Years ago I would have tried to talk sense into him, to prove that I'm right. Now I know better. "You can't reason with mental illness," NAMI reminds us.

It is a fight I would never, never win.

"I know that, Ben. Nevertheless, I'm uncomfortable with the way you're behaving and I'm going to take you home now. I will have you come back another time."

"Oh. Okay." That's all he says.

Something is wrong. So wrong. There's only one possible explanation. "Ben, are you taking all your meds?" I ask.

"Of course, Mom! I would never wean myself off meds without having a plan to do so. I know it's dangerous to stop all at once."

And that's how I know for sure that Ben is, somehow, not taking his medication. Two tip-offs: first, when Ben says things like "a plan to do so," that overly proper grammar almost always signals that he has entered a "superiority" state of mind; second, he is simply protesting way too much. He has implemented his own plan; I feel it in my bones.

"Okay, Ben," I say. "Let's go back to your house, then." I say these words calmly, as I've been taught, but it is with the numb calm I remember from the times in the past when Ben was close to needing to be hospitalized. It's a tone of voice usually reserved for medical patients; a clinical distance that cushions me in my disappointment and fear. *Not again. Please, not again.*

I take him home to Harrison House and alert the staff. "Something's up," I tell them.

"Are you sure?" they answer. They've never seen Ben's full symptoms; they don't know the relapse signals the same way I do.

"I *wish* I were not sure," I say. "But I am. Make sure you watch him when he takes his meds. Please."

Since being placed at Harrison House, Ben has left the care of the ACT team that placed him here; he is assigned to a team for higher-functioning patients. He has seen his new caseworker only sporadically, his new psychiatrist even less frequently. I call and alert them, too; I get the same response: "Are you sure?"

Yes. I am sure. One week later Ben's symptoms get worse. His blood tests show levels of his meds that are no longer therapeutic. We find out that, somehow, he was only taking his meds every other day—a self-imposed weaning. Ben finally admits the truth. "It was just so I could see if I need them anymore."

This is common; many patients try it. I know this; I hate this. It is *dangerous*. The providers say, "We're so sorry we didn't believe you." More supervision is implemented. Now they make Ben sit in the office for an hour after meds, to make sure he doesn't spit them out or throw them up. He swings back to better functionality again, for a while. We've narrowly averted another hospitalization—for now.

And, fortunately, Ben's symptoms subside and he returns to what is now deemed normal for him. I've accepted that this is nowhere near what "normal" was before his illness, but I'll gratefully take it.

Now, though, a new factor enters the picture: Ben's compliance—or, what is the latest term?—his "concordance"—is now in question. He's back to thinking that his meds are not necessary—not even just to keep him out of the hospital, not even just "because those are the rules to stay in Harrison House."

It's a fact of recovery that sometimes there is relapse. Sometimes it happens because the prescribed medications just stop working as efficiently; perhaps there needs to be an adjustment in dosage or in the combination of medications. Sometimes it happens because of stress; Ben had a very hard time staying stable, for instance, after the sudden death of one of the staff members of Harrison House.

Often, though, the relapse happens because the ill person stops taking his or her meds. There are many reasons for this, and many ways to accomplish it. If you live alone, you simply stop; if you live in a supervised situation, you may pretend to take them by hiding them in your cheeks or slipping them into a pocket, taking only some of the pills. Then there's the technique of forced vomiting after medication time, a kind of "medication bulimia." However it happens, the reduction of dosage without doctor's approval is almost always an experiment that fails. Relapse can land patients back in the hospital in record time. Providers and families must always be on the alert for signs of impending relapse and reverse the situation as soon as possible.

Ben will take a huge step toward managing his own illness when he finally takes ownership of it. This is the most difficult leap to make. If it was hard for me and my family to accept the fact of Ben's illness, just imagine how difficult is must be for Ben to accept it. Schizophrenia probably seems like a life sentence to him—to constant medication and its side effects, to being different from all of his peers.

I think of the story of Helen Keller in *The Miracle Worker*, how she behaved herself so well with her teacher Annie in the little cottage they shared for a few weeks. Helen learned to fold napkins, eat with a fork, and behave in a civilized manner. She learned to sign, even in her sleep. But she still didn't get it. She hadn't had the "Aha!" moment that would serve as the bridge from pleasing Annie to really wanting the knowledge that was waiting for her and to understanding why it would change her life. That moment happened at the water pump, when Helen got the connection. "Water." The long-forgotten sound of the word. Words. Other words. Signing. Meaning. Connection. That was when her new life really began.

For Ben, that "Aha!" moment will make all the difference. All the people I know who are recovering from schizophrenia to the point where they can manage their illness without supervision, hold jobs, socialize, live on their own—they all can recall when they "got it." I think Ben is starting to get it; he is still very young, especially since he is still somewhat "frozen in time."

The golden year ends with this disappointing glitch, but I try to remind myself that it was also full of so much improvement. Maybe we got lucky; maybe we got smart and caught the problem before it could get out of hand. *Maybe*, I pray, *this won't happen again.*

This near-miss is a painful reminder that Ben isn't really out of the woods, no matter how well he's been doing. Perhaps he never will be, no matter how much I want it to happen. The scars heal, but they heal thicker each time. It takes a bigger shock to get through to me. But it can still hurt like hell. This illness isn't going away; it will always hover, like a vulture, over his life.

CHAPTER GUIDEPOSTS

Some Reasons for Medication Noncompliance

- Lack of insight into illness (biological—the brain is impaired).
- They believe they don't need it anymore ("I feel fine now").
- They think they never needed it.
- They don't like side effects (weight gain, sexual performance, sedated feeling).
- "If I don't take meds, then I'm not sick" (wish not to be ill).
- Power play between caregiver and ill person.
- Complicated regimen—having to be home to take medication.
- Forgetfulness.
- Fear of becoming medication-dependent.
- Feeling different from everyone else.

What You Can Do

- Watch for signs of relapse, return of symptoms.
- Call doctor, request evaluation.
- Call caregivers, if applicable, and alert them.
- Be aware of any increased stress in relative's life, and reduce if possible.
- Know your limits and what you'll do if they are not met.
- Increase supervision of medications if you can.

An *"I" statement* is a very specific, direct statement that begins with the word *I*. It is frequently used in an attempt to be assertive without putting the listener on the defensive. It can be used to take ownership for your own feelings and actions instead of blaming them on the other person.

Reflective responses acknowledge and show empathy for the other person's feelings. What he or she experiences is real to that person, even when a mental illness is present. It can be helpful to reflect back to the speaker what you heard or what you imagine that person might be feeling, so the speaker feels heard and understood. This step establishes some empathy in the communication, so the person is not put immediately on the defensive.

HOSPITALIZATION NUMBER SIX

Still, here we are again: hospitalization number six. I hate this. I never wanted to see Ben this way again, ever. It has been more than eighteen months since he was last admitted on the night of the blackout. He will go to the psych floor as soon as a bed opens up; right now, though, he's still in the ER, in a small room with two other men who were also admitted overnight. Each is on his own small cot. Each man talks to himself. They do not talk to each other.

Since the incident in December when we caught Ben cheeking his meds, things have never been as consistently good as they were last year. Ben's behavior has been erratic, the dosages he has kept in his system uncertain. He tried another semester in college, and was writing beautiful, coherent pieces in English Composition on his good days. In fact, he was getting an A in the course so far. His final project involved interviewing me about the day he was born, and finding a newspaper from that day in order to discover a parallel he could draw from the two sources. He was almost finished with this project.

Earlier in the month, though, he slipped back into odd behaviors; he missed some classes and assignments. I went to talk with his professor, who told me that he thought Ben was "a wonderful, creative writer who just needed some more self-discipline to reach his full potential." He had no idea that Ben suffered from mental illness.

But yesterday, Cameron called me from Harrison House. Ben's behavior had been so odd that morning that they'd begged him not to go to school. "It would be social suicide, Ben," they'd told him. "Your friends will not want to see the way you're acting." They couldn't stop him. "Nah, thanks, I'm fine," Ben had responded, in the high-pitched voice that signaled something was most definitely not fine.

By that night, Ben was back in the hospital. He'd been discovered on someone's porch, singing. It's still unclear why he was there. All I know is that the homeowner got scared, called the police, and Ben was brought into the ER for evaluation. They found his home address in his wallet and called us at home late last night. Ali answered the phone. "It's the hospital. Ben's there." She handed the phone to me and walked out of the room.

"We think your son might have taken LSD," the admitting nurse said. "He's hallucinating."

I imagined what Ben might be saying, might be doing. It could easily be mistaken for a bad acid trip, I supposed. "No," I said. "If you test him, you'll find he's clean. He has schizophrenia and has been off his meds." I've said that so many times now, it rolls right out of my mouth.

"Oh, that explains it then," she replied. Later tests confirmed this: there were no illegal drugs in Ben's system. But there were also very low levels of the medications he *does* need to function in this world.

By the time I see Ben in the morning, he is still waiting to be admitted. Thanks to an anti-anxiety drug administered the night before, he slept all night on the ER cot. He needed it.

This drug, Ativan, is also a disinhibitor, I find out. When I walk in today, Ben is babbling to himself quite a bit. "Mom!" he calls out, when he sees me. "Hi!" His joy at seeing me is so genuine, so open, that I almost forget why he's here. I return his huge bear hug, and sit down next to him. Then I see that his eyes are *too* animated, almost wild. He doesn't look dull anymore. Everything about him seems exaggerated. Everything is just too *big*.

This is sometimes one of the reasons that people in Ben's situation stop taking their meds. At first, it feels *great*; they get the energy back that has been clouded by the feeling of sedation that comes along with what the rest of us see as sanity. The only problem is that the euphoria doesn't remain in one place; it doesn't take long before it builds into mania, psychosis, and—usually—hospitalization.

There's a place I go to in my mind when Ben is like this. I don't do it consciously—it's like a primal reaction, a safe zone. It's a place of self-preservation. When I slip into this mode, I find myself treating Ben again as if he were my patient, not my flesh and blood. I am calm. I am inquisitive. I am numb.

I ask Ben why he was found on a stranger's porch last night. "I just went to the wrong address, Mom," he answers. I ask him again, ten minutes later. This time he says that he thought he had found Rachel's house. I still don't know if this "Rachel" is real or imagined; he won't say any more than this.

There's not much I can do for Ben until a bed opens up; I've also run out of conversation. I ask him if he'd like some food to eat from the cafeteria.

"Yeah, Mom, that'd be *awesome*!" he says.

Okay. This much I can do. I can mother him, at least, in this way. And off I go. I need the break from looking at him. I need to breathe.

When I come back with my tray of bagels, cream cheese, and orange juice, Ben is sitting on his cot next to another tray: the hospital has distributed a lunch of chicken and mashed potatoes. Ben has not eaten any meat or poultry for five years, but now he hungrily eyes the chicken. "That smells good!" he says.

"Do you want some?" I ask; I want to see what he does. Ben hesitates, looks at the plate. "No, thanks," he says. "But I'll have some of the potatoes." And then he starts to eat the mashed potatoes—with his fingers.

I cannot believe this. He has *never* done this. I lock the door of my emotional safety zone. *I cannot panic. I am not allowed to panic.* "No, honey," I say. "Not with your fingers." I gently take the plate from Ben, wipe his fingers with a napkin, and give him the meal I've brought from the cafeteria instead.

"Wow, a bagel! Thanks, Mom. You're the best."

He eats. We wait. He sleeps. I wait. Ben wakes up; he looks disoriented.

I look at my son, sleep crusting around his eyes, curly brown hair slipping out of his ponytail. I look right into his eyes. *Maybe, if I look at him—really look at him—I can make contact. Maybe I can get through. Maybe there are no words, but maybe he can feel my love. Maybe he'll know.*

I look at Ben, locking my gaze as long as I can. He looks into my eyes, too; I think, maybe, that we are making a connection. He hasn't looked away. But then—he starts to cry. Not just cry. He starts to sob. Big heaving sobs that distort his face and shake his shoulders. I have not seen Ben cry in at least two years. Schizophrenia has robbed him of big emotions.

Ben holds out his arms to me. "Mommy . . ." he says.

I rush in beside him. I hold him. I soothe him, I pat his back. I hold him tight, I let him go. He cannot stop crying.

Is this a good thing? Is this a breakthrough? Does this mean Ben is feeling things again?

"I made a mistake. I made a mistake," he keeps saying. I don't know what to do. I don't know how to help him, except to hold him.

"Ben," I say, "what mistake did you make?"

"I went to the wrong house," he says, and the sobs begin again. I'm holding a big, man-sized version of my six-year-old son.

After fifteen minutes of this, I have to walk out of the room so that Ben can stop crying. My presence has become a trigger now. My hugs make him cry even more. This hurts.

A few hours later, we are taken upstairs to the psych unit. By now it is late afternoon. I am unbelievably tired, physically and emotionally. I've been up since 3:30 a.m., and my child is falling apart again, moment by moment.

I stay for the intake procedure, the usual questions, the usual requests. Now that Ben's sobbing has stopped, he has returned to an emotion that surfaces when his schizophrenia is unchecked: suspicion. He answers questions, but by now he knows exactly what they want to hear.

The nurse sits across from Ben, with the hospital laptop computer. This system is new, and she has to type in his answers. The process is very, very slow. She asks Ben this question: "Do you ever see things that aren't really there?"

Do you ever see things that aren't really there? How is he supposed to answer that?

I can't stand it. "Excuse me," I say. "Have you ever—even *once*—ever had anyone say *yes* to that question?"

She thinks. "Not really," she says.

Later that day, after Ben is settled and asleep, I try to clean up the mess his psychotic break has left behind. I visit his English professor and tell him that Ben is in the hospital, that his final project may be late. I recover

CHAPTER GUIDEPOSTS

Fear of Success in Mental Illness

People with schizophrenia feel enormous anxiety and insecurity; even though they cannot express emotions, they still feel pain inside. They long for connection, but closeness of any kind feels threatening. . . . Above all, they are wary of risk . . . they greatly fear encounters that might expose the devastated self to the world.*

What You Can Do

Don't criticize. . . . If there is one single standard to work for in your relationship with an individual with a brain disorder, it is to respect, and protect, their shattered self-esteem.

Ask your ill family member what they feel they are ready to do. Plan for progress in small steps that have a better chance for success. Make short-term plans and goals and be prepared for changes in directions, and retreats.†

*NAMI Family-to-Family Education Program, class 7.
†NAMI Family-to-Family Education Program, class 7 handout, "Empathetic Guidelines."

the backpack Ben abandoned in the college cafeteria before heading to the porch where the police picked him up. I wonder what he did, what he said, in school that day; I wonder if the other students will ever accept him again, or if his reputation is forever tarnished. I do whatever damage control I can. After all, I'm still his mother.

ONLY FIVE DAYS TO RELAPSE

Three months after Ben's relapse, it now seems like a mere blip in the recovery process, a glitch in the proceedings. His April hospital stay lasted only fifteen days; Ben was stabilized on medication and released. Since then, he managed to salvage his English Composition course, completing the work he'd abandoned along with his meds. Ben's final essay was less spectacular than the early ones—in fact, it rambled—but he wound up with a B in the class and earned another three college credits.

Once again, he has returned to us, like a photograph emerging from the blank Polaroid pictures of my childhood. That always seemed like magic to me. So, sometimes, does this: Ben comes back to us.

I think back to the day—a little more than a year ago—when I spoke at Bridge House about Ben's recovery. I remember calling Dr. Taylor, Ben's former psychiatrist, to invite him to the ceremony. I told him how well Ben was doing on the Clozaril. It was truly miraculous to me, how the symptoms that I'd seen just months ago had stopped entirely—the twitching, the muttering, the scattered sentences. I wanted Dr. Taylor to hear some good news about Ben, especially since he'd been the one to prescribe Clozaril in the first place.

"I'm so glad you called me," he said. "I'm thrilled for Ben. It's not often I get to hear happy news; thanks for letting me know." Dr. Taylor sounded more casual and friendly on the phone than I'd ever heard him sound before; perhaps this was because Ben was no longer his patient, no longer his responsibility.

I supplied more details about where Ben was living, what we were trying to do for his future. I described the plan we had in mind for Ben's recovery: gradual steps toward progress, with adequate psychological and practical support as Ben became ready.

"That's the right plan," said Dr. Taylor. "I'm really glad to hear it. One word of advice though—off the record." He went on to tell me a story of a patient he knew, without revealing her identity. This woman had done so well on Clozaril that she'd progressed to the point where she was accepting her illness, monitoring her own meds, living in her own apartment, and had held a full-time job for three years.

"Wow," I said. That sounded wonderful. That was what I wanted for Ben; that's where the plan was headed, however long it took. Was it possible that Ben's future could look like that?

"Unfortunately," Dr. Taylor continued, "this all ended when she decided, on her own, to see if she could do it *without* the medication. She didn't tell anyone what she was going to do. She didn't wean herself off gradually; she just stopped taking it."

I'd seen what could happen when Ben refused to take medication in the past, especially if he'd stopped taking it all at once, instead of gradually reducing his dosage. It can be dangerous to both mental and physical health. This time, though, seemed different. For the first time since his diagnosis of schizophrenia, Ben really seemed so much better. *Surely, the longer he stays in treatment, the better his life gets, he'll begin to see that the plan is working. Surely he won't abruptly stop taking his meds.* "So what happened to her?" I asked.

CHAPTER GUIDEPOSTS

Life Course of the Illness

Ten years after developing schizophrenia:

- 25 percent recover completely, usually within the first two years
- 25 percent are much improved; usually they have responded well to medication and continue taking it; they can live independently, have a social life, maybe work part-time or full-time
- 25 percent are modestly improved and respond less well to medication; can lead satisfactory lives with extensive support network
- 15 percent unimproved
- 10 percent deceased, mostly by suicide or accident

Thirty years after the illness begins, the outlook is even better.*

*E. Fuller Torrey, *Surviving Schizophrenia: A Manual for Families, Consumers, and Providers* (New York: HarperCollins, 2001), 130.

"In five days, she was back in the hospital. Five days. And she's having a heck of a time trying to build her life back up to where it was, even though she's back on the medication. Sometimes, it doesn't work as well the second time."

My God. All that work—all that progress—shot down in less than a week? Dr. Taylor continued, "So—let's do everything we can to make sure Ben stays on those meds. It's so important."

I hated this reality check; I'd wanted to imagine that Ben could still be cured. I wanted the doctor to believe it somehow, too. But I knew he'd told me the truth, no matter how much it ruined my fantasy.

POOL PARTY

Ben has now been a resident of Harrison House for eighteen months; for the second year, we've invited his housemates to our home for a pool and pizza party. It's one way for me to give something back to the people who watch over my son on a daily basis. Only five of the current seven residents can make it this year: one has a meeting with his caseworker, the other is back in the hospital for a week. One staff member, Frank, has come along to supervise. I like Frank; he is a former CEO who left the corporate world at the age of forty-three to go back to school for a degree in social work; he now has a much smaller income, he says, but a happier heart.

Ben is a proud host, happy to share his home with the guys. He jumps in the pool right away with Julio, the newest resident of Harrison House. Julio has a history of bipolar disorder and alcoholism; at the age of forty, though, he is finally able to accept his situation and works diligently at his recovery. He and Ben get along well, and I hope that some of Julio's realizations will inspire Ben to see his own situation more clearly. Ernest, a childlike black man in his thirties, has been in Harrison House for two years; he's recovering from depression and drug addiction, but I suspect that he may have other mental challenges as well. I like Ernest; he's always cheerful and sweet. Last week Ben invited him here to try the pool out before the party; Ernest doesn't know how to swim, but that day he bravely allowed my boyfriend Geoff to teach him a few things. Today he stays in the shallow end of the pool, practicing his floating; every five minutes he calls to me the way my children used to when they were young. "Ben's Mom!" he says. "Watch this!"

Henry, an overweight middle-aged man whose face always seems locked in the same neutral expression, is tired; he immediately falls asleep

---

CHAPTER GUIDEPOSTS

Humor can help.

The people I have seen who were the most successful in coping with schizophrenia were those who had retained a sense of perspective and an appreciation of the absurd.

What do I mean by a sense of perspective? I certainly do not mean laughing at a person with this disease. Rather, it is laughing with them. For example, one family in which the son relapsed each autumn . . . had a standing family joke that the son always carved his pumpkins in the hospital.

—E. Fuller Torrey, MD*

———————

*Torrey, *Surviving Schizophrenia*, 322.

---

on a patio chair, his head tilted back against the pillow, and stays that way until the pizza arrives. The fifth guest, Howard, stays under the canopy next to the pool and just watches everyone else. He doesn't say a word; he seldom does. "Howard doesn't like to swim," Ben explains. Howard seems content to sit there in the shade, watching. At least I *think* he's content; it's difficult to tell because his expression, too, doesn't change.

Ben and Ernest decide to have a race—four laps. He looks toward Howard and shouts, "Hey, Howard, we're gonna have a race. Wanna start us off? You just have to count."

Howard speaks for the first time. "Okay, Ben," he says. "One, two three, go!" When the race is over, Ben motions me over to the side of the pool. "I just wanted Howard to feel included, Mom," he whispers.

Later that day, after the guys have all gone home, Geoff calls to ask me how it went.

"Well," I say, "it went fine, but I'm glad it's over." I struggle for the right words to describe this odd party. "It was kind of like a cross between being a Cub Scout den mother and *One Flew over the Cuckoo's Nest*."

Geoff laughs. So do I. Sometimes you've just got to.

20

YOU CAN'T REASON WITH
MENTAL ILLNESS

The lesson I had to learn, over and over again, is one that NAMI teaches frequently: *you can't reason with mental illness.* I wasted many hours trying to find the right words, the right logic, that would reach Ben somehow, turn him back into the person he used to be. It doesn't work. You can't do it. When you are talking to a person deep into symptoms, you're talking more to his illness than to the person underneath it. All you can do is cope, do what must be done, and wait.

Ben has had another relapse; this one lasted much longer than the one in April. While hoping for things to get better for your child, it helps to remember to be grateful for how good things are. And be prepared—they can also get worse. If they do, know that you can climb back out of the hole again—but it isn't easy. It never is. As before, the progress is slow and uncertain. Put one foot in front of the other. Don't look back. Keep your focus, and your belief, on the hope that you'll all come out of this again—somehow. Don't give up.

I'm waiting, for what is now the seventh time, for Ben's discharge paperwork to be completed so I can escort him out of the psych unit and back into the outside world. After so many of Ben's hospitalizations, I still feel like the whole experience is unreal. I know what to do now—stay in touch with the doctors and nurses; visit often but know when to leave; petition for a court hearing if Ben refuses medication; offer to be a part of case management meetings. I'm an old hand at this. It's just that part of me thought we'd never have to go through it again.

What caused Ben to go off his medication this time? True, he'd never quite returned to the same level he'd reached during the "golden year"; still, he was making some progress again, however shaky, in the months following his last relapse. Was he afraid of failure? Is that why he didn't go back to school? Or—was he afraid of success? Was he afraid that, once the world saw that he could accomplish things, we'd expect even more? Or did he suddenly look at those accomplishments—so meaningful to us—and hold them up to the mirror of where he once thought he'd be at the age of twenty-two? With so many of his old friends graduating from college, going off to graduate school, paying rent, planning marriages, did he suddenly ask himself, "What's the point?" Was it easier to let the haze of schizophrenia cloud his thoughts again, so he could live in the world where his delusions felt like a better life?

Any of these answers might be true—*all* of them might be true. The important thing now is that Ben is, at last, stabilized once again on Clozaril; it has, however, been a much longer road to get him here than last time. Underneath it all was a new fear: will the medication work again, after the relapse? And if it doesn't—are there any other options left? I already know the answer to that last question: right now, Clozaril is the only option for recovery for Ben. We've tried all the others.

I recall moments along this latest road through relapse and recovery. The first one occurred in a therapy session. Ben had been transferred to a different case management team after his last relapse, one that was more geared toward young adults. This treatment plan was more hands-on than the one before, and it included family therapy for all three of us.

That morning, we talked about what the past year had been like for all of us. Ali shared how much she misses the relationship she used to have with Ben. *This is good,* I thought. *She's starting to open up to Ben. He's never heard her talk about this.*

Then I heard the sounds of sobbing; to my surprise, they weren't coming from Ali. Ben was crying. I hadn't seen him do this since his last hospital admittance, and that had probably been due mostly to the letdown effect of Ativan. This time, there was no drug I could blame for his tears.

"You don't understand how it feels," Ben cried. "I try to be *good*. I try to be *nice* to everybody. I do what they tell me to. And I just hate my life."

"Ben, honey," I said.

"No, Mom, you don't know. You don't know what it's like to be segregated from your own family, to feel unwelcome. You don't know how much it hurts." He gasped for air. This was not the child I'd thought would open up.

My long-buried guilt came rushing back. *The sad part is—he's right. I had no idea that he was still aware enough, still emotional enough, to be hurt by the way his life has turned out so far. Because, bottom line—this wasn't his choice. To*

*be sick, to be limited, to live in this supervised housing situation, to have to take the
bus instead of a car—none of it was his choice. Ben's right. This sucks.*

But I couldn't change any of it. I had no answers left except to encourage Ben to stay on his meds and build his life back up, one baby step
at a time. Baby steps are so hard when you want to run.

Three weeks later, Ben completely unraveled. He'd been creatively
avoiding his meds all this time, but not always with success because of
careful supervision. Otherwise the fall would have happened much more
quickly.

This later family therapy session brought new symptoms of relapse.
Ben struggled to stay focused. His attention was moving quickly from me
to his therapist MaryAnn to writing on slips of paper from his pocket. He
acted happier than usual, responding quickly—too quickly. His tears a
few weeks ago had been a sure early sign of trouble; this energy surge was
another.

The ironic thing about this energetic Ben was that, for a brief window
of opportunity, I could see the child he had been before schizophrenia
changed our world. The fog over his soul was lifted; the light was back
in his eyes. His face held more expression; the facial muscles no longer
seemed weighted down with apathy. I glimpsed the man Ben could be, if
not for this hated illness. I wished that this stage could last, that somehow
his relapse pattern could freeze here, with Ben *alive* but not yet delusional.
I could live with this. But experience had taught me the truth: in this window, Ben would get to be bright and charming, but he would only be able
to hold that pretense up for so long. The next phase, the slide into delusion,
was waiting in the wings.

Ben said, "I kind of like my meds. They make me feel happy. They're
not so bad."

Whenever he says he likes his meds, it's another clue that he is not
taking them.

Ben stepped out for a cigarette. MaryAnn and I agreed that his excess
energy was indeed a warning sign: he could be nearing another hospitalization if this kept up. I half-hoped for a hospital stay and half-hoped that Ben
would keep his meds down tonight and be better tomorrow.

I left the office and went downstairs to the main entrance where Ben
usually waited for me; he wasn't there. Frantic thoughts tiptoed through
my head: *he ran away, he was mugged, he's hiding from me.* But as I approached
my car, I saw Ben there—clearly having a conversation with someone who
was invisible to me. Ben talked, waited for a response, talked again, nodded
his head, gestured with his arms. Then he spotted me, shouted an overly

jovial "Hi, Mom," and stopped talking. There was no one else anywhere near the car. We got in.

It was an awkward ride back; between our attempts at conversation, Ben sang—too loudly—along with the radio. I dropped him off at Harrison House and told the staff what was happening. With any luck and with careful supervision, he'd be better tomorrow.

The next time I saw Ben was forty-eight hours later in the hospital. He had sneaked out of Harrison House before it was time for his medication that evening and had been missing for forty hours. He had wandered through two towns, in an increasingly confused state. He'd been spotted by the police and managed to hide from them. I'd been turned down by the "Crisis Management Team" when I called to beg for help; budget cuts had forced them to offer help only between the hours of 8 a.m. and 8 p.m. Evidently, it was necessary to time your crisis for daytime hours.

Missing for forty hours. I called every local police department in the area; I called security at the malls, in case he had gone there. Ben had no money. He was not dressed for the cold. He was becoming more confused, I was sure, with each hour that went by. I ran down the list of frightening scenarios for any parent with a missing child—*car accident, kidnapping, robbery victim?*—and the additional ones of a relative of someone with mental illness. *Did he walk into the ocean with his heavy backpack on and not walk out? Is he going for a hike in the middle of the highway? Did he hitch a ride out-of-state?*

Ben was finally found in an all-night CVS, desperate for some food. Because he had no money, he opened a bag of chips inside the store and began to eat them. The clerk called the police, who arrived to find Ben sitting in the aisle, still munching, and dazed enough to cooperate fully while they placed him gently in the back of the squad car and called me. Ben sat there placidly while I worked the phones from home, trying to obtain an order for his involuntary commitment. Finally, an on-call state psychiatrist returned my call, and we got the order. Ben was finally transported to City Hospital, riding in the back of the squad car. No charges were filed, due to Ben's confused state.

The hospital stay, this time, lasted forty-five days. Ben at first refused medication; then he wanted to try some other prescriptions, none of which had any effect. His assigned psychiatrists went along with Ben's wishes; it took a long time for them to discover for themselves what I could have told them—and did—on my first visit. But since Ben was safe and supervised, they reasoned that it might be the best time to experiment again, if only to prove to Ben that Clozaril was his best option.

Visiting Ben was especially difficult this time; it reminded me too much of his first hospital stay, back when all of this pain was new, raw, shocking. After seven times down the same hospital road, I'd built up an immunity of sorts, comprised of all the scars and calluses of my past shocks, disappointments, and frustrations. But I'd hoped with all my heart never to see Ben wandering the hall in circles again, talking out loud to no one, twitching and agitated. But there he was again; it was as if the past two years of recovery hadn't happened at all. *That fast.*

Often, I had company this time when I visited Ben. Sometimes Ali came with me; more frequently it was Geoff, my boyfriend for over a year. Geoff was trying to understand Ben's illness, trying to piece together the stories I'd told him, the episodes he'd missed. Seeing Ben this way was harder for him in a way, because he'd never seen Ben's symptoms before.

Geoff lives logically—he works with computer systems for a living—and he racked his brain to find a way to get through to Ben. He tried to formulate some sensible plan to get him to agree to stay on the meds. I knew Geoff meant well, that he really wanted to find a logical solution, a way to get Ben out of his messy cycle. But the problem is this: the solution may be logical, but mental illness is not.

I'd thought I'd faced most of my fears already, that I was jaded now. But two new fears haunted me. The first was that, even if Ben finally gave in and took Clozaril again, it might not work as well this time. That has been known to happen. The second came up unexpectedly during a hearing to grant me the right to medicate Ben even if he didn't agree to treatment. If I wasn't granted that right, and Ben continued to refuse medication, where would he go? Where would they send him?

When Ben's first fifteen days in the hospital were up this time—his discharge date, by law, unless we took some legal steps to keep him there—he still refused to go back on Clozaril. Ben was in no shape to be discharged. I knew what to do because I'd done it before; I'd done this *all* before. We arranged for a court hearing, as I had during hospitalization

---

CHAPTER GUIDEPOSTS

In most states, the Right to Involuntary Commitment and Right to Medicate last only as long as the hospital stay during which you secured those rights.

number one, to apply for Right to Involuntary Commitment and Right to Medicate; as required by law, Ben stayed in the hospital until the hearing date. We'd bought time, once again.

Yes, I had been here before.

IT COULD ALWAYS BE WORSE

Ben is still in the hospital but has now been back on Clozaril for ten days. This was not easily accomplished, and during the process we were introduced to a new low: the possibility that Ben might have to be transferred out of the hospital and into a nursing home, the only option for long-term care.

The court hearing was held in November, and the judge agreed that we could require Ben to take medication; unfortunately, that decree did not include the right to choose *which* medication he had to take. Ben didn't fight the proceedings this time, but he also would not agree to take Clozaril. "I like the other medications much better," he said.

True, the medication Ben had agreed to take caused no side effects. Unfortunately, neither did it have *any* effect—any effect at all. No wonder he liked it. Ben shook hands all around—the judge, the two independent psychiatrists, his case manager—and left the room. He seemed remarkably unruffled by the fact that he wasn't being discharged from the hospital, that he would have to stay longer.

What is worse, I wondered, *to be in the hospital for the seventh time, or to be so used to it that you no longer mind it? When hospitalization becomes part of the norm of your life?*

"So," I said to the professionals in the room, "what's next?"

"Well," replied independent psychiatrist number one, "clearly Ben is not functional enough to be discharged yet."

No kidding. Sigh of relief from me. "Okay, so how do we get him better?"

"Well," said psychiatrist number two. "If Ben is this ill and refuses to take the medications that work, we'll probably have to transfer him to a different facility where he can be cared for."

A different facility? I knew exactly what that meant in Connecticut. There are few, if any, long-term-care facilities here for people with mental illness; "a different facility" would mean a nursing home. *And if that happens, Ben will be lost—maybe forever.*

In a nursing home, he'd be behind safe walls, but no longer under the auspices of the Mental Health Department. He'd be under the care of the Department of Public Health. Not specialized enough, by far.

I'd read stories in the newspapers about such cases. Patients who don't belong in nursing homes, who need the expertise of mental health workers, are assigned to staff without that training—and the chance of recovery goes down the tubes. Such patients are kept alive, maybe, but they are not kept in hope.

I had not been *here* before. And that's why I started to cry again. My strength, it seemed, extended only as far as the things I'd already gotten used to.

I thought I was immune to this. Emergency rooms. Seventy-two-hour holds. Hospital stays. My son in a police car, an ambulance, in handcuffs. The norm keeps changing, the deeper I get. But this? This I am not prepared for. I'm not prepared to abandon possibility.

A picture of Ben wandering forever in some nursing home, no treatment plan in place to get him out, worked its way into my mind. I forced it out; I wiped my eyes.

"Doctor," I said, "you can try whatever meds you'd like to try with Ben. I predict that none except Clozaril will work, but go ahead and try if that's all he'll let you do. Maybe, just maybe, we'll get lucky and we'll find something else that works. But I will *not* have my son transferred to a nursing home. *I will not.*"

The Chief of Psychiatry called me a few days later to tell me that Ben had decided, on his own, to go back on Clozaril. Ben called me later that day to announce the "good news" about his decision. We're still not sure what changed Ben's mind; perhaps he overheard the plan to stabilize him on the dreaded Haldol as an alternative, or maybe he just needed to feel like he was calling some shots himself. When Ben was a little boy, he always needed to feel in control of his own choices; whenever I'd suggest something, he'd say "I'll think about it," wait just long enough for it to seem like it was *his* idea, and then agree. Perhaps this was the same little boy, now grown, hanging on for dear life to the few decisions he felt he still could control. Maybe he just needed to wait long enough for it to seem like it was his idea to go back on Clozaril.

But I don't care why Ben is cooperating; I'm just so relieved that he is. I didn't have to go to court to force him to change medication, and now I can hope again. In the past few days, I've seen some good signs. During today's visit, Geoff and I notice that Ben is holding a conversation for a bit longer and responding at a more normal rate. It's still an obvious and major effort for Ben to be social, but he tries.

Ben is also a little bit sad; the one friend he had made on the unit this time has just been released. Ben is walking the halls alone once more. I tell the doctor that I think, beyond the huge amount of time it may take for the meds to take effect, that Ben is still a young man who has lost his best friend on the unit, and who is bored. How many times can you walk around the same circular hallway, even if you have a constant conversation going with your voices?

To my great relief, the doctor is open to my suggestion that Ben be allowed to earn the right to go outside for a few minutes each day—yes, even to smoke a cigarette. He needs hope; he needs to see some forward motion. I also suggest he be allowed to "help" the nurses as he recovers, because that often brings out the best in him. This is a good conversation with Ben's doctor; I thank him for listening to me. I'm so grateful that he sees Ben as a person. This seems so rare.

Fourteen days later, Ben is discharged once more. He has responded well to Clozaril, but has a long climb back up ahead of him. I'm happy for Ben. I hope he will try. I hope he will listen. I hope he will let someone help him. I hope, above all, that he has learned a lesson—I hope he stays on the meds. They might not work so well the next time they have to be reintroduced; in fact, we're still not entirely sure how completely they'll take effect this time. We'll just have to wait and see.

So here we are: discharge day number seven. The papers have been signed, the plan is in place. Ben will return to Harrison House and attend an outpatient program for young adults for a few weeks as well. My son comes out to the front desk to greet me, the possessions that have defined his world for forty-five days contained in the plastic bag he carries. He hugs me, shakes hands with the staff at the front desk, and says, "Ready to go, Mom?" One young nurse turns to me with a smile. She says, "Wow, I never realized how much Ben looks like you." The other nurses look at us and agree with her.

"Thanks," I say. "I hear that a lot, but I'm surprised that you're just mentioning it now for the first time."

"I never noticed it before," she replies. "But now that Ben has *expressions* on his face again, I can see it."

I look at Ben; yes, there is some light returning to his face. Some. Ben is coming back, slowly; I don't know how far back he'll come, but at least he's on his way. He won't have to be transferred to a nursing home, lost to us forever. I'll take it.

The nurse presses the security button that will allow the unit door to unlock. Ben holds it open for me, switching the plastic bag to his other arm. We go together, back out into the real world; I hope, once again, that this is the last time Ben has to make this transition. *Let him stay in the outside world, please. Let him build his life, however long it takes.* I pray that he doesn't have to go backward, back to the emergency room, ever again. I don't care if the steps he takes are baby steps—just as long as they go forward, at least most of the time.

21

LOVE, THE POSITIVE "SECOND HIT"

I often think about the "second hit" theory: that the *tendency* toward schizophrenia and similar illnesses may be present in the brain from birth, just waiting to erupt, like a time bomb, at some later date—for males, usually sometime around the late teens or early twenties. The bomb may need something to light its fuse, something to trigger the illness. This can come in the form of stress or a life event, or perhaps even a virus or other physiological change. They call this trigger the second hit. In Ben's case, it's possible that his second hit occurred when William disappeared, leaving Ben with the stress of growing up without a father. Or maybe Ben reacted to a drug in high school, or contracted some virus, subtle but potent to his brain.

We'll never fully know why Ben was unlucky enough to develop schizophrenia. But I do believe this, with all my heart: love can be a "second hit," too—a positive one. Without love, I don't know where Ben would be. Without his *own* loving nature, I don't know what forms his delusions might have taken; without the love and support of his family, I don't know where his illness would have led him. To the streets, among the homeless? To prison? To a nursing home, permanently? So many of the mentally ill are found in these places. I know this much: if my love can keep Ben safe, can prevent him from homelessness and hopelessness, then he will be all right. I will always do everything in my power to keep fighting for him.

We sit across from each other at Captain's Pizza, my son and I. His curly dark hair is pulled back into its customary ponytail, but it appears to have been freshly washed. His clothes, too, are clean—and it's nice to see him in something other than the two outfits he lived in for two months in the hospital. He has been out for two days.

275

We order food, and Ben asks the waitress for some paper so we can play Hangman while we're waiting. For thirty minutes or more, we have an actual conversation. There are no empty pauses. Ben tells me that he took the bus to the mall yesterday to replace his PlayStation 2, which evidently had been stolen from his room while he was away. He even saved money by buying a refurbished model—making sure there was a warranty, yet. This from the person who, ten days ago, could barely keep track of the beginning of a sentence once you got to the end.

Ben asks me what I plan to do about my job hunt; I have left the radio station and am planning my next career move. He actually listens and responds to my answer. The waitress notices nothing out of the ordinary. In fact she may even think Ben charming; he is, certainly, polite and sweet. Nothing to distinguish us from any other mother and son in the place. Such joy, again, in being ordinary.

I feel a knot unravel slightly in my stomach. A feeling of fullness rises through my abdomen toward my heart; this has nothing to do with food. I think it is composed of hope, but also a resistance to it—if you hope, you can be disappointed. But I choose hope, and I focus on gratitude. I have this visit from my child. He is not gone for good.

After we eat, Ben goes outside to smoke a cigarette. I pay the bill and look out the window before going out the door myself. Ben is out there smoking—and also muttering to himself and twitching. *How exhausting is must have been for him to refrain from his self-talk for so long*, I realize. The miracle remains, however, that he evidently was able to distinguish the appropriateness of when and where to give in to his inner world.

And the greatest gift of all is this: he made the distinction and acted on it. I think Ben did this for me. Along with all the medications, programs, advocacy, therapy, there is always, underneath, the tremendous need for love . . . and the power of it. Not enough by itself, perhaps, but this one ingredient can make all the difference. Love is the second hit that can continuously relight the fuse to recovery.

If I can't yet get a glimpse of my child's future, then I will settle for a glimpse of the past. The fantasies I had of the man he would grow to be, based on the child he was, may never come true. But his future, redefined by this illness, is still also directed by the person he was and is. He's still in there, under his symptoms: the loving, sweet nature and the quick, insightful mind. It is also shaped by the people in his life: his providers, his friends, and—mostly, I believe—his family. Our love is still powerful, our support still essential.

Then there are the things that keep me going when Ben takes a few steps backward: acceptance, hope, and gratitude. As long as Ben is alive and hopefully stable, then there's a chance that he can have a better future. Someone, somewhere, may invent a treatment that will help him still more. Until then, we are ever hopeful, ever vigilant, in awe of the power of love.

And, now, we see what tomorrow brings. I know that wherever Ben is today, halfway back from the dark places, it's still a far cry from the days when I was trying desperately to somehow force him back to normal, when I had no idea what was happening or how frightening the next symptoms could be.

22

NO SECRETS: FIGHTING STIGMA

Four more months have gone by since Ben's second relapse. He is, again, back on Clozaril, and it's working. *Thank God.* There was a chance it might not take a third time. I have no idea what we would have done if that were the case. In about a week, he'll be twenty-four years old, and we can celebrate his birthday, with the family, out in a restaurant if we want to. I am, again, so grateful.

Ben and I spent the afternoon shopping and hanging out. We've been to the shoe store, the bagel shop, and the neighborhood supermarket—and in every single place, he was appropriate and friendly. I cringed when he took off his socks at the shoe store; his dirty toenails embarrassed me but not him. I let it go: *pick your battles.* His being out of the hospital, almost normal again, was more important. Always that see-saw of comparison to balance the situation: if he could be so much worse, he could be so much better. *He used to be . . .* Those are the thoughts I make myself push away. They are of no use to me now.

This, then, has been a great day. Ben joked with me. We laughed. He helped me put the groceries away. We cooked together—a big pot of vegetarian chili. He listened to directions, but he also added his own creative spin to the spices. We baked cookies. It was an ordinary afternoon. But to me, the miracle this time is enhanced by the fear that preceded it: the fear that the Clozaril might not be so effective after this last relapse.

It's still taking time; we have to be patient. Some days are better than others; some times of the day are better than others. Tonight, Ben has come to see me and Geoff in a variety show at our temple to raise money for a charity. He is falling back into some symptoms because it's late and he's tired. We're seated with some people who haven't seen Ben since his bar mitzvah more than ten years ago; I can see them warily glancing Ben's way whenever he talks a little too loudly or twitches. Four months back on the Clozaril is no guarantee of consistency, or even that he'll ever go back to where he'd been before his relapse, but he's still doing very well—in my eyes. The others at the table don't see what I see.

When Ben leaves the table for a moment, this is what I tell them: "I know you haven't seen Ben for a few years, so I want you to know what's going on. Ben has developed a disability, and you might see a few strange things that he can't help right now. You might see him twitch—kind of like Tourette's—or he may mutter under his breath. Don't worry. He's completely harmless, he's still Ben, and he's really happy to be here and to see you all." I do not say the word *schizophrenia*. If anyone asks, I will. But this is good enough. They get it.

I can see my friends relax, and looks of empathy cross some of their faces. "Don't worry," one of them says to me, "we'll watch out for him. Go on backstage; he'll be fine." Fear and uncertainty have turned to sympathy and support. If I hadn't been honest, if I hadn't brought the subject up, this would not have happened.

Sympathy is hard to come by when your child has a mental illness. Understanding usually has to come along with it, and mental illness is only just starting to be spoken about in an honest way. Some celebrities in recovery from mood disorders—such as depression and bipolar disorder—are starting to speak out, which helps. But schizophrenia, a thought disorder, seems to be the last holdout.

If Ben were in a wheelchair, he'd have a similar problem; misconceptions and lack of acceptance of anyone who is different extend everywhere in the world of disability. If he'd been born with a mental challenge, such as Down syndrome, there would be a different set of preconceptions. Our situation would be different, of course—my family would never have had the chance to know Ben without this condition, so maybe we wouldn't focus on what we'd lost. Then again, we'd never have had those years with Ben when he was well. No matter how useless it is to compare one emotional pain to another, we do it sometimes anyway. In the case of mental illness, though, comparison with other possible scenarios—and any parent can tell you that the real or imagined dangers in raising children are numerous—consistently brings up one painful consistency: where there is mental illness, there is a special brand of stigma.

If Ben's life had been changed physically when he was in his teens—if he'd been hurt in an accident or diagnosed with cancer—we'd have gone through many of the same stages of recovery, from denial, through anger and bargaining, to eventual acceptance. We might, however, have been spared the unwelcome presence of stigma. Throughout Ben's illness and recovery, we've also faced blame, judgment, misconceptions, and preconceptions. Some of the stigma has come from within our family—some of it, before I learned better, came from inside of me.

Mental illness remains a shameful secret within many families, and for good reason. The media still portray mental illness only in its most dramatic form. I seldom read about someone who is living with schizophrenia, bravely winding his way through the complicated path to a more normal life. The news that gets attention comes from the small percentage of the mentally ill who become suicidal or violent when their delusions take control. Where is the story about my friend Bill, who after twelve hospitalizations went on to obtain a certificate in human services and now coaches others with mental illness to get their lives together? Where are the stories of the dozens of consumers who volunteer their time to share their experiences in NAMI's In Our Own Voice presentations, or teach others in Peer-to-Peer, the consumer version of Family-to-Family?

Ben has a disability; this is the truth. His future will most probably be different because of it. When people who don't know about his schizophrenia—people I've just met, or friends I haven't seen in a long time—ask me what he's been doing, this is how I explain it, as a disability that has made his life path a little different from the norm. This would be true no matter what kind of disability he had, physical or mental. I don't offer any more information than this, unless they ask me more questions; I do this not to hide the truth but to wait for the invitation of their interest. At some point, though, I know that the sympathy in their expression may quite possibly turn cold. If they are not educated about mental illness, they may take refuge in the familiar stance: they try to place blame. I see it in their eyes sometimes; they think, *This could never have happened to my child.* I know this because I used to think the same thing, before I knew better. Mental illness doesn't choose its victims; it randomly strikes the unlucky, even though genetics does sometimes skew the odds.

It is what it is.

I do everything in my power to help my child, to love my child, to remain, as Ben once wrote in his Mother's Day poem, "the railing in his stairwell." But I no longer blame myself for his illness as I once did; nor, more importantly, do I blame Ben. I know that in trying to place blame, I attempt to locate a hint of control over the uncontrollable. The only thing I wish I could have changed was the ability—the knowledge—to recognize what was happening to Ben sooner than I did. I wish, too, that the "experts" had been able to do the same, that treatment could have begun earlier.

But it didn't. And now—yes—it is what it is. The reality of our family life now includes the presence of the judgment of others, the ones who don't know better simply because they've never had to learn about it. I envy them.

I remember once, before recovery, before Ben's first hospitalization but after we'd finally named his illness, when I reached out to close relatives for help. Even though I knew that Ben had schizophrenia, I still hoped that a united family front could help keep his unpredictably severe mood swings under control. I asked for support in an intervention of sorts, for someone to back me up in a confrontation with Ben. I wanted someone else, someone close to us, to say to him, "You can't talk to your mother like that!"

One relative had said yes right away when I called. "What can we do, where, and when? Of course we'll support you."

Inspired and reassured, I then called another relative. The answer came reluctantly but clearly: "I'm sorry, we really can't get involved. We have to protect our own family, and I don't think it's a good idea for Ben to perceive us as on your side."

I could not believe what I was hearing. "Why?" I said.

"It could be dangerous."

Dangerous? "How can you say that?" I said. "You don't even really know Ben anymore. You haven't spent any real time with him."

"Look," he said. "I don't know how to say this except to say it. Ben has been so strange over the past few years, and it's been going on for a long time. That's why we've had to choose not to see him a lot. I'm so sorry to have to say this, but it's the truth."

"But I'm only asking you to sit with me and *talk* to him! Like a family intervention," I said.

"Yeah, but who knows what can happen? What if he shows up at our door, months from now, with an ax or something? What if he decides to be mad at us for siding with you? I'm really sorry, but I have to protect my family. We can't help you. Good luck."

I hung up the phone, in shock. That was my first taste of the fear that surrounds mental illness, especially when the facts are not clear. Certainly, there was fear for me: fear that Ben wouldn't succeed, that he'd never have the kind of life he'd always wanted. Of course, there was loss and sadness, already. But was he an ax murderer? Was he about to send a bomb to someone in the mail?

No. No, he isn't. No matter what, that just isn't in his nature. He fights with words, with ideas, with desperation, with arguments. But not with weapons—never with weapons. Don't they know that?

And then I started to get angry. Really angry. At the injustice. At the ignorance. And at another loss. I mourned the loss of my fantasy of family togetherness, of shining white family knights coming to my rescue. I wasn't at all sure it would have worked, anyway. Even with the right timing, the right words, the right support. It had been a nice dream, that's all, another straw to grasp at while the haystack fell apart.

Eventually I worked my way through the anger and loss and landed at forgiveness. I called my relative and, using carefully rehearsed words, told him and his wife that I understood that they had done what they thought was best for their family. "I think you have some misconceptions about schizophrenia, though," I said, "and if you ever want to learn the facts I'll be glad to share them with you or give you some information. Meanwhile, I've already had enough loss. I don't want to lose you, too. I love you." But I knew I would never turn to them for help again.

It's not entirely their fault; old misconceptions die hard. I still have to stop myself, when I pass someone on the street who is shabbily dressed, filthy, and muttering loudly, from thinking the old thoughts: *Why don't you get some help? Come on, get a job!* I know better than this, but the thoughts still pop up before I can stop them. It's hard not to judge people who have mental illnesses. In truth, it can be hard to even *like* them sometimes. Physical illness steals from your body but leaves your mind intact; mental illness does the opposite. Although, technically, it *is* a physical illness—a disease of an organ called the brain—it can be hard to feel kindly toward a loved one who's irrational, moody, unpredictable, or lost in his own world. It often seems as if the mental illness has stolen the very soul of someone you love. It makes you wonder where that person has gone, if you'll even see that person again.

Acceptance is one of the final stages of recovery for family members and also for the person who has the illness. Often, family members reach that stage first; that's how it is for me and for Ali. Ben has his own road to follow that will, hopefully, lead him to acceptance someday; sometimes I see signs that he is beginning to accept his illness and also that he's scared to believe it. When he finally gets there, that realization will spur him on to take responsibility for his own life; it will help him manage his illness without the constant supervision he now requires.

That day will be easier to reach if the stigma of having a mental illness is eased. The more people speak out, learn, teach, and accept, the easier it will be to tell the truth. When Ben can say to a new friend, "Remind me to take my meds at nine," when he can excuse himself from a noisy room because the stimulation is too high for him to focus, when he can tell an

---

CHAPTER GUIDEPOSTS

Myth: The Mentally Ill Are Violent

People with a mental illness are generally not violent—nor are they psychotic killers, as the media frequently portrays them. There is no higher incidence of violence among people with mental illness than among the population in general. This common myth has done a great disservice to people suffering from schizophrenia, most of whom are very withdrawn and quiet.*

---

*Rebecca Woolis, *When Someone You Love Has a Mental Illness: A Handbook for Family, Friends, and Caregivers* (New York: Tarcher, 1992), 22.

---

employer why he was in the hospital without causing fear in his workplace, then we will have gotten somewhere. And so will Ben. This—I repeat—is not his fault. And it is manageable. The more understanding there is, the easier it will be for Ben to accept what has happened to him. He won't tell me this, but I know—I *know*—how terrified he is to be different, to lose friends, to not be considered for a job, to walk in the door at college that says "Disability Services." People just don't get it. So they are afraid—and Ben is afraid to accept it, too.

Until then, all we have to work with is our own acceptance, which is easier to maintain when things are going well with Ben. When they are not, I have my mantra: *it is what it is*. Wherever reality is, at that moment, is the starting point for the next thing you have to do.

Underlying all these formal attempts to spread the word about mental illness, to chip away at the stigma born of a plethora of misinformation, is a constant mission for me: to help Ben be accepted in this world, to have a place in it, *as he is*. That is why I wrote this book: not just to share my story with families who may be experiencing a similar situation, but for the ones who are not.

LIGHTEN UP:
HUMOR, THE ULTIMATE ACCEPTANCE

I sit in the audience at the Long Wharf Theatre in New Haven, Connecticut, watching the MOTH Festival. This is a storytelling event; the man at the microphone balances himself on his crutches as he speaks. He has cerebral palsy; neither clear speech nor standing for long periods of time is easy for him. He speaks of his school years, of the stigma associated with not only his misunderstood disability, but also of the pain of hiding the fact that he is gay. And we, the audience, are laughing with him. We are laughing together at his story; we are unified by his humor. His disability no longer feels like a separation, because he has found the humor and is sharing it with us.

Months later, I sit next to Nellie at a NAMI educational conference. Nellie has bipolar disorder; she has her medications all lined up next to her plate of French fries so she'll remember to take them right after lunch. She is not the only one at our table with a display of meds beside her. Several of us are talking about how to reach the general public with positive messages about mental illness. Nellie says, "If I could say one thing to the world, it would be this." We all turn to look at her. "I would say," she continues, "*lighten up*. I'm not dead, for God's sake. It's not the end of the world."

One of the most effective tools for acceptance, surprisingly enough, is humor. A sense of humor is the ultimate sign of acceptance. When you can laugh about something—not *at* something—you've come a long way toward accepting it. Many of the participants in Family-to-Family are shocked the first time they're able to laugh about the pain they've gone through, but it almost always happens. In community, there is healing— and part of that healing is laughter.

I once attended, in 2001, a meeting of Schizophrenics Anonymous. This group is based on principles similar to the twelve steps of Alcoholics Anonymous. After a lengthy conversation with Charlie, the founder of the local chapter, I was granted permission by the group to sit in. The week I went, there were about seven or eight people attending, in various stages of recovery. They asked me to share my perspective as the mother of someone with schizophrenia, and they spoke of their own paths toward recovery.

Afterward, we all went out for pizza—because, as Charlie told me with a smile, "We need to practice socializing, you know." They got the joke. "Besides, the pizza's only two dollars a slice," said Bill, another group member. I loved these people. They even joked about their *past*. They shared a genuine laugh over things they had once believed about themselves: that they had "known everything," that they were meant to be elected president. This was the first time I had ever heard these stories told with any humor inside the tragedy. It felt like the ultimate acceptance, being able to laugh with each other about it. They had found community, and they had found laughter.

Humor can also serve to make outsiders more comfortable about what has happened to Ben, to our family. During Ben's last hospital stay, he often slipped into psychosis when he was refusing his medication. During one of these periods, I took refuge at the front desk as Ben paced around the hall for the fifth time in ten minutes. One nurse told me something I'd heard before, at other hospitals: that Ben, even without medication, was still a nice guy. She said, "You know, your son is probably the *nicest* psychotic person we've ever come across." To my surprise, that made me laugh out loud—right through the pain of seeing Ben in the state he was in. Once I started laughing, the other nurses joined me. That exchange gave me some kind of hope along with the unexpected laughter. I felt, at that moment, that Ben was not lost. He was still here; he was still somehow human again.

Today, whenever I tell that story, I always get a laugh; more importantly, however, I see the listener visibly relax. When I can find my sense of humor, if I use words that are less self-pitying to describe what has happened to Ben and how things are, then the air between us becomes warmer, the listener more receptive. The walls come down with the use of humor, if it's based in truth. It's true that, when Ben is lost in delusion, it's hard for him to tune in to what I'm saying because "there's a whole entertainment center going on in his head that's much more interesting that his mother"; it's true that hosting a pool party for Harrison House is like a cross between being a Cub Scout den mother and stepping into *One Flew over the Cuckoo's Nest*. If I find solace in finding the humor, maybe that's just my way of finding acceptance within my own heart. But there's a bonus: it seems to make others more accepting, too.

Sometimes, I can even joke with Ben about his behavior. Once, in our local Starbucks, I caught him in self-talk when he thought no one was looking. When I gently reminded him that he'd agreed to keep these behaviors for times when no one could see him, he said, "Okay, Mom." But then he playfully poked me and added, "Hey, it could be worse. I could have been *shouting* inside Starbucks. At least I have *some* self-control!" and we laughed. Together, we laughed. It's progress.

As with all humor, though, timing is everything. Both of you have to be ready, and sometimes you have to dig deep to find it. Grief has to be absorbed first, and that takes time. I certainly wasn't ready to laugh when I was lost in the confusion of counting hospital stays, unsure what new symptoms would appear, wondering if Ben would ever—*ever*—begin to get better. It's hard to laugh while you're stuck on the ride that won't stop.

But, when you're ready, humor can make you feel like you've been welcomed back into the world. And, somehow, being able to laugh brings strength, hope, and understanding.

23

NEVER GIVE UP HOPE

It's time for the curtain call at the end of a play reading in a professional theater workshop in Norwalk, Connecticut. I take my place in line for bows—and so does Ben. He spent the day with us in rehearsal, writing down directions and altering his performance accordingly; he hit every cue in performance. No one in the audience has any idea that he has schizophrenia. They also can never know what a feat of focus it has been for Ben to remain alert and present for so many hours on end. The next day, he will sleep until late in the afternoon from the physical exhaustion of the mental effort. But right now, he is flushed with happiness. He did it. My heart is huge with love and pride.

Ben has stayed out of the hospital now for over five years. He has been at Harrison House for six years, and he has been clean and sober for even longer than that. He avoided going back to college after his relapse; I think he'd been embarrassed by it, though I learned not to ask why. I just waited until he was ready to return. And he is now back in school, taking six credits at a time, and he has made the dean's list every semester. That, I never thought I'd see again.

It took many months after Ben's seventh hospitalization for the muttering under his breath to stop, and I feared it might never go away. Ben still doesn't agree—at least out loud—that the medication helps him, but he has said that it "seems to keep him out of the hospital." Baby steps. We've not been free of ups and downs, or of Ben's wish to not have to take medication at all, but—still—so far, so good.

The Clozaril still seems to be healing Ben—or, rather, the fact that he hasn't had a psychotic break in a few years, because of the medication, may actually be helping his brain cells to heal from the damage his episodes caused.

I work, gently, at freeing Ben from the idea that he takes medication "only to please you, Mom." It's hard to say what I know I must— "Don't take it to please *me*, Ben. If I weren't here, would you stop taking it?"—because I'm still so afraid that he'll see that as permission to stop and that he'll wind up back in the hospital. And yet, if he always gives me the responsibility for his recovery, he'll never fully participate in it himself. It's a delicate balance.

That attempt at balance is always present. *How much do I help him? How much do I let go?* That is parenting, mental illness or not. And it's damn hard.

Someday, Ben would like to graduate to a more independent living situation. He attends group and does his chores at Harrison House, and he especially loves when it's his turn to cook. He asks me to find vegetarian recipes for him. When Ben is ready, he can move on to a place with less supervision—after one or two years on the waiting list.. But he isn't ready yet; I suspect that part of him has become quite used to his life, just the way it is. And we still have to factor in the fact that Ben may not be retaining the full dosage of his medications. When he slips, someone has to catch him.

It's our new normal.

Every time Ben has another hospitalization, I am told, his baseline changes.

A baseline is the level of functioning that providers aim for in treating someone with mental illness. It changes with each episode that requires hospitalization—and it's usually lower each time. The goal is to try to keep the consumer at the level of functioning he or she attained in order to be released.

Twelve years ago, when Ben's symptoms began, that baseline might have included the ability to succeed in school, to go on to college.

Ten years ago, when he was in programs for teens who need help, the baseline might have included the ability to get and keep a job, the ability to return to college part-time.

Six years ago, after the psychotic breaks that maybe—just maybe— could have been prevented if Ben had been accurately diagnosed earlier, it might have meant he could learn to budget his money, teach others to write poetry, go on vacation with his family, rebuild friendships.

After his two relapses, we reduced our hopes: maybe he could manage volunteer work, remember doctors' appointments, go out in public, and keep his response to "inner stimuli" under control while others are in the room.

So the fact that he was in the wedding party at his sister's wedding in the fall of 2010, as well as best man at my wedding to Geoff the previous August, is memorizing a monologue for his college play, drove me around to work after I had hip surgery, and is working with a job coach to practice interview skills—well, it's amazing.

If you met Ben today, you would find him pleasant, sweet, and intelligent. You might think he lacks maturity for someone his age—but you might also think he's just a free thinker, or typical of any twenty-eight-year-old who is trying to find his own way in the world. After all, how are you to know that his brain was asleep or busy with other matters, during so many of the years when he should have been having the experiences that would have cemented his maturity: graduating from high school, dating, having relationships, working summer jobs? How could you know that he was "frozen in time" by the onset years of his illness, that he's struggling now to, slowly, catch up?

You might notice, too, that he's a little bit—well, *distant*. His face used to be more alive, but how would you know that? You'd see eyes that are, perhaps, a bit dulled; you'd see a smile that is, sometimes, slow to form. On his good days, you might find him, at worst, lacking in animation.

If it's not one of his best days, though, you might also notice that every once in a while, Ben needs to step aside and be alone. If you follow him, you might see him twitch a little bit. He may mumble quietly to himself. But then he comes back and acts normally. Sometimes he's just really tired and needs to sleep all afternoon.

If that happens, the thing is: so what? On these days, every so often Ben has to retreat to his inner world, especially if the stimulation around him is overwhelming. You and I can turn down the volume on some of the things we want to tune out. Ben, most of the time, cannot—or it takes so much effort that he needs a break. But the minute you engage him, he'll come right back to you. Ben needs you.

Lately, the good days far outnumber the ones where these symptoms appear.

In fact, I'm happy to say that I haven't seen one of those bad days for months. Still, what goes around might very well come around again. I can never relax, never say we're out of the woods for good. And so if you see Ben twitching—or anyone with schizophrenia doing something similar—know that there's a person in there.

Is this enough? Hardly—but it will have to be enough for now. For, if Ben can get *here*, maybe he can go on from here. In the meantime, we all—his family, his team of providers, his friends—want to keep him alive and keep him from another episode if we can. There's evidence that every psychotic break can cause brain damage, measurable loss of brain cells. I will do everything in my power to prevent this from happening again.

Of course, there isn't that much in my power. If I could secretly lace his cigarettes with just the right amount of Clozaril . . . if there were an injectable, long-acting form of it . . . if there were a better medication . . . if research would find a better way . . . until then, I will do whatever I can. I will love him with all my heart; his sister loves him with all her heart. His stepfather Geoff and new brother-in-law, Marc, who never knew Ben in earlier days, have grown to love him too—and accept him for who he is, inside and out. And we will never, never give up hope.

This is what I want you to know. Ben has changed, yes—but he's still here, and he's still valuable. *His life has value.* He has love, kindness, talent, dreams, ability, humor, and a need for love and acceptance. He needs friends; he needs family. He needs community, and he needs to be included in this world. If he needs to take medication twice a day, and that medication makes him need twelve hours of sleep at night, he is still capable for the other twelve hours in that day. When Ben is taking his meds, he can react. And learn. And grow.

But the medication is just the foundation of his recovery. Consistency is the key—consistency in taking the medication, and in its effectiveness alone. But there is so much more to recovery. Ben comes alive when he spends time with his friends, the ones who still accept him the way he is, even if Ben himself can't fully accept it yet. He also comes to life when he helps someone else, or when he arrives at his agency "practice job" and feels useful. He's at his best when involved in real-life activities: a movie, Thanksgiving dinner, basketball in the driveway, watching Shakespeare in the Park, going bowling with his cousins. He needs what we all need: friends, family, activity, and purpose. He needs love.

My dreams for Ben are smaller now. Some have come true: we've been able to include Ben in family vacations again; all five of us actually boarded a plane this year for my nephew's wedding in the Midwest. Two years ago I could not have risked that—Ben's mumblings might have frightened someone, and he might have been escorted off the flight. But this year it went off without a hitch. Ben gets up every day with purpose: either school or an AA meeting or volunteer work. I hope someday he can work part-time and can drive his own car once again, have the dignity of earning his own money. Perhaps he might take the NAMI training to become a Peer-to-Peer facilitator; maybe he will tell his story to others who will benefit from hearing it. I've seen others with schizophrenia get there— I know others who take their success all the way to earning a doctorate. I've also seen the ones who seem lost forever—wandering the streets, trapped in prisons, barely functioning in nursing homes. Ben may be one of the lucky ones. If I have anything to do with it, he will be.

Ben is in there; Ben is *here*. He is my son, and he has people who love him. He's a person—a person with a past and, God willing, a future. He has potential. See him.

There's so much in him that is worth knowing. So much courage, courage he doesn't even know he has.

I am proud to be his mother.

After six decades of progress, mental disorders remain unacceptably common, causing more disability in people under age 45 than any other class of non-communicable medical illness.

—National Institute of Mental Health

Severe mental illness research funding at the National Institutes of Health (NIH) lags significantly behind that of other chronic illnesses, despite the burden posed by these brain disorders and the existing research opportunities.

—NAMI Policy Research Institute,
"Roadmap to Recovery and Cure," February 2004

The End

RESOURCES

AN IMPORTANT ACKNOWLEDGMENT

Almost everything I learned about Ben's illness was, at the very least, sparked by my experience with NAMI's Family-to-Family Education Program. This free twelve-week class gave me the basic—and often painful—facts about schizophrenia and its effects, and then inspired me to act on what I learned and to learn more. I am proud to have taught this program more than a dozen times and to have trained others to do so. To Dr. Joyce Burland and all who have volunteered to help others by teaching Family-to-Family—bravo, and thank you.

If you love someone with a mental illness, I cannot urge you strongly enough to learn about NAMI, become a member, and clear your schedule for the next twelve-week Family-to-Family course offered in your area. The life you save may be your family's. Without NAMI, Ben's story—and that of my entire family—might have been entirely different. We had to learn the truth of his illness to know how to help ourselves—and Ben.

Beyond NAMI, keep learning all you can. It will empower you to keep going, hang on to hope, accept reality, empathize with your loved one, and handle the inevitable setbacks.

SOME OF MY FAVORITE BOOKS, AND WHY

There are many excellent books besides these (and some awful ones). This list should give you a start.

Adamec, Christine. *How to Live with a Mentally Ill Person: A Handbook of Day-to-Day Strategies* (New York: Wiley, 1996). This book is exactly what the subtitle says it is—it is full of practical suggestions, from how to recognize symptoms to what to do to plan for your relative's future; very empowering and positive in tone, while extremely realistic.

Amador, Xavier. *I Am Not Sick, I Don't Need Help! How to Help Someone with Mental Illness Accept Treatment*, 10th Anniversary Edition (Peconic, NY: Vida Press, 2007). Amador is a psychologist and also a sibling whose older brother suffers from schizophrenia. Want to understand why your relative denies his illness? Want a plan to deal with medication noncompliance? This is a great book that combines science and personal experience.

Earley, Pete. *Crazy: A Father's Search through America's Mental Health Madness* (New York: Putnam, 2006). Earley looks at his son's schizophrenia and the system of mental health care in the United States through the eyes of an investigative reporter; why psychiatrists sometimes can't help, the problem with confidentiality laws and "patient's rights," the history of deinstitutionalization.

Moorman, Margaret. *My Sister's Keeper* (New York: Norton, 1992). The sibling point of view is shown from the author's own experience.

Schiller, Lori, and Amanda Bennett. *The Quiet Room: A Journey out of the Torment of Madness* (New York: Warner Books, 1994). This story is told from many points of view—patient, family members, and doctors—in alternating voices. Schiller spent many years in hospitals and was treated with Clozaril when it was finally approved; scenes from this book still both haunt and inspire me.

Steele, Ken, and Claire Berman. *The Day the Voices Stopped: A Memoir of Madness and Hope* (New York: Basic Books, 2001). Steele's insider view of schizophrenia, truthfully told; it includes his pain about his family's rejection of him, and it helped me to vow to never abandon Ben. Steele later devoted his life to helping others stay on track in recovery.

Temes, Roberta. *Getting Your Life Back Together When You Have Schizophrenia* (Oakland, CA: New Harbinger, 2002). Simple guidelines and facts for the person who has been diagnosed and is ready to help take charge of his or her own recovery; the facts about schizophrenia are explained simply and it is written in a very conversational style. It includes a helpful chapter for family members as well.

Torrey, E. Fuller. *Surviving Schizophrenia: A Manual for Families, Consumers, and Providers* (New York: HarperCollins, 2001). Everything you ever wanted to know about schizophrenia—and some things you never knew you needed to know—but didn't know where to ask; also includes a great list of best and worst books ever written about schizophrenia, plus websites and other resources.

Wager, Pamela Spiro, and Carolyn S. Spiro. *Divided Minds: Twin Sisters and Their Journey through Schizophrenia* (New York: St. Martin's Press, 2005). Identical twins each write the story from unique points of view: the "well" twin, who is now a psychiatrist, and the "ill" twin, who is an award-winning poet and describes periods of psychosis in remarkable detail. An interesting view of the ambivalence of sibling experience, from pride to guilt to resentment.

Woolis, Rebecca. *When Someone You Love Has a Mental Illness: A Handbook for Family, Friends, and Caregivers* (New York: Tarcher, 1992). Once again, a practical and well-laid-out guide with easy-to-read chapter guideposts, from understanding treatments and the course of mental illness to dealing with housing, jobs, and stigma; excellent appendix about medications, and resource directory.

ORGANIZATIONS, WEBSITES, AND OTHER HELP

National Alliance on Mental Illness (NAMI)
Colonial Place Three
2107 Wilson Blvd., Suite 300
Arlington, VA 22201-3042
Main: (703) 524-7600
Member Services: (888) 999-NAMI (6264)
Information Helpline: (800) 950-NAMI (6264)
www.nami.org

National Institute of Mental Health (NIMH)
6001 Executive Blvd.
Bethesda, MD 20892-9663
(301) 443-4513
www.nimh.nih.gov

American Psychiatric Association
1000 Wilson Blvd., Suite 1825
Arlington, VA 22209-3901
(800) 368-5777
www.psych.org

National Alliance for Research on Schizophrenia and Affective Disorders (NARSAD)
60 Cutter Mill Rd., Suite 404
Great Neck, NY 11021
(516) 829-0091
www.narsad.org

National Mental Health Association (NMHA)
2001 N. Beauregard S., 12th Floor
Alexandria, VA 22311
(800) 684-NMHA (6642)
www.nmha.org

OTHER HELPFUL WEBSITES

www.schizophrenia.com—information, resources, success stories and more
www.schizophrenia.ca (Schizophrenia Society of Canada)
www.na.org (Narcotics Anonymous)
www.SAnonymous.com (Schizophrenics Anonymous)
www.bringchange2mind.org—to reduce stigma of mental illness

OTHER PUBLICATIONS

Schizophrenia Digest (www.schizophreniadigest.com). Excellent for family members as well as consumers; strategies for coping, success stories, latest news, and research.

New York City Voices: A Peer Journal for Mental Health Advocacy (www.nycvoices .org). Started by the late Ken Steele (see books) in 1995. This is "a journal where mental health consumers, ex-patients/survivors, family members and professional helpers can let their voices be heard, providing mutual support for living the most empowered and independent lives possible."

ACKNOWLEDGMENTS

From the time I sat down to write the first chapter of *Ben Behind His Voices* to its final draft, there were many who contributed, directly and indirectly, to the progress of this book. Thanks to Jessica Bram and the members of her creative writing class for making me complete one chapter per week, and encouraging me to continue after the class had ended. There were a number of editors, proofreaders, and friends who read early editions and provided helpful feedback and encouragement: Paul and Marilyn Pastore, Lucy Hedrick, Doris Eder, Pete Eldridge, Chris Morehouse, Linda Appleman Shapiro, Dr. Thomas Smith, and my wonderful husband Geoff (even if he did need a week recovering from surgery to find the time to read it). Thanks to everyone in NAMI, from the national office down to every local affiliate, for fighting the good fight on so many playing fields to advocate for those with mental illness and their families. To the members of the Family-to-Family classes I taught and trained: thanks for sharing your stories and lives with each other and with me. Your courage is remarkable.

To my wonderful agent, Claire Gerus, my gratitude and warm hugs. Claire took a chance on an unknown author and never wavered in her belief that this memoir would and should find its way to the right publisher, someone who would fall in love with its message. That turned out to be Suzanne I. Staszak-Silva, senior acquisitions editor at Rowman & Littlefield Publishers. Thanks, Suzanne, for your feeling—and your faith—that Ben's story was worth putting into print, and thanks to all the R&L editors and designers who put their talented hands and minds into its final production.

Thanks to my children, "Ben" and Ali, for allowing me to write about their lives, their courage, and the love that kept us going. Thanks to the friends and family, old and new, who never gave up on Ben, even when that belief was so hard to find.

ABOUT THE AUTHOR

Randye Kaye is a professional voice talent, actress, broadcaster, and speaker. She served more than twenty years as a major radio personality in Connecticut, and she continues to work in theater, TV, film, commercials, narrations, audiobooks, and more. She is also the Connecticut trainer of Family-to-Family educators for the National Alliance on Mental Illness (NAMI) and a diversity trainer for the Anti-Defamation League (ADL). Randye is a member of the Screen Actors Guild (SAG), the American Federation of Television and Radio Artists (AFTRA), Actors' Equity Association (AEA), the National Speakers Association, and Mensa. You're invited to follow her blog at "No Casseroles for Schizophrenia."

www.randyekaye.com